From the Air Force to College

From the Air Force to College

Transitioning from the Service to Higher Education

Jillian Ventrone and Andrew Hollis

ROWMAN & LITTLEFIELD
Lanham • Boulder • New York • London

Published by Rowman & Littlefield
A wholly owned subsidiary of The Rowman & Littlefield Publishing Group, Inc.
4501 Forbes Boulevard, Suite 200, Lanham, Maryland 20706
www.rowman.com

Unit A, Whitacre Mews, 26-34 Stannary Street, London SE11 4AB

British Library Cataloguing in Publication Information Available

Library of Congress Cataloging-in-Publication Data Available
ISBN 978-1-4422-5523-4 (cloth : alk. paper)
ISBN 978-1-4422-5524-1 (electronic)

∞™ The paper used in this publication meets the minimum requirements of American
National Standard for Information Sciences—Permanence of Paper for Printed Library
Materials, ANSI/NISO Z39.48-1992.

Printed in the United States of America

Contents

Preface

The Post-9/11 GI Bill is a highly sought-after veterans' benefit. Many individuals opt for military service mainly so that they can earn a debt-free education through this benefit. Airmen can not only earn this benefit, they can also, to further their career and education goals, take advantage of the many education and training benefits available while on active duty.

Navigating the world of higher education and the opportunities available while in the service can be difficult. *From the Air Force to College: Transitioning from the Service to Higher Education* offers accessible information that guides airmen through the maze of possibilities and assists them in getting the most out of their available choices. Taking advantage of these opportunities can enhance an airman's promotion potential and create better career possibilities for him upon separation from the service.

Introduction

The Air Force can be the initial platform of a lifelong career pathway for individuals interested in serving one contract or for those who stay on active duty for a full career. The education and certification options available to airmen can enhance the career prospects of those who choose to take advantage of the benefits, but learning about and navigating the possibilities can be difficult. *From the Air Force to College: Transitioning from the Service to Higher Education* is designed to help readers navigate this process and to assist them throughout their Air Force journey, including individuals who are just about to join, active-duty airmen, and those preparing to transition back into the civilian sector.

This book serves as the go-to guide for those who are actively seeking opportunities to further develop their education and improve their current and future career prospects. The Air Force offers many different opportunities for career enhancement and self-betterment, but if an airman does not know whom to seek out for advice, the process can get complicated. In addition, deciphering the world of higher education and navigating the available active duty and veterans' benefits is challenging. Incorrect choices can mean extended periods of time backtracking later on or running out of payment options. Reading this book will help you make well-informed choices and reinforce your confidence in the decisions you make.

The first-hand stories outlined in this book demonstrate how many service members have already achieved successful educations and careers through the advice of the authors and the listed programs. Readers will gain a more realistic perspective on pursuing their own goals based on these stories. Names and ranks have been changed to protect their identities.

The Air Force does not have a manual that airmen can reference for all of their academic needs, but this book fixes that gap. Whether one is interested in an enlisted-to-officer pathway that requires education, or in a certification that relates to an Air Force Specialty Code (AFSC), or in vocational educational options, *From the Air Force to College: Transitioning from the Service to Higher Education* can serve as a valuable treasure trove of information and as a tool to launch one's career.

For an airman who has never received counseling regarding his education or available benefits, this book can serve as the reference manual that guides him through his preparation and helps him navigate all of the possible funding options. Many extra free resources that have proved useful for the service members with whom we have worked with over the years are also included within the book, and these might help to enhance an airman's education or career prospects.

Some of the information delivered in this book is reprinted from the Army version, *From the Army to College: Transitioning from the Service to Higher Education.* Much of the information provided is applicable to service members from each of the different branches.

Chapter 1

Get Going on Your Education

Making knowledgeable decisions regarding education must be a priority for active-duty personnel and veterans, but many have a difficult time creating a plan of attack. School is a foreign environment and getting started is often the hardest part. This chapter offers airmen advice on the steps that must be taken to initiate the process with confidence.

GET GOING ON YOUR EDUCATION

While it might initially seem daunting to get going on your higher education academic pursuits, proper preparation will save you much heartache at a later date. Service members are often not able to allocate enough time between mission demands, deployments, and military job training to conduct meaningful research. Understanding what to look for is the initial hurdle; it is a big one, but once you clear it everything else will begin to fall into place. This chapter will help you organize a plan while familiarizing you with the different options available for school. Referencing this book along your trip down the pathway of higher education should make the voyage much less stressful.

Returning to school after being in the military can seem like an intimidating experience, but it will be worth your while. Many service members entered the service because they did not feel that college was the appropriate pathway for them at the time; however, many airmen do tackle college during their first enlistment and learn that it is an attainable quest. Airmen can set almost any academic goal and achieve it given the proper support.

Active-duty airmen can visit the education centers on most bases for assistance with their academic decisions. After reading through this book, make an

1

appointment with an academic counselor at the base where you are stationed. He or she will help direct you through the process of getting started. The counselor can also act as your guide along your educational pathway. If you ever feel that your chosen pathway is not progressing properly, the counselor should be your first go-to individual.

If still on active duty, there is a specific pathway to be eligible for Tuition Assistance (TA). The section on TA in the chapter "Cost and Payment Resources" (chapter 7) will cover the steps required to be eligible to receive funding through this program in an in-depth manner. If you are preparing to transition off active-duty service, make an appointment with a counselor to receive assistance in understanding your GI Bill benefits and how to activate the benefit process. The counselors can also help you prepare for your new mission, higher education.

If you are a veteran and are located close to a military base (any branch), contact the base education center for assistance. If you are not located near a military base, call the veterans' representative at the school you are thinking about attending. He or she should be your initial point-of-contact for everything at the school. These individuals are often veteran students at the school and have already been there and done that, so they know how to get you started along the proper pathway.

The following checklist will help you structure an educational plan. Take the time to write down your answers and review the information.

1. What do you want to be when you grow up? (This is still a difficult question for many of the career service members whom I counsel.)
2. What type of school should you attend—traditional or vocational?
3. Do you need a two-year or a four-year institution?
4. Have you picked a school already?
5. What are the institution's application requirements?
6. Have you collected your required documents?
7. Have you applied to the institution?
8. How will you pay for your schooling?

Let's sort through the list to help you start making decisions.

WHAT DO YOU WANT TO BE WHEN YOU GROW UP?

If you know which career you would like to pursue, you are already a few steps ahead. If not, try a self-discovery site such as CareerScope (http://benefits.va.gov/gibill/careerscope.asp), Kuder® Journey (http://www.dantes.kuder.com/), or O*NET OnLine (http://www.onetonline.org/). The sites are free and might help you narrow down possible career fields to fit your personality type, especially Kuder® Journey which offers three personality-based assessment tests and offers recommendations based upon the results. Researching different career possibilities, including income levels, job openings, and required education levels, usually helps airmen begin to develop interest in a specific pathway. More information on these sites can be found in chapter 3, "Research Tools."

If you have no idea which career pathway to take, starting at the local community college is often the best bet. Attending a community college may help you test the waters. Declare for an associate degree in general studies and use the elective credits to try different subjects. Elective credits are built into degree plans and offer you freedom to pursue topics outside of your declared major. Many community colleges offer vocational classes; if you think that might be a viable pathway, you can add some of these classes. The academic counselors at the community colleges can also help you choose the right career.

Check out Air Force Credentialing Opportunities Online (AFCOOL) (chapter 5) if you are interested in reviewing civilian sector careers that are similar to your Air Force Specialty Code (AFSC). AFCOOL lets you track a pathway from your AFSC to career selection and includes all relevant credentialing information, such as the type of credential, renewal information, potential apprenticeship possibilities, and costs. Sometimes researching AFSC-related pathways in the civilian sector can help you develop ideas about possible career pathways. I have worked with service members in the past who used the COOL sites for research and found careers of interest that they had previously not been aware existed.

WHAT TYPE OF SCHOOL SHOULD YOU ATTEND: TRADITIONAL OR VOCATIONAL?

If you have chosen a specific career, you also need to decide upon the type of school necessary to achieve the appropriate degree or certification. Education that is traditional in nature, such as criminal justice, engineering, or business, will require a traditional degree path at a regionally accredited institution of higher learning. Traditional in nature educational pathways typically require classroom-based learning. Online learning for traditional degrees is becoming more commonplace; however, strictly online learning while on the Post-9/11 GI Bill will result in a reduction of your housing stipend. The online-only housing stipend rate under the Post-9/11 GI Bill is currently set at

$783.00 (http://www.benefits.va.gov/GIBILL/resources/benefits_resources/ rates/ch33/ch33rates080115.asp) for the academic year 2015–2016. Veterans must take at least one credit every semester through the face-to-face format in order to receive the full housing stipend under Post-9/11. The level at which this amount differs from the full housing stipend under Post-9/11 will vary depending upon the location of the school.

Education that is vocational in nature might require a nationally accredited vocational school, but not always. Vocational training is more hands-on in nature and usually offers streamlined curriculum. Vocational pathways focus on the subject you chose to study and often do not require a full round of general education classes.

The different types of schools that you can select from for your educational pursuits are discussed in chapter 4 of this book. Always check at your local community college to see if it offers the vocational education you are interested in pursuing. Oftentimes, community colleges have apprenticeship or on-the-job training (OJT) programs attached to their vocational training options. State community colleges hold regional accreditation which enables students in many of the vocational programs to still be earning transferable college credit.

DO YOU NEED A TWO-YEAR OR FOUR-YEAR INSTITUTION?

Does your educational pathway require a two-year or four-year degree? If in doubt, check O*NET OnLine, or contact the schools in the area to enquire about the level of degree offered for that particular field of study. O*Net gives information on the different educational levels along with corresponding national wages or the wages for a selected state.

Most vocational pathways require either a one- or two-year certification. Sometimes employers will even demand a traditional associate degree. Typically, a two-year school is sufficient. Check the offerings at your local community college. Community colleges are in tune with the needs of the local community; meaning, that if the local population has a great demand for welders, the school will most likely offer a welding pathway.

Most career fields that are traditional in nature (think white-collar work) require a four-year bachelor's degree or a graduate-level degree. Oftentimes, a quick search of the educational requirements on a job announcement will give you a good idea of the academic demands of that particular field. For example, if you are interested in becoming a computer engineer, job announcements might stipulate a bachelor's or master's degree in computer science, computer engineering, or electrical engineering. Now you know what your minimum educational requirements will be if you decide to pursue a career in that field.

HAVE YOU PICKED A SCHOOL ALREADY?

If you have a school (or schools) that you are interested in attending, check to see that it is accredited and offers the degree you would like to attain. If so, the first phone call you make should be to the veterans' representatives. They should be able to answer all of your questions. If not, they will direct you to the appropriate individuals. Accreditation, which is covered in chapter 4, can be extremely important for career viability and should be given top priority in your school selection.

Here are a few questions to ask the veterans' representatives:

- What are the admissions requirements? Are they flexible for veterans? Do you need an SAT or ACT? What are the admissions deadlines?
- Will the school accept military transcripts
- Is the institution a member of Servicemembers Opportunity Colleges?
- Which GI Bill is best for the school: Montgomery GI Bill (MGIB) or Post-9/11?
- Will you have to pay out of pocket for tuition or fees above the amount the GI Bill will cover?
- Does the school approximate how much money books will cost yearly?
- Where are veterans buying their books? Through the bookstore or online? Is there a book exchange or rental program for veterans on campus?
- What veteran services are offered at the institution or nearby?
- How far away is the closest VA center (http://www.va.gov)?
- How many veterans attend the school?
- Does the institution have a student veterans' organization?
- How can you find other veterans who need roommates (if applicable)?
- Does the school have a veterans' center, and what resources are available in the center?
- What helpful hints can they offer pertaining to your attendance at the school?

If you are trying to decide between two schools, hopefully, the answers to these questions will offer more guidance.

If you do not know where to go to school, read on for more advice. College Navigator, which is discussed in the "Research Tools" chapter (chapter 3), can be incredibly helpful for conducting school searches. Remember: when in doubt, the local community college is a safe bet, and getting started should be the goal.

If you have narrowed your search to a few schools but are still unsure which one to choose, make a quick campus visit, check the application process, and review the time-line restrictions. Oftentimes, settling on a school requires a leap of faith, but many small, often overlooked, factors can help guide your decision. For example, if you are about to deploy and are indecisive about choosing between two different schools, the school that offers the smoothest registration process or the most online support might be a better choice. Service members have to consider time spent and mission demands because pursuing education while on active duty remains an off-duty benefit.

WHAT ARE THE INSTITUTIONS' APPLICATION REQUIREMENTS?

Depending upon the type of school you choose, it might have stringent application requirements, or it might be quite lenient. Application requirements can help you eliminate schools if you missed deadlines or do not possess the materials required for submission—for example, an SAT or ACT score, or letters of recommendation.

If you choose a four-year university or college, you should know that the institution is likely to require SAT or ACT scores and a formal application process. If you opt for community college, you can avoid a long application process and transfer to a university after acquiring a predetermined amount of college credit. The amount of credit you will be required to finish prior to being eligible for the transfer process will be based upon the transfer requirements of the institution where you are trying to finish your bachelor's degree. If you are pursuing a vocational degree or certificate, you should know that vocational schools typically have open admissions similar to community colleges.

If your transition from active duty to veteran is quick, the open admissions process with a local community college can be a less stressful transition into higher education. As long as you follow an appropriate course of study, dictated by an academic counselor at your school, you should not need to worry about the transfer process until a later date. The counselors will tell you which classes you are required to take to be eligible for transfer, and they will be listed on an academic degree or transfer plan.

HAVE YOU COLLECTED ALL THE REQUIRED DOCUMENTS?

Prior to applying, verify with your school of choice which documents you will need to provide. Is an ACT or SAT required? Do you have proof of residency? Have you applied for your GI Bill and received your Certificate of Eligibility (COE)? If you plan to attend a university, you might need a completed application, submitted test scores, letters of recommendation, an application fee which is sometimes waived for veterans, and transcripts. Open admissions institutions such as community colleges and vocational schools usually require a completed online application and proof of payment such as the COE for GI Bill or a TA voucher for active-duty personnel. Visit the "Cost and Payment Resources" chapter of this book (chapter 7) to learn how to apply for your benefits.

HAVE YOU APPLIED TO THE INSTITUTION?

Complete the required application process using all applicable documents. This process is usually online and can take quite a bit of time. Most sites will save your information for a certain number of days if you are unable to finish in one sitting. The "Admissions Process" section in chapter 4 of this book offers detailed guidance for this area. Many of the service members I (Jillian) counsel request help with this process, especially because a personal statement essay section often appears in one of the steps.

HOW WILL YOU PAY FOR YOUR SCHOOLING?

This is the time to pay good attention to your funding possibilities! When discussing funding options for education, GI Bills are best for veterans, TA is best for active-duty service members, and Federal Student Aid (FSA) is a possibility for both. MGIB and Post-9/11 are not the same. Both help with academic funding, but the two bills work in sharply different ways. Veterans who use either bill will find that a great many expenses are still left uncovered.

Active duty and veterans can apply for FSA for extra help. Veterans also have unemployment as an option. Check out your state's Department of Labor for more information regarding unemployment eligibility and possibilities. Many of the active-duty service members I work with are awarded Pell Grant money through the Free Application for Federal Student Aid (FAFSA) and Pell Grants do not need to be repaid. The "Cost and Payment Resources" chapter (chapter 7) offers detailed information about funding your education.

Here is a recap of the checklist provided above:

- Choose a career.
- Find a school.
- Organize your finances.

If you are undecided on a career, get started on general education classes at the local community college. Exercising your brain is never a mistake.

Chapter 2

Educational Concerns for Active-Duty Personnel and Veterans

Educational needs can vary greatly per person and change based upon your service status. Airmen must identify their needs first, then search for an institution that can fulfill them. Consider what types of flexibility you are looking for in an institution and evaluate the possibilities using the resources offered in this book before making a final decision.

ACTIVE-DUTY PERSONNEL AND VETERANS' EDUCATIONAL NEEDS

Service members' needs vary greatly compared to the civilian population. Determining the types of needs you might have prior to settling on an institution will allow you to make a preemptive strike on any service-related issues that might occur upon your transition off active duty. Picking an institution that can cater to these needs or is located in an area where your needs can be met is imperative for creating a positive learning environment. For example, if you are a veteran with medical concerns, you might want to choose a school that is located near a VA hospital or medical center.

If you are pursuing school while on active duty, consider your occupation, the position you currently hold, the amount of free time you have, location concerns, learning styles, Internet availability, and any personal needs you might have before you begin searching for an institution. Understanding these needs will enable you to make a well-informed choice. While you can transfer schools if your initial choice is not a good fit, you always run the risk of losing credit in the transfer process and having to backtrack. Veterans using a GI Bill only have a limited amount of GI Bill benefits to use. Losing college credit during a transfer from one school to another could set you back on your overall progression to degree completion. The GI Bill may give you the ability to complete a debt-free education if you can plan your academic career accordingly. Use it wisely after educating yourself about higher education or vocational training and learning how your available veterans benefits work.

Just as all of our personal needs are not the same, all schools are not the same. School offerings will vary by the levels of education, resources, or support systems they can provide. Picking the right institution for you is a personal process and, in most cases, will require quite a bit of research. Understanding what your needs are prior to beginning will significantly reduce the amount of time you spend conducting your searches.

Active-duty service members need great flexibility with their learning environment. Often, they require a school that offers a wealth of online courses and degree offerings, expedited semesters (eight weeks instead of the traditional four months), military familiarity, understanding professors, coursework that does not require Internet connectivity, and an academic counselor who will always be available. Each of these items is necessary in order for the population to achieve academic success while still maintaining mission demands and promotion requirements.

If you are considering online courses as you feel that your current position does not leave you enough time to attend school, be careful. While this option might offer you more convenience, your grades could suffer, and you might create unneeded and unwanted stress for yourself. Distance learning is not an easier pathway. Online courses require the same amount of work as their face-to-face counterparts. Potential barriers include not having easy access to your professors and minimal class interaction. You need to have solid reading comprehension skills, the motivation to work independently, and the ability to organize on your own in order to process information and keep track of deadlines.

Most online courses also have mandatory check-in days and times. If you are considering online courses, make sure to determine how the online classroom environment at your chosen institution works. If the school requires mandatory check-in times and you cannot make them, you run the risk of either failing the class or receiving a reduction in your grades for failure to adhere to school or class policies.

If you are in the middle of work-ups for a deployment or already deployed, check to see if the institution offers classes that do not require any Internet connectivity. This is not a common pathway for schools to take for their course offerings, but sometimes it is possible. For example, Coastline Community College in California offers a program called Pocket Ed. Pocket Ed courses are strictly offered in entry-level general education subjects. Currently, nine different subjects are available: biology, personal financial planning, geology, U.S. history, Western civilization, cinema, mass communication, psychology, and sociology. Courses begin at the start of each month and students have three months to complete the work. Proctors for exams can be service members at the E-6 rank or higher and they must outrank you by at least two ranks or they can be officers.

If you need to attend school in a face to face setting because it is better for your learning style, check to see that the school you choose maintains the flexible classroom offerings you need to be successful. Does the institution offer weekend, evening, or hybrid classes? Does it offer classes on your base? What are the professors' contact policies regarding their active-duty students? Lastly, what can the school offer in the way of support services?

Military students require high levels of flexibility by both the institution and its professors. Given deployments and permanent change of station (PCS) moves, airmen need to know that the school they have chosen will assist them at every turn no matter what type of situation arises. For example, what happens if you are deployed and lose your Internet connection for several days? Will the professor take your assignment late without penalizing your grade?

If you are not able to attend class face to face because of your current duty assignment and don't feel confident about pursuing online coursework, but you still want to make progression toward a degree, consider other options. If you know which school you will ultimately attend, call and ask if that institution accepts CLEP exam results (see chapter 8). Taking and passing CLEP exams could assist you with your academic progression even though you cannot currently attend classes. If you need to take an entrance exam such as the SAT or GRE, you may want to begin preparing for the exam. Check with the base education center to determine testing dates and times and ask for available study materials.

Try to discuss any concerns you might have regarding each class with the professor at the start of the course, not when the course is half way through. Most will understand and try to make accommodations, but usually not if you approach them right before an assignment is due or right before the class ends. If that pathway does not work, try talking to your academic counselor. This is why it is imperative that schools with significant military populations maintain veteran-only academic counselors who understand service members' special needs and know how to help in any situation.

Unfortunately, I often hear from service members that they cannot locate the academic counselor at their school. Some schools put people in these positions who are not trained, do not understand the special needs of the military population, or do not hold the proper level of education. In these schools, these positions tend to turn over often, and students might find themselves with a new counselor so frequently that the individual does not understand their concerns.

Always ask any school you are interested in attending if they have policies regarding deployments. Schools with clear policies will not require any guesswork on your part. For example, some institutions will allow students to finish courses remotely if an unforeseen deployment arises. During such situations, well-trained academic counselors can assist you in finding options that might enable course completion to occur in a timely manner. At a minimum, they can give an active-duty service member a clear chain of command to contact when in need of assistance.

Service members' educational needs can vary greatly depending upon their long-term military goals. Airmen who plan on staying in the military for long-term careers are usually aiming for degree completion. Those completing only one enlistment are usually aiming for solid transfer credit to take with them and shorten the time they will need to spend in school upon their separation.

Degree requirements can be restrictive. Some degrees are difficult or impossible to find in an online format from a reputable institution, for example, the engineering and science fields. If you are considering a degree that might limit how much of your education you can complete while on active duty, you might consider completing as much of the degree as possible in an online format, such as all of your general education classes or elective credit. Upon separation from the service, you can tackle the courses that must be completed in a classroom environment.

Be careful of taking elective credits while still on active duty. Many schools will offer you elective credit based upon receipt of your DD214. Why take credits that might be awarded to you at a later date or not necessary? If you know the institution you want to attend prior to separation, you can either contact that institution's veterans department and ask if the institution will confer credit in this manner, or look up the degree requirements to determine if a requirement exists. If the school awards credit for military training, stay away from the elective classes until a counselor tells you that you need them. More information on this topic can be found in chapter 8, "Prior Learning Credit."

Credit transferability is a sticky topic. Several concerns should be considered before moving forward if you are pursuing transfer credit. Ultimately, credit acceptance is up to the final institution you will attend for graduation. Schools usually consider the accreditation of the prior institution and specific program requirements when reviewing credit brought in from other institutions. Some schools have preexisting transfer agreements that will create a low-stress transfer pathway at a later date.

Some state schools have developed programs to show students how credits transfer between the institutions, such as ASSIST in California. ASSIST (http://www.assist.org) is a cooperative project between the University of California school system, the California State University system, and the state community colleges that allows students to compare class transferability by course of study, department, or general education/breadth agreements. These are commonly called articulation guides, and checking if the school is part of a particular system will allow you to choose intelligently when taking classes to transfer.

Classes do not always transfer for the credit they were originally intended to fill. You must also keep an eye on how many credits an institution will accept. For example, Arizona State University (ASU) will transfer a maximum of sixty-four lower-division semester hours (i.e., 100- and 200-level classes) from a regionally accredited community college (https://transfer.asu.edu/credits), although some exceptions apply for veterans. If you intend to transfer to ASU to complete a bachelor's degree, taking more than sixty-four lower-division credits from the school you are currently attending would be unproductive. Try your best not to find yourself in a situation where credits will not transfer or might need to be repeated.

Consider a few questions before moving forward in this situation:

- Always check the institution's accreditation. I cannot emphasize this point enough. Chapter 4 in this book reviews the different types of accreditation and concerns to be aware of prior to selecting an institution. If you make the wrong choice, you might have to backtrack later. This could cause you to run out of GI Bill benefits and have to find alternate funding for your schooling.
- Consider the state you come from or intend to move to before choosing a school to attend. Many schools have satellite locations in other states or at military installations. If you can find one from your state, in most cases it will be better for your needs.
- If you know which institution you would like to attend after separation from the military, check whether the school offers online classes.

If feasible, it would be best to start while on active duty at the school where you intend to finish when you are a veteran. Many schools, including state-based two-year and four-year institutions, offer online classes and are approved for Tuition Assistance (TA). Marshall, Central Michigan, Pennsylvania State University, and many other institutions offer strictly online master's degrees. Colorado State University, University of Massachusetts, and University of Maryland are a few of the big four-year universities with fully online bachelor's degrees that are TA approved. Many community colleges offer fully online associate degrees, such as Central Texas Community College, which is located on several military installations. Check the Department of Defense Memorandum of Understanding website (http://www.dodmou.com) to see if your school is approved for TA. Attending a school online that you can continue to attend once separated will make your transition much easier, and you will not run the risk of losing credits during the transfer process.

- If these options are not possible, contact the school you are interested in attending upon separation and ask if it has transfer agreements with any particular schools. Most big universities are fed by local community colleges, and most community colleges offer online classes. Usually, big state universities have transfer agreements with the local state community colleges.
- Check with the local education center to see which schools have a presence on the base.

Veterans' educational needs have been the topic of much discussion. The Post-9/11 GI Bill has allowed today's veterans more flexibility than ever before, and schools across the country have had significant increases in their veteran student populations. Unfortunately, veterans of the current conflicts face transition issues that pose many difficult challenges. Schools that recognize these challenges and tailor services on the campus to meet the special needs of their veteran populations should be recognized for their support.

Be careful when choosing a school that claims it is veteran friendly. A study conducted by the Center for American Progress determined that the criteria for listing schools as "veteran friendly" on some websites and media outlets are unclear. Schools should offer you a proper academic pathway as well as veteran-based support. Be leery of any institution that claims it is "veteran friendly" but cannot back it up with concrete proof.[1]

Ask about campus support services for veterans. You should look for veteran-only academic counselors, VA services on the campus or nearby, nonprofit veteran assistance such as American Veterans (AMVETS) or Disabled American Veterans (DAV), student veteran organizations such as the

Student Veterans of America (SVA), financial aid support, unemployment support, contact with off-campus services that specialize in veteran outreach, and a significant student veterans' center that is consistently manned. The center should be prepared to handle or refer to the appropriate agencies any problem that comes its way.

Many academic institutions, including ASU, host the Veterans Upward Bound (VUB) program on their campuses (https://eoss.asu.edu/trio/vub). The VUB program is designed to encourage and assist veterans in their pursuit of higher education. The federally funded program aims to increase and improve qualified veterans' English, math, computer skills to assist with literacy, laboratory science, foreign language, and college planning skills. All of the courses are free and ASU offers courses daily on three of the school's campuses. Check the national VUB program website (http://www.navub.org/) to find out if your school offers the program. You can also find the specific VUB office for your particular state by finding your state on the dropdown menu toward the top left corner of their main website to enquire into the services they provide.

School location is important for veterans for many reasons other than the Monthly Housing Allowance (MHA) attached to Post-9/11. Usually, in a traditional higher education environment, we live where we go to school. This may not be the case for many veterans. Often, veterans are older and have families they must support while they pursue higher education. Sometimes jobs dictate where we can live, and driving long distances to get to class may add unneeded stress to an already stressful transition. If you have already chosen the place where you would like to live, or are still on active duty, try to find a school within a decent driving distance. Check for veteran services offered around the school, because if you need help, you may not want to drive one hundred miles to get it.

The setting of the school's location is also important. If you need the night-life of a city or if you need a fast-paced lifestyle, you should take that into consideration. If you prefer something without many distractions, consider a quieter institution in a small-town location. You can also check to see if the veterans' center at the school has a designated veteran-only study space allocated for quiet study time. Pay attention to the region as well. If you are a veteran exiting the service without any college credit, you will be spending four years at this institution. If you hate cold weather and snow, you might not want a school in a northern region of the country.

Class availability is imperative for veterans for reasons such as MHA amounts under the Post-9/11 GI Bill and socialization. Both of these subjects are extremely important to consider when thinking about your transition to school. Many schools offer veterans early bird registration to assist them in achieving a full-time schedule of classes that are required for their degree plans. If a full-time schedule cannot be met, then veterans using their federal benefits will begin to see a reduction in the amount of money they receive. The MHA and degree plan requirements under Post-9/11 are addressed in the "Cost and Payment Resources" chapter.

Isolation can become a concern for transitioning veterans who face an unknown civilian population that doesn't operate in the regimented fashion they are used to in the military. Airmen who isolate themselves run a great risk of facing difficulty in the transition process. Making contact and developing relationships with other veterans at the school is a good way to combat this issue. According to a study conducted by the Defense Centers of Excellence:

> Peer supporters "speak the same language" as those they are helping as a result of shared experience(s), which fosters an environment of credibility and trust. Importantly, peers tend to interact more frequently with service members than do chaplains or members of the medical community. As a result, peers are most likely to notice changes in behavior and personality of an individual.[2]

Even if you do not believe that isolation will become a problem for you, consider two reasons to pay attention to the situation anyway.

1. You should always have preemptive precautions set in place. Remember, prior, proper, planning.
2. You might be able to help another veteran who is not in a positive mental health frame of mind and needs assistance.

Airmen should review the following checklist with a veterans' representative at the school they plan to attend:

- Make contact so you have a face to put with the name.
- Explain your situation and ask for helpful hints for anything you may need.
- Ask about housing and where you can find other veterans for roommates.
- Find out what services the school has set in place for its veteran population. Maybe the school has a veteran-only student body (president, vice president, secretary, etc.) that helps plan social events or promotes veteran well-being at the institution.
- Determine where the closest VA center is located.
- Ask about student veteran organizations (such as SVA) available on campus.

- Find out about the institution's veteran population. How many veteran students attend the school? Does the school/vet center host any veteran-only events?
- Ask whether veterans receive early admission.
- Ask whether there is a veterans' academic counselor.

Veteran interaction on campus is important for veteran success. Many veteran departments at schools actively participate in community events involving veterans or invite agencies such as the Veterans of Foreign Wars or the American Legion to visit their campuses. This is a great way to meet new friends and help your peers. Interaction is not solely for you to create a school support web and make friends. Networking with other veterans is a great way to keep in touch with other people who have shared similar experiences. Sharing experiences with those who have "been there, done that" may help you reintegrate faster into civilian life. This network can also be an amazing tool later for job searches and entrepreneurship possibilities.

Most schools will have a Veterans' Services Office, which is often where you will find military-specific counselors and peer groups made up of other veterans. For example, the University of Alabama has an office specifically for veterans entitled the Center for Veteran and Military Affairs. The school also offers a Career Transition Assistance Program specifically for veterans, which focuses on job search skills and utilizing prior military experience to maximize success upon degree completion. The center features a Family Assistance Program that is meant to offer support for any aspect of a veteran's life, including spousal job searches, assistance in finding housing, day care, and navigating both the campus and local community in search of resources.[3]

Researching the topics mentioned above may help you understand the school's overall culture and attitude toward its veteran population. If the school does not seem to have many veteran services in place, you may want to consider other options. Schools should provide veterans a multitude of support services in case they face unforeseen issues while transitioning and need help.

The VA recognized the need for veterans to hear transition troubles and successes from peers and created a website to help. Make the Connection (http://maketheconnection.net/) helps veterans through shared experiences and support services. The site contains resources and videos from veterans who have faced issues and offers advice based on personal experience. Local resources such as VA chaplains, veterans' centers, outpatient clinics, and PTSD programs can be found here as well.

Chapter 3

Research Tools

Before you decide which school to attend or decide on a specific career pathway, you need to make yourself aware of all your available options. Using the free research tools outlined in this section will enable you to find a school that will meet your academic and career needs, as well as useful career-based information. These sites are not foolproof, but are a good start. Each tool offers invaluable information in the different levels involved with planning your future, whether that is a long-term career in the Air Force or a civilian sector route. Using all of these sites and cross-referencing the information will benefit the overall organization of your profession. If possible, always check with an academic counselor aboard the base where you are stationed for information relevant to your needs. For example, if you are a Tuition Assistance (TA) user, you will need to determine if the institution you have selected is approved for TA.

- College Navigator
- O*NET OnLine
- DANTES College & Career Planning Counseling Services, powered by Kuder® Journey
- CareerScope/My Next Move for Veterans
- VA Education and Career Counseling Program (Chapter 36)
- Counseling Services

COLLEGE NAVIGATOR

http://nces.ed.gov/collegenavigator/

College Navigator offered by the National Center for Education Statistics is a beneficial tool for both active-duty and transitioning airmen. The free site enables users to search schools based upon very detailed criteria. Searches may be saved for future reference and dropped into the favorites' box for side-by-side comparison. Comparing schools side by side enables users to determine which school better suits their needs. For example, I (Jillian) searched Point Loma Nazarene (PLNU) and Loyola Marymount University (LMU) in California to determine which of the two private schools would be less expensive. After dropping both schools into my favorites' box, I selected the compare option in that section. The side-by-side comparison tool listed PLNU's current tuition rate for a student who lives off campus at $48,794 and the LMU's rate for the same student at $58,742. I still need to go directly to both schools' websites for more information, but my initial search is demonstrating the vast difference to me in yearly costs between the two institutions. I understand that the Post-9/11 GI Bill currently will only cover up to $21,084.89 (http://www.benefits.va.gov/GIBILL/resources/benefits_resources/rates/ch33/ch33rates080115.asp) per academic year for a private school, and I know further research would be required to determine whether LMU or PLNU is a viable fiscal option for me as a veteran student. My next step would be to determine if either school is participating in the Yellow Ribbon Program (chapter 7) through the VA.

College Navigator allows detailed searches in fields such as distance from ZIP codes, public and private school options, distance learning possibilities, school costs, percentage of applicants admitted, religious affiliations, specialized missions, and available athletic teams. This way, users can narrow down selections based upon specific needs. For example, if I were interested in attending a school with a Christian background as part of my learning, I could click on the religious affiliations tab at the bottom of the search section and add that criterion to my list.

Beginning each search within a certain number of miles from a ZIP code will enable you to limit the search results that show up. If the selection is insufficient, try broadening the distance a bit prior to removing all of the other parameters you deem important. Many schools offer some degree of online schooling as part of the learning environment. If you are open to online learning, you may find that you can still attain all of your search parameters comfortably even if the school is a bit further in distance.

A generic initial search on College Navigator might resemble this:

1. State—California
2. ZIP code—90290, with a maximum distance parameter set at fifteen miles
3. Degree options—business
4. Level of degree awarded—associate
5. School type—public

Results demonstrate that four schools meet my (Jillian's) search criteria: Los Angeles Pierce College, Santa Monica College, Los Angeles Valley College, and West Los Angeles College. Because each of these institutions met my initial search criteria, I might want to narrow the mileage to a selection closer to my home base, or look for other, more particular areas that demonstrate the differences. These areas may include the student population, programs offered, and veterans' department structure. I may find that the veterans' department is nonexistent, which would not inspire my confidence in the institution's ability to take care of my unique needs.

Beginning in 2009, schools have been required by the Department of Education to compile three pieces of data to allow students to better analyze the costs and value of attending a particular school. College Navigator provides graduation/retention rates, median borrowing rates, and the cohort loan default rates. Checking this information will give potential students better insight into an institution's value.

The site also tracks the graduation/retention rates of first-time and full-time students who graduate within a 150 percent of the time from beginning their degree. According to the American Council on Education (ACE), graduation rates "are an obvious, commonsense indicator of how well an institution is serving its students. After all, what better evidence could we have than the percentage of those students seeking a degree who actually receive one?"[1] More information on why graduation rates matter and why they don't matter can be found here: http://www.acenet.edu/the-presidency/columns-and-features/Pages/Why-Graduation-Rates-Matter%E2%80%94and-Why-They-Don%E2%80%99t.aspx.

This may only capture a very specific or small population at a particular school. If a student were to be classified as a transfer student, he or she would not be captured by this number. If a school you are considering attending has particularly low graduation/retention rates, it would be wise to contact the institution and inquire about this issue.

The median borrowing rates are the median amount of debt that the student population is taking on to attend that institution. The cohort loan default rates are the number of students that attended the school and defaulted on their loans after leaving the institution. Sometimes listed schools will have high median borrowing rates and high cohort loan default rates along with low graduation/retention rates. Some might assume that this means that the institution may not be providing educational value to the student when he or she attempts to attain employment. This could cause trouble for that student if he or she is not able to afford school loans after graduation.

Unfortunately, these numbers are complex and only provide one small piece of the overall puzzle when assessing whether a particular institution is the right choice for a student. Talking to a counselor at the school and investigating the responses offered about these concerns can help a potential student better understand what the statistics may mean. Make sure to speak with an educational advisor at your base, or if you have already moved out from the base, give the advisor a call to set up a distant counseling appointment. Counselors who work for the AF can give you unbiased information regarding the results of your institutional search. Remember when you call a counselor at the school that that individual works for that particular institution.

O*NET ONLINE

http://www.onetonline.org/

O*Net OnLine is a career occupation website that enables users to complete detailed research on any careers they might be interested in pursuing. The career departments on the military bases use O*Net OnLine for résumé development. The site details areas such as career fields, needed skills, income possibilities, work contexts, and required education levels.

To research a potential career on O*Net OnLine, enter the name in the upper right-hand corner under the "Occupation Quick Search" tab. For example, I (Jillian) entered civil engineer. Upon clicking the link, I was taken to a page that listed civil engineering along with numerous other possibilities that are similar in nature: wind energy engineers, traffic technicians, construction and building inspectors, and civil drafters. This option enables users to research a broader base of potential career pathways prior to settling on one.

Occupations listed as "Bright Outlook" have growth rates that are faster than average in that field and are projected to have a large number of job openings during the decade from 2012 through 2022. These fields are also considered new and emerging, meaning they will see changes in areas such as technology over the upcoming years. Offering several different occupations under one particular search enables users to broaden their horizons and complete numerous searches that are similar in nature.

Clicking on one particular career pathway will allow you to find the national and state-based median wages for the chosen occupation—for example, the search I conducted under civil engineer listed the national median wages at $39.45 hourly or $82,050 annually. The projected annual growth rate is between 15 and 21 percent. Also listed are the majority of industries where civil engineers are finding employment—in this case, professional, scientific, and technical services.

Last, schools that offer the proper education pathways can be searched by state. Unfortunately, the school search cannot be narrowed down further by location, type of institution, or other minute detail. For more detailed searches, return to College Navigator.

DANTES COLLEGE & CAREER PLANNING COUNSELING SERVICES, POWERED BY KUDER® JOURNEY™

http://www.dantes.kuder.com/

DANTES College & Career Planning Counseling Services is available to service members for free, whether you are still on active duty or already separated from the service. Four main areas of education and career research and planning are available on the site—assessments section, occupations, education and financial aid, and job/job search.

Airmen can conduct inventory assessments that enable them to see their areas of strength and weakness. This gives test takers insight into career fields that match their personality types, thereby offering a broader base of potential careers to research. Background information on the careers can be researched to determine whether users are interested in pursuing the option further. Under the education section, users can match the requisite type of education to the chosen vocation as well as find schools that offer the desired degrees.

Résumé building and job searches can be conducted through the site as well. One interesting tool Kuder offers is the ability for users to build résumés and cover letters, attach other needed or pertinent information, and create a

URL that hosts the information to submit to potential employers. This allows multiple pieces of information to be housed in one place in a professional manner for viewing by others.

CAREER SCOPE® AND MY NEXT MOVE FOR VETERANS

http://www.gibill.va.gov/studenttools/careerscope/index.html
http://www.mynextmove.org/vets/

CareerScope hosts an interest and aptitude assessment tool similar in style to DANTES Kuder. CareerScope is hosted by the VA on the main GI Bill web page. The free site assists service members in finding and planning the best pathways for those transitioning off active duty and into higher education. Assessments are conducted directly through the site, and a corresponding report interpretation document demonstrates how to interpret assessment results. The easy-to-understand site is a valuable research tool both for those who have already identified which career pathway they want to take and for those who are still undecided.

VA EDUCATION AND CAREER COUNSELING PROGRAM (CHAPTER 36)

http://www.benefits.va.gov/vocrehab/edu_voc_counseling.asp
http://www.vba.va.gov/pubs/forms/VBA-28-8832-ARE.pdf

Although it is not widely known, the VA offers free education and career counseling advice. The counseling services are designed to help service members choose careers, detail the required educational pathway, and assist in working through any concerns that arise that might deter success. Veterans should refer to the website for eligibility, but the main determining factors are that the veteran must:

- Be eligible for VA education benefits (or dependents using transferred benefits) through one of the following chapters: Chapters 30, 31, 32, 33, 35, 1606, or 1607;
- Have received an honorable discharge not longer than one year earlier; or
- Have no more than six months remaining on active duty.

Fill out an application that can be found at the website listed above and return it to get the ball rolling. Airmen who have already separated from active service and are not located near an Air Force base will find this to be a solid outlet for assistance.

CAREER ONE STOP

http://www.careeronestop.org/

Career One Stop is one of my (Jillian) go-to sites for career exploration, and is the first site I visit when I work with military students who are interested in apprenticeship programs. The site holds valuable information regarding topics other than apprenticeships as well. It is a comprehensive career exploration site. Career One Stop has six main sections for exploration:

- Explore careers—learn about career fields, explore different industries, take self-assessments, and research different job skills.
- Job Search—information on relocating, wages and salaries, benefits, unemployment insurance, and paying for education or training.
- Find training—information on traditional education and apprenticeship program, conduct a search for community colleges, find credentials, and research employment trends.
- Resources For—find special tips on veterans' reemployment.
- Toolkit—samples and formats create a cover letter and thank you note, and find out how to get ready for an interview.
- Find Local Help—workforce services in different locations.

If searching for information regarding apprenticeships programs, click on the "Find Training" tab, then under the "Types of Training" section click "Apprenticeship." This page hosts two links titled "Apprenticeship USA," which takes users to the DOL page regarding apprenticeship training, and "Apprenticeship Finder," which allows users to search for specific programs or by city, state, or zip code.

Use the state-based search option to find a program in the state and county of your choosing. For example, Staff Sergeant Bowen is from Maryland. He would like to participate in an electrician registered apprenticeship program. He clicks on the "Apprenticeship Finder" tab, then inputs his state. At this point, each state will have designed its own points of contact, so the directions will vary, but he needs to find the link to search for apprenticeship programs. So, Staff Sergeant Bowen clicks on "Find an Apprenticeship" at the top of the page and then "View Links to Program Websites." On this page, he can search for the appropriate link for an electrical program and the contact information. He can also click the "Veterans ReEmployment" link, which is found by hovering on the "Resources for" tab at the very top of the main page and clicking on "Veterans." Here, he can input his particular MOS and find occupations he may be qualified for, or nearly qualified for, based on the specific military training he received in the Air Force.

THE DEPARTMENT OF LABOR

http://www.dol.gov/

The DOL is a one-stop shopping place for many topics, but I use the site for information regarding unemployment, registered apprenticeships, and career exploration. On the main DOL page, under the "Popular Topics" tab, I use "Unemployment," "Training," and "Veterans' Employment" tabs the most.

Most of the service members I (Jillian) work with are eligible for unemployment upon separation from the service. The DOL website is a good place to start looking for initial information regarding the benefits. On the corresponding page, the "Unemployment Compensation for Ex-Servicemembers" tab has eligibility information regarding the benefits, a fact sheet, and a link that allows users to search for specific State Workforce Agencies.

The "Training" section has a tab on the right-hand side of the page for information on apprenticeship programs. This page holds information that allows an individual to familiarize oneself with apprenticeships and the process of participating. The DOL is a good place to begin a search for a specific program in a specific location. Read the Fact Sheet before clicking on the "Office of Apprenticeship" tab that will take users to the main page regarding registered apprenticeships. Anything you need to know about an apprenticeship program can be found here: http://www.doleta.gov/oa/.

The "Veterans' Employment" section has a wealth of information that is relevant to most veterans. Topics such as apprenticeship information, veterans' preference, and employment assistance are covered. Information on the Uniformed Services Employment and Reemployment Rights Act (USERRA) can be found here as well.

BUREAU OF LABOR STATISTICS
OCCUPATIONAL OUTLOOK HANDBOOK

http://www.bls.gov/ooh/

The Bureau of Labor Statistics (BLS) Occupational Outlook Handbook is a resourceful tool to use for career exploration prior to starting on your education journey. Conducting career research before starting school will assist you in making a more knowledgeable decision regarding your education. Search career fields by pay levels, educational requirements, training requirements, projected job openings, and projected job-growth rates. You can research various career sectors or find out what are the current fastest growing job fields. If I wanted to find out the level of education required to be a petroleum engineer and how much money they make, I click on the "Architecture and Engineering" tab and scroll down (the options are in alphabetical order). Here, I can view a short job summary, see that the field requires a bachelor's degree, and learn that the median pay in 2012 was $130,280. Clicking on the link takes me to a more in-depth information regarding the career field. Lately, many of the service members I counsel are asking about petroleum engineering education pathways. While I can see on this page that petroleum engineering has a faster than average growth rate (26 percent), I think the pay scale is what attracted them!

COUNSELING SERVICES

When you begin your education journey, you will undoubtedly find a plethora of options available and it can become overwhelming. You will realize that there are plenty of companies that seek profit from your educational pursuits. The AF offers free, nonbiased professional counseling to you through your education counselors aboard the bases, and it is a solid place to begin your planning. The counselors can be an extremely valuable asset to you at this stage. It is in your best interest to know how to use the base education centers and understand the role of the academic counselors. The counselors work for you, not for the colleges on base. Understand that their mission is to keep your best interests in mind, not the interests of the colleges.

Education services offices are located in all major Air Force installations. The education services personnel provide information on educational opportunities and counseling services to all Air Force members assigned to the base, including active duty personnel, DOD civilian employees, adult family members, and military retirees. They are also adept at providing additional support to Air Force Reservists, Air National Guard, and other sister service members. Education services personnel are the liaisons between the students and all education opportunities providing services to people on the base.

Counselors can show you college and degree options offered at your location. Since there are typically four to eight on-base colleges offering both undergraduate and graduate programs at each major installation, with many offering accelerated courses on eight-week terms in a variety of formats to include lunch, evening, weekend, and online, there is something to meet everyone's needs. Counselors can assist you in finding study material, direct you to where you can buy books, help you receive tutoring, assist in helping you determine your academic and future career goals, and form your education degree plan. The education center can schedule your education-based exams, including CLEP and DANTES. TA training and tuition assistance requests for each course are approved through the center as well. Financial aid, scholarships, commissioning opportunities, the various GI Bill options, VA education programs, and Troops to Teachers all fall within the realm of the services provided at the education centers.

I (Andrew) have a very high regard for my first education counselor because she had a profound impact on the direction of my life at the time. I remember our initial conversation like it was yesterday and have referred to it many times over the years. When I arrived at my first duty station (Wurtsmith Air Force Base, Michigan) in 1988, I was fresh off of completing Basic Military Training and my twenty-six week, four-day technical training course for Offensive Avionics Systems Maintenance. The base leadership made the education office a mandatory place to go to for newcomers. I failed to understand why at the time; I had no interest in college and merely sought a stable job upon entering the Air Force. During the conversation with my counselor, she used some terms (italicized below) that I was unfamiliar with, but later I came to place quite a lot of value on them.

I remember my counselor handed me a two-page report and congratulated me on all of the college credits that I had accumulated to that point in my career. She seemed genuinely impressed and I was quite surprised, but yet to be convinced this was meaningful to me. I really just wanted to go to work on that airplane that I had waited so long to get my hands on. She laid before me a Community College of the Air Force (CCAF) catalog that exhibited all of the requirements for an associate in applied science degree in avionics systems technology. Throughout the conversation, she would point at various aspects of the degree as if to say "you are here."

She explained that by attending technical training (affectionately known as tech school) every day for twenty-six weeks, I had completed all of my technical core and technical elective portion of my degree requirements. She stated that Air Force tech school was just like going to college—the instructors who taught at the school were required to have a degree and the curriculum had to be certified for college credit worthiness.

My counselor went on to explain that I had to complete training for my five skill levels and that training would satisfy the internship portion of the degree. Afterward, I needed to complete five classes in general education; oral communication, written communication, college mathematics, social science, and humanities. Fortunately, she claimed, all of the classes were offered on base at Alpena Community College. Furthermore, TA would make the pursuit of my degree very inexpensive. She then transitioned to a different aspect of the conversation. Her posture changed slightly, she paused, looked me in the eyes and said, "Andrew, wouldn't you like to be a college graduate and earn an associate in applied science degree from the Community College of the Air Force?"

She had captured my attention at this point, although this was a totally new concept for me, since I never considered pursuing college before. I had no reason to; my father and grandfather didn't even graduate high school. But, the proposition sounded like a good deal at the moment. "What do I have to do?" I asked. She sprang into action, enrolling me into the CCAF (CCAF now automatically enrolls all enlisted airmen) and helping me complete a Pell Grant (FAFSA) application. I ended up receiving two Pell Grant checks for $550 each to help fund my degree, and that exceeded my out-of-pocket costs at the time.

I eventually completed my degree and wish that I could correctly portray how amazing it made me feel. When I joined the Air Force, I needed direction. I was full of self-doubt and lacked self-confidence. Now I was a college graduate and hungry to take on additional challenges and pursue self-development. I proudly displayed my diploma in my work center and could hardly wait to tell my dad and anyone else who would listen. My educational journey was really in its infancy at that point and I have since added a few more advanced degrees, but none more important. The first degree served as a stepping stone for bigger things to come. Thanks to the influence of my first education counselor, my degree from the CCAF positively changed the course of my life by giving me the confidence and focus to do more. So very much more.

The bottom line here is that education counselors are very important people; treat them well and respect what they have to say, because it can be a life changer!

Chapter 4

What Should I Look for in a School?

Service members often have unique personal needs that should be taken into account when they create plans to pursue education. Since schools are not all the same, airmen must be vigilant and not commit to a pathway that might not be a good match. One airman's best possible choice for an institution might be the worst possible choice for another. This chapter outlines important institutional factors that will assist you in making an educated decision. The following topics are discussed:

1. Types of schools
2. School accreditation
3. Admissions requirements
4. Admissions process
5. Standardized admissions tests

TYPES OF SCHOOLS

You have learned about the tools available to help assist in your research; now you need to know what to look for during the search. Schools serve different purposes depending upon the type of institution. Understanding the differences will help you make a more educated and empowered decision.

In most cases, career choices determine the type of institution we should attend. For example, are you taking a vocational or traditional pathway? Do you need a two-year degree or a four-year degree? If two years are sufficient, then you can eliminate most four-year universities from your search. Narrowing your search by a few key factors will help in the selection process.

Technical schools, community colleges, universities, public and private, not-for-profit and for-profit schools have different guiding factors and structures. This section offers brief explanations of the types of schools and how to choose the one that best suits your needs.

Two-Year Schools

Two-year schools are community colleges (CCs) or technical schools. Most are state based, but not always. CCs offer the following:

- Associate degrees
- Transfer pathways to universities and colleges
- Certificate programs
- Vocational programs which might include apprenticeship opportunities
- Open enrollment, which is especially good if you had trouble with your high-school GPA
- No SAT, ACT, or essay required
- Significantly cheaper tuition and fees than universities and colleges

Oftentimes, two-year community colleges can cost students less money and help lessen the financial burden a college can place on a veteran before he moves on to a four-year institution. Students can spend up to two years at a community college before a transfer becomes necessary. Many CCs offer specific transfer pathways into the four-year schools located in the state and sometimes for institutions located across the country as well; these pathways are prearticulated with the four-year schools and state the conditions under which credits or degrees (typically A.A. or A.S.) will transfer.

Because community colleges are usually found in numerous locations throughout each state, they are easy to find and often near your home. The open-enrollment policy makes for a stress-free transition from active duty and is the fastest way to start school. Most of the service members I (Jillian) assist opt for a community college when they are on a time crunch because of deployments or training. Sometimes it is the only pathway, especially if university admission deadlines have already passed.

Most CCs offer vocational programs that require an associate degree or a certification process. Many of the vocational pathways also have available significant hands-on learning options, such as apprenticeship programs or on-the-job training options. Attending a vocational program at a state CC gives you a safe, regionally accredited option to transfer credit if you decide later to pursue a bachelor's degree at another regionally accredited school.

Always check with the specific school about the program you would like to attend. Some programs, such as nursing and radiologic technologist, are often impacted. This means that there are more students than spots available, so acceptance may be delayed. Sometimes, a nearby for-profit school may offer more than enough seats for their students in these types of programs, but you are usually paying a higher premium in tuition for this luxury. Knowing the differences between the types of schools that are available to attend allows you to make the best decision possible.

Community colleges frequently offer internships and apprenticeships within the surrounding community. These programs may help you gain employment at a faster rate, generate work experience for a résumé, upgrade your current status within a particular field, or credential you for a specific career. Oftentimes, these pathways are attached to an associate of applied science (AAS) degree. AAS degrees do not require students to take a full course of general education subjects. Typically, they will only require basic freshman-level math and English courses. While this degree does not necessarily preclude transfer to a four-year school, that is not the intent. They are career-based degrees as opposed to designated transfer pathways to a four-year institution.

Four-Year Schools

Colleges and universities are four-year schools. Each state has a state university system, but not all colleges and universities are state based, as you will read about them in the next few paragraphs. Four-year schools can offer the following:

- Bachelor's degrees
- Research institutions, centers, and programs
- Financial aid—four-year colleges can be very expensive
- On- and off-campus enrichment opportunities, such as study abroad and guest lecture series
- Various fields of study that offer a wide range of job opportunities
- Broader range of course selection than community colleges

- Large, diverse campuses, and populations at some of the bigger universities and state schools; smaller campuses and smaller, more familiar class sizes at smaller liberal arts colleges
- Competitive admissions process

Many universities also have graduate schools, where students can continue their studies to obtain advance degrees such as an MA, PhD, MD, JD, and others. Before going to graduate school, however, students must finish their undergraduate coursework (some schools do have specialty combined programs), and another admissions process is necessary for acceptance.

Attending a university can sometimes be overwhelming. Classes can be so large that you never have a one-on-one conversation with your professor, which sometimes makes students feel anonymous. Finding your niche might take some time in a large population, but it will afford you more opportunities to interact. Large institutions usually offer numerous degrees and classes to choose from; smaller liberal arts colleges may be a bit more specialized.

If you feel that a four-year institution might be too much, too soon or simply do not have the time to organize all of the required admissions documents, starting at the local community college might be the best option. Many civilian students take this path for the same reason. Community colleges are also beneficial for students who might need more one-on-one attention during their studies, or simply have not been to school in a long time and feel safer in a smaller, less competitive environment. Whatever the case, arm yourself with information before making a decision. Sometimes, a visit to the campus will settle the issue. The school should be a comfortable fit because you will be spending a significant amount of time there.

Study abroad can be a fun option. Many service members opt for this option, some are interested in cultural exploration, and others are married to foreigners and intend to live in their spouse's home countries. Whatever the reason, preparing correctly for study abroad takes some time depending upon the option you chose. If you opt for study abroad period that is sponsored by your US-based institution, your school will convert the credits earned abroad to reflect credit just as you would earn through another course offered within the parent, US-based school. Many foreign schools are able to take your GI Bill benefits. Check the GI Bill Comparison Tool (http://department-of-veterans-affairs.github.io/gi-bill-comparison-tool/) to see if the institution you are interested in attending participates.

Attending a foreign institution for your entire degree seeking pathway could potentially cause you trouble down the road. Most foreign schools do not abide by the regional accreditation that is preferred for traditional education in the United States. Make sure to find out if the degree can be translated in the United States prior to committing to attending a foreign institution. Information on foreign degree or credit evaluation can be found on the National Association of Credential Evaluation Services (NACES®) website (http://www.naces.org/). If the degree from the foreign institution you are considering attending cannot be evaluated by US standards, you may run into difficulties later. You run the risk that a potential employer may not value your degree or that an advanced degree program may not recognize the level of education you have achieved.

Public Schools (Universities and Community Colleges)

Public schools, often referred to as "state schools," are typically funded by state and local governments. In-state residents pay lower tuition charges than out-of-state students. Some schools' out-of-state tuition charges can total an extra $10,000 or more per academic year. Sometimes state schools have reciprocal agreements with schools in other states that allow for reduced out-of-state tuition charges—for example, the Midwest Student Exchange Program (http://msep.mhec.org/) MSEP, based in the Midwest, has nine participating states with over one hundred schools that charge undergraduate students a maximum of 150 percent of the in-state tuition charges and private schools that offer a 10 percent reduction in tuition.

State schools offer a wide range of classes, degree options, and degree levels, and oftentimes state residents get priority admissions. Class size at state schools can be a concern. Sometimes, upward of 250 students may be enrolled in a lecture class. This can make it difficult to interact with professors or staff.

Most states have a flagship university with smaller locations available throughout the state for easier access. In some instances, students attending state universities cannot graduate in the standard four-year time frame because mandatory classes are often full, although, many institutions now offer priority registration to veterans and active duty. This enables veterans to maintain full-time status while using their GI Bills so that they also rate full-time benefits.

Also keep in mind that public schools are not specifically profit-driven and can therefore fall prey to many of the ills that affect any state-administered institution, such as a large amount of bureaucracy. This of course does not mean you should avoid public institutions. Just be prepared to research as much as possible and be your own best advocate when seeking assistance and help. If you have sent an e-mail or called an advisor at the school and have not received a response, ask to speak to a supervisor and let your concerns be known that you are not receiving the assistance you require.

Private Schools

Private schools do not receive funding from state or local government. They are financially supported by tuition costs, donations, and endowments. They may be nonprofit or for-profit in nature, traditional, or nontraditional. Private schools usually charge students the same price whether they are in-state or out-of-state residents. The cost of private school tuition is often more than resident tuition at a state school, but not always. Many private schools offer scholarships and grants to greatly reduce the tuition costs. Usually, private schools have smaller class sizes than public schools, which can mean greater access to your professor. But, since they are typically smaller than state schools, they often offer a smaller variety of degrees to declare as a major when compared to a public university. Private-school acceptance may be less competitive than state acceptance, but not in top-tier or Ivy League institutions. Some private schools have religious affiliations, are historically black or Hispanic-serving institutions, or are single-sex institutions.

Think about the tuition costs of a private university similarly to the sticker price when buying a car. Unlike public schools, which are required by the state government to charge a specific price, high prices at private schools can sometimes be overcome. Sometimes schools offer students who might not otherwise be able to afford the tuition an institution-based scholarship in order to secure a particular student's acceptance. Typically, these are not traditional scholarships, but they enable private schools to reduce the amount of financial burden on an individual through in-house benefits. Veterans are an often sought-after population by institutions of higher learning, so consider speaking with an admissions counselor at a school before you rule it out based on the cost being above the Post-9/11 GI Bill allowable amount. The amount of tuition paid by a student can vary greatly, but the cost of college is also exploding. Talk to the counselors and the financial aid department during the process, it may save you thousands of dollars in the long run.

For-Profit Institutions

The difference between for-profit and not-for-profit is in the title. For-profit schools are operated by businesses, are revenue-based, and have to account for profits and losses. According to a recent government report on for-profit schools, the "financial performance of these companies is closely tracked by analysts and by investors"; this means that the bottom line is always revenue.[1] For-profit schools typically have open enrollment. Open enrollment can be helpful when you are transitioning from the military and have many other urgent needs at the same time. Open enrollment means that everyone gains entry to the school. That may prove disastrous for an individual who is not ready for the demands of higher education, but if the student is well prepared, it might provide a good pathway.

If you are looking for ease in the transition process and flexible class start dates, for-profit schools can offer you that benefit. Usually, they have classes starting every eight weeks, or the first Monday of every month, with rolling start dates.

Be informed when choosing your school. The College Board reported average costs of published state-school tuition and fees for 2014 at $9,139, and average private-school tuition and fees at $31,231.[2]

For-profit institutions have come under fire recently by Congress for several different concerns, including their intake of Federal Student Aid (FSA) and GI Bill money. If you would like more information on these concerns, see these three websites:

1. https://www.insidehighered.com/news/2012/07/30/harkin-releases-critical-report-profits
2. http://www.gpo.gov/fdsys/pkg/CPRT-112SPRT74931/pdf/CPRT-112SPRT74931.pdf
3. https://www.sandiego.edu/veteransclinic/index.php

Veterans should be concerned about private-school cost because the average cost for 2014 was significantly higher than the current Post-9/11 payout of $20,235.02 for the academic year 2014–2015 (the school year 2015–2016 has the Post-9/11 GI Bill private school rate set at $21,084.89). If you decide on a private school that charges tuition and fees above and beyond the Post-9/11 payout amount, check to see if the school is participating in the Yellow Ribbon Program (YRP). The YRP, which is explained in-depth in the "Cost and Payment Resources" chapter (chapter 7), may help you close the tuition gap.

Not-for-Profit Institutions

According to the National Association of Independent Colleges and Universities, "private, not-for-profit higher education institutions' purposes are to offer diverse, affordable, personal, involved, flexible, and successful educations to their students."[3]

Not-for-profit private schools sometimes offer flexible admissions for veterans that many state institutions cannot. Offering flexible admissions to veterans is a school-specific benefit, and veterans should address that option with their preferred institution.

Private, not-for-profit schools can have tremendous name recognition, such as Harvard and Yale University. On a smaller scale, many private, not-for-profit colleges and universities are well known within our own communities. For example, in my (Jillian's) hometown of Chicago, three well-known private, not-for-profit schools are DePaul University, Loyola University, and Columbia College. Each of these schools enjoys an excellent reputation, has a comprehensive veterans' department, and is well known throughout the Midwest.

Attending this type of school is typically a safe pathway, especially when listing your school on a résumé. Be aware that private schools can be very expensive, and the cost can sometimes be prohibitive. For example, DePaul is roughly $35,700 (http://offices.depaul.edu/student-financial-accounts/cost-of-attendance/tuition/Pages/tuition-2015---2016.aspx) per academic year.

The good news is that many private schools also participate in the YRP. For example, DePaul participates with unlimited spots and $12,500. As you will read in chapter 7, which addresses the YRP, this means the VA matches that amount, and you end up with an extra $25,000 on top of your private school maximum allowable rate of $21,084.89 (school year 2015–2016) under Post-9/11. Basically, your tuition is covered. Make sure to determine whether the school is participating in the YRP and in what manner before committing to attend.

Vocational-Technical and Career Colleges

Vocational-technical (votech) schools and career colleges prepare students for skill-based careers in technical fields. Many technical schools are state run, subsidized, and regionally accredited. Credits from these schools are generally accepted elsewhere. Career colleges are private, usually for-profit institutions, and they mostly hold national accreditation. Credits from these schools may not be widely transferable.

Programs at these schools can run anywhere from ten months to four years, depending on the skills required to finish training. Many have rolling admissions. Programs often run year-round, including the summers, in order to get students into the workforce faster.

Typically, in a votech-based program, general education classes such as English and math are not necessary. Program completion results in a certificate of completion or an associate degree in applied science. The associate in applied science will require entry-level math and English classes. Votech schools focus directly on the task at hand, meaning training in a need-based skill and preparing students for a career.

If you have decided to take a votech pathway, research the school's cost, credentials, faculty, program requirements, and student body prior to committing to a specific institution. Cost is important: the GI Bill has a set maximum amount it will pay for private school. Find out whether you will also be eligible to apply for FSA, but remember: you are mainly interested in the Pell Grant. You can find more information regarding student aid in the "Cost and Payment Resources" chapter (chapter 7).

Determine whether the school is licensed by the state and which accreditation it holds. If the program requires licensing by the state, but the school does not have the proper licensing agreement, you might not be able to sit for the state exam. Why go through a program that does not allow you full completion and credentialing? That could translate to a lower-paying job, or the inability to get hired in your field.

Ask about the professors' backgrounds and qualifications. Find out if you will be able to apply any military credit toward the program and if the program includes on-the-job training or internship possibilities. Visit the campus to determine what type of equipment you will be trained on and review the faculty setting. Check the school's completion rates, meaning how many students graduate and whether they graduate on time. Last, verify that the school offers job placement services. Find out the following:

- What is its rate of placement?
- Where are students being placed?
- What positions are they getting right out of school?
- How much money are they earning?

Usually, a phone call and follow-up school visit are required to fully understand the program benefits. Remember that vocational fields prepare students for specific career pathways, so transitioning later to a different pathway will require retraining.

Votech schools usually hold national accreditation. In the accreditation portion of this chapter, I (Jillian) explained the difference between regional and national accreditation. Nationally accredited programs' credits usually cannot transfer into a regionally accredited school, although some exceptions exist at schools that hold dual accreditation. For this reason, always check the local community college for similar programs. Many community colleges offer vocational programs that can be converted later to transferable college credit.

ACCREDITATION

Accreditation is an often overlooked topic that service members need to consider prior to making a final selection on an institution of higher learning. Most service members I counsel are not aware of the different types of accreditation that schools may hold, but should take the time to research the topic. Selecting a school with the wrong type may cause an airman significant backtracking at a later date.

The United States does not have a formal federal authority that oversees higher education. Each individual state exercises some level of regulation, but generally speaking, colleges and universities have the ability to self-govern. Accrediting organizations were born to supervise and guide institutions of higher learning in order to assure students that they were receiving valuable education. The organizations develop and maintain specific standards for participating schools that hold the institutions accountable for the quality of education they are delivering. The standards, "address key areas such as faculty, student support services, finance and facilities, curricula and student learning outcomes."[4]

Accredited schools participate in accreditation voluntarily and must adhere to the accrediting bodies' standards. Having accreditation is like having quality control for higher education, and when searching for schools, it should be an important factor to consider. Students who attend accredited universities and colleges have a greater chance of receiving a quality education and gaining credit for their degrees. If a school does not hold accreditation, you will most likely not be able to apply for federal or state-based financial aid. Credit hours earned from nonaccredited schools will not usually transfer into accredited institutions and will not be recognized for entrance into most master's degree programs. Those who need to pass licensure examinations for certain professional fields might not be allowed to sit for the exams if they attended nonaccredited institutions. You also run the risk of any potential future employers not accepting your degree. Ultimately, attending an accredited institution means that "a student can have confidence that a degree or credential has value."[5]

Education is an investment. Be an informed consumer before making a decision. Also, be careful when conducting research with schools. Not every institution is as it appears. Speaking with an academic counselor on an AF base will help you make solid decisions regarding your educational pursuits. AF academic counselors work for the AF, not one particular school. This way you can be sure you will receive fair and unbiased assistance in selecting a school.

Typically, students need to look for institutional accreditation and possibly programmatic accreditation. Institutional accreditation means that the college or university as a whole is accredited. This enables the entire school to maintain credibility as a higher learning institution. Only regional or national accrediting agencies can give institutional accreditation.

The degree you choose will dictate the type of accreditation you will need. Degrees that are traditional in nature require regional accreditation. Degrees that are nontraditional in nature might, but might not, require national accreditation. Traditional in nature degrees encompass such topics as education, engineering, business, anthropology, and criminal justice. Nontraditional education encompasses subjects that are more vocational in nature, such as welding and electrical work.

Every single state school (state community colleges, state colleges, and state universities) in this country holds regional accreditation. The Post-9/11 GI Bill is used most effectively at a state school. New legislation was passed in 2014, The Veterans Access, Choice and Accountability Act (https://veterans.house.gov/the-veterans-access-choice-and-accountability-act-of-2014-highlights), which enables veterans who attend any state institution that accepts the GI Bill to receive the in-state tuition rate as long as they are using their GI Bill for payment and enter the institution within three years of separation from the service. This means that if you attend a state school and finish your degree in the allotted thirty-six months, nine months per year over the course of four years, you will not pay a dime for tuition. Free school—what's better than that? Do not panic if you are intending to pursue a private school or if you are intending to pursue a degree that will require more than four years to finish, as other options do exist.

Regional accreditation is the most widely recognized and transferable (credit hours) accreditation in this country. There are six regional accrediting bodies in the United States. The accrediting bodies are based on the region of the country:

- Middle States Association of Colleges and Schools (MSCHE): http://www.msche.org/
- New England Association of School and Colleges Commission on Institutions of Higher Education (NEASC): http://cihe.neasc.org/
- Higher Learning Commission (HLC): https://www.hlcommission.org/
- Northwest Commission on Colleges and Universities (NWCCU): http://www.nwccu.org/
- Southern Association of Colleges and Schools Commission on Colleges (SACSCOC): http://www.sacscoc.org/
- Western Association of Schools and Colleges (WASC): http://www.wascweb.org/

Regional accrediting organizations review schools in their entirety. Both public and private and two- and four-year schools can be reviewed. Holding regional accreditation should allow credits to transfer smoothly between different member schools depending upon the established transfer criteria at the receiving institution. Remember: ultimately, the college or university you are trying to transfer into has a final say on credit transferability.

Schools that hold national accreditation typically offer educational pathways that are more vocational (nontraditional) in nature. This type of education might lead to a completed apprenticeship program or certification. Vocational education is a means of training future workers with skills more directly relevant to the evolving needs of the workforce. These types of career fields are more hands-on and technical in nature. Many nationally accredited schools can offer students successful pathways to promising careers. The programs are designed to get students into the workforce as soon as possible, and can usually be completed in two years or less, significantly faster than a four-year bachelor's degree.

Students do not need to attend a nationally accredited institution to receive vocational training. Many local state community colleges offer nontraditional education and often have apprenticeship or on-the-job training programs offered in addition to the educational classes. This might be a better pathway if you are unsure of your future career demands. Credits from a state community college are more widely transferable than credits from a nationally accredited institution because they hold regional accreditation.

There are available options for airmen interested in vocational/technical degrees. For example, if a recruit wants to be a welder, he or she has several attractive options available through the Air Force. By attending the structural apprentice technical training course, students learn various aspects of professional welding including metals layout and fabrication, oxyacetylene welding, metallic arc welding, and inert gas welding. Students earn fourteen SHs from the initial course, ten additional hours from the qualification I course, and five more hours with the qualification II course. This credit, coupled with the CCAF Internship, can accelerate the completion of the associate in applied science degree in metals technology from the CCAF.

If an airman elects not to complete the degree but still wants to pursue a certification, he or she has several more options available through Air Force Credentialing Opportunities Online. As of June 2015, six welding-related certifications are available ranging from the entry-level Certified Welder certification to the advanced Certified Welding Inspector certification. Funding for the exams is provided through AFCOOL.

Airmen in the Air National Guard and Air Force Reserve may choose to attend a state community college for a program, enabling them to have more flexibility at a later date if they decided to pursue further education. For example, if he completed a certificate program in welding at a state community college he would retain a greater chance of transferring those credits toward an associate degree in welding at a later date.

Sometimes, institutional accreditation is insufficient and programmatic accreditation is also necessary. Programmatic accreditation is specific to a department within an institution, and is often needed for certain degrees above and beyond the institutional accreditation, such as nursing, business, and engineering. Programmatic accrediting organizations focus on specific courses of study offered at a college or university. Attending a program that maintains programmatic accreditation can help your degree be more effective (as in getting you a job!) or make earned credit hours more transferable. If you are not sure whether your degree requires programmatic accreditation, search CHEA's website: (http://www.chea.org/Directories/special.asp) for further information.

Choosing a school with the right type of accreditation is important. Credits from a regionally accredited institution usually transfer into a nationally accredited institution, but credits from a nationally accredited institution almost never transfer into a regionally accredited institution. The exception would be if a student was transferring into an institution with dual accreditation, but there are very few in the country. This means that a rigorous search for qualifying information must be made in order to determine the proper academic pathway for an airman's selected career.

In these cases, looking at programmatic or specialized accreditation may be more important than institutional accreditation, or in other words, regional or national accreditation. For example, programs such as diagnostic medical sonography and radiologic technologist require specific programmatic accreditation. Attending an institution that has the correct programmatic accreditation, such as through the Commission on Accreditation of Allied Health Education Programs and the Joint Review Committee on Education in Radiologic Technology for the programs listed above, might be more important than attending an institution that has the most transferable credits. It would depend upon your future career demands. If you do not foresee yourself continuing on for an advanced degree in the field you are pursuing or in a different field altogether, then gaining the most transferable college credits might not be your goal. But, it is very hard to see many years into the future. For me, making the safest decision possible would hopefully eliminate problems in potential future demands for schooling based upon unforeseeable changes in career fields.

To search for a specific school's accreditation or a particular program of interest, go online (at http://www.chea.org/search/default.asp) and agree to the search terms. You can also complete a search of the national accrediting agencies that the U.S. Department of Education considers reliable (go to http://ope.ed.gov/accreditation/) or on College Navigator (http://nces.ed.gov/collegenavigator/).

ADMISSIONS REQUIREMENTS

Admissions requirements at each school will vary depending upon the type of school, specific degree requirements, and the school's ability to offer flexibility to service members. Some, such as community colleges and many vocational schools, maintain open admissions. Others, mainly four-year institutions of higher learning (universities), have a predetermined set of admissions qualifications that can be quite rigorous. This section will discuss the possible requirements for admission into colleges and vocational schools.

State-based Community and Technical Schools

Entrance into the local community or technical college is typically much less stressful than entrance into the four-year universities. Attending community college is a great way to get started with school for those who have little or no time to prepare the required documents or manage application deadlines. This is a beneficial option for service members who often have little time between returning from deployments and transitioning off active duty. Community colleges also do not have the same rigorous admissions requirements that universities demand from potential students. This allows students who lost their time to prepare due to mission demands to still get going on their educations without a delay.

State-based community and technical colleges may offer or require the following:

- Open admissions
- Acceptance, in most cases with or without a high-school diploma or GED
- Early registration for active duty and veterans
- An application fee
- Registration deadlines
- Special entrance criteria (prerequisite classes) and a waiting list for start times in specific, high-demand impacted programs (too many applicants and not enough available open spots)
- English and math placement tests to determine proper level placement
- Admissions application, typically online, that only takes a few minutes
- Supporting documents—for example, high-school transcripts, military transcripts, and proof of residency
- Proof of immunizations

Four-Year Colleges and Universities

Four-year institutions of higher learning usually have selective admissions with application requirements and deadlines. Be sure to read the section on the Air University Associate to Baccalaureate Cooperative and General Education Mobile in chapter 5 in conjunction with this section as the information offered might assist you with this process. Some may offer veterans flexible admissions, but, in most cases, veterans will follow the same pathway as civilians. A written timetable of deadlines for all materials can be obtained by contacting the school and checking the admissions sections of the website. Be prepared to spend a fair amount of time preparing.

College and university admissions may require the following:

- An application (in most cases, this can be done online)
- Application fees
- ACT and SAT test scores (see the "SAT and ACT Study Help" section in this chapter)
- Essays
- Letters of recommendation
- A college pathway in high school, meeting minimum subject requirements

- High-school and college transcripts
- Minimum high-school GPA
- Minimum high-school class rank
- Demonstration of community service; military service may fulfill this requirement
- Proof of immunizations

Vocational-Technical and Career Colleges

Depending upon the program to which a student is applying within the school, admission requirements may vary. In certain fields, such as nursing, entrance exams may be mandatory. Exams can include physical fitness tests, basic skills exams, and Health Education Systems, Inc. (HESI) entrance exams.

It is always better to research carefully the career pathway and determine whether the certification or license from a career college is valid. Oftentimes states have mandatory requirements pertaining to the fields of education taught at a technical school, and students need to verify that the school meets these standards. For this, refer to the state government website; many have a state-approved program list right on-site.

Typically, admissions are open with a few minimum requirements, such as the following:

- High-school transcript and diploma or GED
- Completed admissions forms
- An interview
- Statement of general health
- Any mandatory subject-specific exams

THE ADMISSION PROCESS

Most schools generally follow the same admission process even though the requirements can differ drastically from school to school. Whether a student is an incoming freshman, a transfer student, or an applicant to a vocational school, the pathway to gain admittance will follow the same route, but it may vary in difficulty. Prospective students at schools with an open-enrollment policy will normally have a less intensive pathway to admittance. Students pursuing schools with selective admissions will spend more time preparing.

The student follows a typical pathway:

1. Pick a school or schools, call the veterans' representatives, discuss admissions requirements, and decide on an institution
2. Apply (usually online)
3. Receive acceptance
4. Apply for tuition assistance (TA), the GI Bill, or FSA and register for classes (choose classes based on a degree plan)

Pick a School

The students should contact the veterans' representatives to initially get an idea of a school's perspective toward its veteran students. The vet reps have been there, done that already. If there are any tricks to gaining admission, they will know. Also, it enables the student to identify himself or herself as a veteran, active duty, or military spouse. The admission's pathway, cost, and required documents may be different from those for the civilian population, and the vet reps will be able to guide the students in their quest for the appropriate resources.

Students should request pertinent information, either paper-based or online resources. It is good to have all relevant information, including application and registration deadlines, financial aid time lines, class start dates, dorm-based information (if applicable) or in-town housing options, and who will be the point-of-contact for GI Bill concerns and Certificate of Eligibility (COE). This topic is covered in depth in the "Cost and Payment Resources" chapter (chapter 7).

Contacting the veterans' department of the school of choice should be a top priority. Difficulty in reaching representatives is not a good sign. The veterans' department at the school is the student's support system. If it is not possible to find anyone prior to attending the institution, how difficult will it be to find a rep later after admission? Check the Comparison Tool on the VA website (http://department-of-veterans-affairs.github.io/gi-bill-comparison-tool/) to know how many individuals have used GI Bill benefits at that school. A high number may be either a good or a bad sign. Schools with high numbers demonstrate that they are familiar with the process, but may be overworked. Consider the goals and the need to receive answers.

The Federal Trade Commission recommends questions for service members (and civilians) to ask schools before making a final decision. More information on these questions can be found here: http://www.consumer.ftc.gov/articles/0395-choosing-college-questions-ask#servicemembers.

Apply

Once research is completed and a particular school or schools has been selected, it is now time to apply. Verify with the vet reps whether the application fee needs to be paid; many schools waive the fee for active duty and veterans.

Check the school's website prior to applying. In most cases, schools have an application checklist on their admissions page. This should help in preparing all relevant documents such as transcript from the CCAF, DD214, personal statement, SAT or ACT scores, or immunization records in advance.

Oftentimes, the application checklist for a four-year college or university does not list a personal statement, but later the school might surprisingly request one. Personal statement length requirements range from 350 to 3,000 words. Some institutions list very specific essay prompts they want to follow instead of writing a generic personal statement.

Writing a personal statement should not be nerve racking, although many service members feel tremendous stress during the experience, most just trying to find a starting point. Once it is started, the veterans will find the experience to be a good precursor for their new college life. College does require a fair amount of writing. Additionally, remember that every veteran will have very unique experiences that the typical applicant will not have. Try to impress on the school how these unique experiences will help make the school a better place on admission. Most schools would be lucky to have an airmen as a student with a real working knowledge of what it is like to be an adult who has lived past the age of eighteen and endured the rigorous demands of work.

Here are a few steps to guide the veterans or airmen to write a personal essay.

Step 1

If you are having trouble starting, try brainstorming. I recommend sticking to topics around your military experience. Think about your time in the service and the accomplishments you achieved. Consider the following topics:

- Why did you join the Air Force?
- What do you do in the Air Force?
- Be prepared to illustrate the accredited and highly specialized technical training, including special duties such as recruiter school.
- Where were you assigned and how did you to put that training to use? Did you go anywhere interesting to conduct that training such as an overseas deployment?

- Have you visited interesting cities for training or deployment? Where? What did you do while deployed?
- Did you deploy to a war zone? How did it make you feel?
- Did you meet people from other countries on deployment or overseas assignment? What were the cultural differences?
- Did you deploy with other branches? What was that experience like?
- Did your deployments or combat experiences help shape the decisions you are making now? Is that why you are pursuing higher education?

Keep in mind that you are talking to a board of civilians who may not share the same experiences as the typical student. Explain what it meant to be a highly skilled Air Force technician, supervisor and problem solver. What did it mean to lead others in life and death situations and live with the consequences? Relate to your experiences as a human being tasked with these responsibilities. Do not underestimate the value of your life as an airman. Many people who have never served in the military may not be able to relate to the level of responsibility unless you can explain it well.

Step 2

Next, typically you can pick a subject and narrow the talking points. Sometimes it helps to brainstorm topics on paper that interest you to see if subjects overlap. Many airmen feel that they do not do anything exciting in the military, which is definitely not true. Everything service members do is exciting to civilians. Where else can you see these types of activities? Maybe it is all in a day's work for you, but civilians find it fascinating.

Step 3

Once you settle on a topic, write it down on a piece of paper. Think about the topic, and write brief statements about everything that comes to your mind surrounding it. For example: I joined the Air Force after I graduated high school because I come from a military family.

- Work
- Training
- Adventure
- Education
- Patriotism
- Security
- The War

Once you have drawn up a list, you need to add more layers to discuss. Here is an example:

- Work: productive suffering, meaningful work equals personal satisfaction, physical work, community environment
- Timing: graduated high school or college, came of age, rite of passage
- Patriotism: American flags, pledge of allegiance, 9/11 firefighters, serve my country, family military history, higher calling
- Security: airports, military bases, national events, worldwide, job security, pay, career
- Deployment to combat zone, serve my country, combat veteran, benefits, test of strength and willpower, face the unknown, perseverance

Step 4

Think about the notes you have written. Narrow your subject or topic by eliminating areas that don't seem to fit. For example, I (Jillian) don't think the section on security follows the theme of the other topics. When I review each section, it seems that I joined the military after high-school graduation because it is a rite of passage that occurs in my family. The Air Force taught me good work values and community involvement. I was able to participate in the defense of my country, which bolstered my perseverance to succeed. Somehow, the security section does not seem to fit with the rest, so I am eliminating it.

Step 5

- Organize your thoughts in a good writing order, and start to think about expanding the topics into a paper format.
- Patriotism: American flags, pledge of allegiance, 9/11 firefighters, serve my country, family military history, higher calling
- Timing: graduated high school or college, came of age, rite of passage
- Work: productive suffering, meaningful work equals personal satisfaction, physical work, community environment for the greater good
- The War: participate, serve my country, benefits, test of strength and willpower, face the unknown, perseverance

Now you need to determine why this experience shaped your current perspectives on education and organize the thoughts you listed in a logical written order. You should also start thinking about your career goals, your character strengths, and why you have chosen this particular institution. Below, I have labeled each group in the order I feel it belongs to be able to write an effective personal statement.

- Patriotism: American flags, pledge of allegiance, 9/11 firefighters, serve my country, family military history, higher calling (2)
- Timing: graduated high school or college, came of age, rite of passage (1)
- Work: productive suffering, meaningful work equals personal satisfaction, physical work, community environment for the greater good (3)
- The War: participate, serve my country, benefits, test of strength and will-power, face the unknown, perseverance (4)

Before you begin to write your essay, you need to consider your audience. Here are a few questions to consider while writing:

- Who will read this essay?
- What does the reader already know about this subject, and why is it important?
- What do I want the reader to know about this subject?
- What part of my topic is the most interesting?

Your reader could be a dean at the school, an academic counselor, a professor, or the like. Most likely, this individual has no knowledge of your topic if you write about a particular military experience, but do not discount the fact that he could also be a veteran. You need to explain why this experience shaped your decisions moving forward. You want him or her to see you in a different light than other applicants. You want your essay to stand apart and be more memorable than all of the others. Make sure to pick a topic that you can write about easily and that will attract interest.

Essay Example

After graduating high school in June of 2004, I enlisted in the U.S. Air Force. After watching the terrorist attacks on New York on September 11, 2001, I knew I could not ignore the pull I felt to participate in the effort my country was making. I also come from a long line of service members, and following in their footsteps seemed a natural thing to do.

On completion of my Air Force technical training in aviation maintenance technology, I was assigned to Nellis Air Force Base to work on the F-16 Falcon fighter aircraft. Working on the world's most technologically advanced aircraft with airmen who were considered masters in their field was prestigious and exciting. I learned to work in a team environment, be detailed orientated, and be highly efficient with the resources allotted to me. Within this training environment, I learned how to respond during high-stress situations and mastered my responsibilities.

Both Iraq and Afghanistan were combat-laden hotspots at this time, and I was soon sent to Iraq to assist with the mission. The year-long deployment to Iraq shaped my perspective on hard work and dedication to the mission. I knew that if I did not fulfill my responsibilities my mission and fellow airmen would suffer. The preparation and training we went through as a group prior to deploying paid off when we needed it most.

Iraq was a meaningful experience for me. It taught me to consider my actions as an integral player in the overall mission, regardless of my own personal considerations, because I had signed my name on the dotted line and had agreed to this position. Although I love the Air Force, I am ready to pursue the second chapter of my life, a bachelor's degree in electronic engineering. Using the hands-on skills I learned repairing aircraft will enhance my education and diversify the classroom learning environment. My time in the service taught me what it takes to succeed, teamwork and willpower, and I am willing to share my work ethics with those around me.

I chose to attend XYZ University because of its reputation as a leader in the field of community involvement and its excellent electronic engineering program. The university offers a holistic approach to the education of its students, and I feel my background will be respected and put to use to increase the effort and learning of my peers. The university's Veterans' Center offers numerous services to assist me should I need anything and offers many opportunities for veteran interaction. I hope that XYZ University will take the time to consider me as a prospective freshman student. If selected for admission, I know that working together with my professors, we can make the classroom a more productive and challenging place for learning.

After writing the essay, please contact CCAF to send the official transcripts to the school immediately. Although many schools will take these at a later date, the earlier it is submitted, the faster the application process.

Apply for FSA (see chapter 7, "Cost and Payment Resources"). If applying to multiple schools, say, list all of them on the federal aid application. This might lead to federal money for education expenses that does not need to be paid back!

Receive Acceptance

Most open enrollment schools quickly offer official acceptance. Schools with selective admissions often send official acceptance after many months. Check the school's website for reporting dates, or ask the veteran representatives. I have found a few schools with selective admissions that are able to give almost immediate acceptance or denial to veterans—for example, DePaul University in Chicago and Robert Morris University in Pittsburgh.

In most cases, the acceptance letter or the student account website will give information on the next steps to complete. These steps may include payment of fees for a spot in the school or for on-campus housing. This is typical for face-to-face schooling. Most active-duty service members pursuing school will not face these extra fees. Determine the final date for reimbursement of these fees as this will help when choosing another school at the last minute. This way, it is not possible to lose the money.

Apply for Tuition Assistance, GI Bill, or Federal Student Aid

After receiving school acceptance letters and after deciding on an institution, it is now time to activate the GI Bill or apply for TA to pay for the schooling. If the airmen or veteran is still on active duty, then contact the local education center to enquire about TA. However, if separated, or soon will be, it is time to activate the GI Bill. If eligible for both MGIB and Post-9/11, the "Cost and Payment Resources" chapter will help in deciding which one to choose. The veterans' representatives at the school of choice should be able to help as well, but many schools will naturally prefer the Post-9/11 because the school is paid directly. Be sure to consider the cost–benefit analysis of attending any particular school, since the Post-9/11 is not always the best entitlement to use. The section in chapter 7 titled "Activating Your GI Bill" will explain how to get the benefit started.

If veterans or airmen have a state-based benefit that pertains to their specific situation, then they may need a bit more one-on-one help to determine the best pathway. Review carefully the explanation in chapter 7 of the benefits available before committing to either federal GI Bill. In some states, veterans can bring in more money by double-dipping on state-based educational benefits and MGIB than those strictly under Post-9/11. Again, if it is not possible to decipher the best pathway, contact the veteran representatives at the school of choice for advice on what other veterans have chosen. Never guess about the benefits: it is possible to miss out on hundreds of dollars every month.

Now is the time to apply for the FSA. Remember, TA and the GI Bills only go so far. TA does not cover books, computers, or tools, and it is capped at $250 per semester credit hour. FSA money can help bridge any gaps.

Register for Classes

Next step is to meet with an academic counselor in order to choose the appropriate classes for the degree. If attending school online, oftentimes the academic counselor will e-mail a degree plan on request. The degree plan lists every class that has to be taken to attain the declared degree or certification.

Typically, degree plans will also reflect any credits the school applies to the degree program based on the information provided in the transcript from CCAF. Most schools will not inform the student of the evaluation outcome until the end of the second class, so more guidance may be needed from an academic counselor prior to class selection for the first term. Starting with general education subjects is a safe route since most of the time military credits only knockout elective credits. General education subjects in a traditional degree pathway are always necessary and outside of using College Level Examination Program (CLEP) exams, these classes must be taken.

Always be aware of the registration deadlines. Check with the school to see if the institution offers early registration for active duty or veterans. This is an especially crucial step for veterans using their GI Bills. The VA will only cover classes listed on the degree plan (just like TA). Early registration allows veterans to pick classes before the civilian population. Every class should be open. If these deadlines are missed, there may be trouble getting into the classes that are needed to maintain full-time status according to the VA (full-time status = full-time housing allowance on Post-9/11). If the final deadline is missed, it is possible to lose the spot at the school.

Veterans will most likely need to produce a copy of their DD214 to the veterans' department at the school to prove benefit eligibility. It is a good idea always to keep a copy on hand along with the student identification number. Active duty may need a copy of their orders to be on the base where they are currently stationed. Oftentimes, the local community college will want to see a copy of these orders in order to grant the service member instate tuition. Spouses may need a copy of the orders as well as their dependent identification card in order to receive the instate tuition rate. The spouse should have access to a copy of the orders just in case the veteran is deployed. Spouses using transferred Post-9/11 benefits should keep a copy of the service members' DD214 if they have already separated.

Previous school transcripts have to be sent to the new institution for evaluation. In most cases, the transcripts go from the old school directly to the new one in order to remain official. It is usually a smart idea to have a couple of spare sets of transcripts on hand. Once a transcript is opened, it is no longer considered official, so order an extra one. Take a copy of the transcript when meeting with the academic counselor. They will guide the class selections prior to evaluation of the official transcripts. No point in taking a class that has already been taken!

When the students are ready to matriculate, at a community college, it might become necessary to take the math and English placement tests to determine the starting point for these two classes. If the student scores below college freshman level, the school will place him or her in remedial classes. This is not a big deal, but it can slow the student's progress. These classes will help boost the baseline skill level and help the student to be more successful in future classes. To boost the math and English skills prior to taking the placement test, see http://www.petersons.com/DOD and click on the "Online Academic Skills Course (OASC)" link. The same Peterson's website also hosts the College Placement Skills Testing (CPST) program, which was designed to help students score better on college placement tests. Testing into freshman-level math and English helps the student to avoid remedial coursework. Matriculation usually requires an orientation session. Some schools offer the orientation in an online format; others require the students to physically attend classes. The academic counselor will inform the student when the paperwork has been processed and the official degree plan is on file. The student has now matriculated.

All of the initial hard work to start school is done at this point. Now is the best time to prepare for everything else. A veteran may need housing. Again, check with the vet reps for recommendations. Some service members find roommates through the vet reps, the Facebook page for veterans attending the school, or the student veterans' associations.

Start by checking out all of the veteran services offered on the school campus or in the surrounding areas. Knowing where the services are located may save heartache and time later on. Some of the services offer outreach; some might be strictly for socialization or networking. Take advantage of both.

If a veteran has served in a combat zone, find the closest VA Vet Center at http://www.va.gov/directory/guide/vetcenter_flsh.asp. The Vet Centers may offer eligible veterans counseling, outreach, and referral services to help with postwar readjustment to civilian life. Research the VA service at http://www. vetcenter.va.gov/index.asp.

Student veteran organizations that are school specific operate on many campuses. Usually, their information can be found on the school's website. Student Veterans of America (http://www.studentveterans.org/) connects veterans through social media outlets to offer support and promote student vet success. Participating in an organization can help veterans integrate into their local veteran community. Veterans who seek out other veterans typically have higher success rates. Veterans who isolate themselves may have difficulty transitioning.

SAT/ACT

Depending on the school, an ACT (www.act.org) or SAT (www.collegeboard.org) score may be necessary for acceptance. Many schools offer veterans flexible admissions by bypassing these exams and accepting writing samples and/or placement tests instead. To determine individual requirements, call the veterans' representatives at the school. Typically, a quick call can supply you with all the required application materials.

If the school requires an ACT or SAT score, develop a plan of attack. Application deadline dates, test dates, and study resources need to be located. To find the required application dates, check the school's website and contact the vet reps. In some cases, schools can accept scores for veterans at a later date. Many institutions are aware that service members often have a difficult time testing while on active duty because of mission demands.

Test dates can be tricky. ACT and SAT tests are only offered on specific dates on Air Force bases. Airmen need to book an appointment through their education centers and clear the time with their supervisor. Make sure to leave plenty of time to prepare appropriately. If possible, SAT and ACT exams should not be taken at a moment's notice.

Always check with a school to determine which test the institution accepts, then focus on that particular test for preparation. Some schools will take either; in that case, students may want to take both and submit their best score.

Defense Activity for Non-Traditional Education Support (DANTES) will pay for the SAT and ACT exam provided the member take the exam at their military education center. When testing at a base, list the school's name or leave it blank. If taking both the SAT and the ACT and submitting the top score, do not list the school's name on the test application. If listing the school's name, the scores will go directly to the institution. If *not* listing the school's name, the scores be sent from either organization later. Scores are always kept by the individual organization that administered the test, such as Collegeboard for the SAT scores. These can be found, and sent to the future school by finding the military score request form. It may require an additional fee.

If opting for sending scores to a school or schools during test registration either on the base or off-base, then the student will receive four free score reports for ACT and SAT. If deciding on waiting and sending the scores after determining the results, then each SAT request will cost $11.25 (http://sat.collegeboard.org/register/us-services-fees#) and each ACT request will cost $12 (http://www.actstudent.org/scores/send/costs.html). I recommend that you take both tests, wait until your scores are posted, and then pay to send whichever test produces the most competitive results.

If airmen are not satisfied with their scores, they may retest the ACT and SAT off-base during the next test date with no waiting period. On base, a six-month waiting period applies. Airmen receive one free test on the base while in the AF.

SAT and ACT scores are not returned immediately. Typically, when testing on a base, test scores take approximately eight to ten weeks to be delivered. However, scores can be viewed earlier on the SAT and ACT websites. ACT multiple-choice scores are typically reported within eight weeks (http://www.actstudent.org/scores/viewing-scores.html); essay scores, roughly two weeks later. SAT scores (http://sat.collegeboard.org/scores/availability) take approximately three weeks to be posted online.

SAT and ACT are not exactly the same test. The chart below demonstrates some of the differences. For more detailed explanations of the tests, visit the SAT and ACT websites. The biggest difference is that the SAT tests the ability to apply knowledge while the ACT tests the current level of knowledge on subjects.

Table 4.1 shows that the SAT does not test science, but the ACT does. Specific science knowledge is not necessary to take the ACT; it tests reading and reasoning skills. The SAT has a stronger emphasis on vocabulary, and the ACT tests higher-level math concepts than the SAT (trigonometry).

The optional essay on the ACT is not factored into the composite score. The essay is scored separately. The SAT essay is required and factored into the writing score.

The ACT keeps each subject area separate, whereas the SAT subject areas move back and forth. This may be difficult for some test takers.

Remember that free test preparation for military and dependents for both SAT and ACT can be found at http://www.petersons.com/dod. Khan Academy (http://www.khanacademy.org) has free test preparation help for the SAT math section. Check YouTube as well for more SAT and ACT videos.

Numerous test preparation companies offer classes, but no reimbursement is available for these options. These programs offer structured classroom

Table 4.1   SAT and ACT Comparison Chart

SAT	ACT
Test covers: reading, vocabulary, grammar and usage, writing, and math (includes essay) Three main components: critical reasoning, mathematics, an essay.	Test covers: grammar and usage, math, reading, science reasoning, and an optional writing section (check with school) Five main components- English, mathematics, reading, science, and an optional essay (check if school demands essay)
Test timeframe: 3 hours 45 minutes	Test timeframe: 3 hours 30 minutes (4 hours with essay)
Format: multiple choice and grid-in	Format: all multiple choice
Guessing penalty of a quarter-point	No guessing penalty
Measures student's ability to: draw inferences, synthesize information, understand the difference between main and supporting ideas, vocabulary in context, apply mathematical concepts, problem-solve, interpret charts, communicate ideas, revise and edit, understand grammatical structure.	Measures student's: written and rhetorical English, mathematical skills, reading comprehension, interpretation, analysis, reasoning, problem solving, writing skills stressed in high school and entry-level college classes
Scoring: Penalty for guessing. Maximum score 2400, each section is worth 800. Average score in 2012 was 1498, critical reading 496, mathematics 514, writing 488.	Scoring: ACT assessment only counts correct answers. Composite scores range from 1 to 36, sub scores from 1 to 18. The composite score is an average of the four subscores. National average in 2012 was 21.1

environments and curriculum that may help some service members, but classes do not emphasize an individual's strengths and weaknesses as a self-paced program would. Just remember that self-paced means self-motivated. The students need to organize their time and effort.

GRADUATE RECORD EXAMINATION (GRE)/GRADUATE MANAGEMENT ADMISSION TEST (GMAT)

For attending graduate school, the institution of choice might require a GRE or GMAT score. Always check with the school to determine which standardized admissions test is required for your graduate school program. Traditionally, the GRE is taken for most graduate degrees outside of business, and the GMAT is taken for business school. Only the university and college can tell you exactly which test the institution will demand, but taking the GRE might open more options.

Currently, the GRE costs $195 and the GMAT is $250. It is possible to receive reimbursement from DANTES for taking these tests. It is also possible to receive reimbursement through the GI Bill, but it will reduce the remaining benefits. If the veteran is still on active duty, it is best to go through DANTES and save all the education benefits.

In the past few years, the GRE has become more widely accepted for admissions to business schools, and many top-tier universities, including Yale, Harvard, and Georgetown, have jumped onboard. Princeton Review has a link that lists more than seven hundred schools currently accepting the GRE for business school (http://www.princetonreview.com/uploadedFiles/Sitemap/Home_Page/Business_Hub/Opinions_and_Advice/MBAAcceptingGRE.pdf). Try an initial search, and then cross-reference with the institutions that interest you. If the institution of choice accepts either, try taking a practice exam for each test first (check both websites). It is good to take practice tests as it might help in finding out the student's aptitude for one more than the other.

Free Test Preparation

- GRE: http://www.ets.org/s/gre/pdf/practice_book_GRE_pb_revised_general_test.pdf
- GMAT: http://www.mba.com/us/the-gmat-exam/prepare-for-the-gmat-exam/test-prep-materials/free-gmat-prep-software
- Georgetown University: http://www.youtube.com/watch?v=xFyqJSucqSo
- Other: http://www.khanacademy.org/ (SAT/GMAT math)

Reimbursement while on Active Duty

To receive reimbursement through DANTES for either the GRE or the GMAT, visit your local education center for the correct forms, or follow these steps:

1. Visit the following link and download the appropriate reimbursement form: http://www.dantes.doded.mil/_content/exams_reimbursement_form.pdf
2. Sign up to take the GRE or GMAT. The applicant is responsible for all testing fees upfront.
3. Receive official GRE or GMAT scores (about two weeks).
4. Fill out the appropriate forms and return them to the Education Center's Test Control officer within ninety days of testing.

Veterans' Reimbursement

Veteran's reimbursement is through the GI Bill, www.gibill.va.gov, or 1-888-GIBILL-1. The process differs for each test. Under the MGIB the cost of each test will be deducted from the over worth of the MGIB, which currently stands at $64,404 (as of October 1, 2015). Therefore, if the test costs $250, only $250 will be deducted from this amount. If working with the Post-9/11, the benefit is slightly less generous. For every test paid for, the student will lose one month of the benefit, even if the test costs $50. Visit http://www.benefits.va.gov/gibill/licensing_certification.asp for more information.

Chapter 5

Air Force-Based Education and Credentialing Programs

Since its inception, the United States Air Force (USAF) has recognized the positive effects of education on Air Force personnel. The USAF continually establishes and refines an array of programs to attract the highest caliber of recruit possible to meet the demands of a changing Air Force as well as the needs and desires of its personnel. Offering these unique and prestigious programs provides options for those looking to further their education. One of the most notable and prestigious programs is the Community College of the Air Force (CCAF). This chapter reviews the CCAF as well as the programs that fall within its parameters.

The following topics will be covered in this chapter:

- The CCAF
- Combat Wounded, Ill, and Injured Airmen (Wounded Warriors) and the CCAF
- Accreditation
- The CCAF System
- Education Services and Academic Policies
- Air University Associate to Baccalaureate Cooperative and General Education Mobile (GEM)
- Air Force Professional Credentialing and Certification Options
- Air Force Credentialing Opportunities Online (AFCOOL)

THE COMMUNITY COLLEGE OF THE AIR FORCE

Many consider the CCAF the pride of the Air Force enlisted airmen. The concept of the CCAF is unprecedented for an enlisted military force. While it is one of several federally chartered degree-granting institutions, it is the only two-year institution in the world exclusively serving and awarding regionally accredited degrees to enlisted personnel. Surveys conducted at basic military training demonstrate that 97 percent of airmen entering the Air Force desire an associate degree or higher degree. Moreover, education is consistently ranked as a primary reason airmen choose to join the Air Force. The CCAF is fulfilling this recruitment tool by offering regionally accredited associate in applied science degrees after students successfully complete a degree program designed for an Air Force specialty.

The Air Force takes pride in improving the capabilities of both its airmen and its mission through education. The CCAF has a dramatic impact on both. The oral communication (speech) requirement is a prime example. For example, in order to graduate from any CCAF program, all students are required to successfully conduct a formal speech class to satisfy an oral communication requirement. This terrifies many CCAF students because of their fear of public speaking. The majority of students will delay completing the speech requirement until the very end; however, the time and effort spent satisfying this requisite class is a good investment for all since students who take this class become more proficient in this skill area. Being adept at public communication is a definite benefit for their military careers and for the overall mission of the Air Force.

After every graduation, the CCAF conducts a student and supervisor survey to gauge effectiveness of the degree programs from the perspective of the graduates and the program supervisor. Students and supervisors consistently state that of all courses taken toward completion of their chosen degree, the speech class was the most beneficial. Data from the May 2014 report indicates that 68 percent of the graduates valued the oral communication more than any other course they had taken. Because of this, students may want to consider taking the required speech class earlier in their educational timeline. Data from the same survey demonstrated that 29 percent of the students proclaimed that the degree they earned from the CCAF made them the first person in their family to earn a college degree. This data mirrors previous survey results and affirms that an associate degree from the CCAF remains a remarkable catalyst for its intended purpose—deliberate development of enlisted airmen.

CCAF BACKGROUND AND HISTORY

The CCAF is a unique combination of on-duty and voluntary off-duty education with classes and times that offer flexibility in order to meet individual and mission needs. The college currently has 68 associate in applied science degree programs aligned to one of five career areas—aircraft and missile maintenance, electronics and telecommunications, allied health, logistics and resources, or public and support services. Air Force personnel earn some of the college credit applied toward these degrees simply by training and performing their respective jobs.

The impact the college has had on the Air Force is remarkable and the programs offered by the CCAF have seen a dramatic growth in popularity. In 2014, the CCAF had 23,157 total graduates; 64 percent more graduates compared to a decade ago. The percentage of active-duty Air Force personnel serving in 2004 with a degree from the CCAF was just over 17 percent. Currently, 31 percent of active-duty airmen have attained their degree, representing an increase of 13 percent in a ten-year period.

The certification programs offered through the CCAF are equally impressive. The college has awarded over 26,000 instructor certifications and over 14,000 professional manager certifications. More information pertaining to these types of programs can be found later in this chapter in the section titled "CCAF Specific Certifications."

CCAF Mission

"Offer and award job-related associate in applied science degrees and other academic credentials that enhance mission readiness, contribute to recruiting, assist in retention, and support the career transitions of Air Force enlisted members."[1]

CCAF Vision

"The community college of choice, providing a path to higher learning for those with a calling to serve."[2]

CCAF History

The CCAF concept evolved in the early 1970s as a means of gaining recognition for highly technical Air Force training. Led by General George B. Simler, Commander of Air Training Command, Air Force visionaries recognized the need to enhance the skills of noncommissioned officers as technicians, leaders, and citizens. Representatives of the Air Training Command, Air University, and the Air Force Academy held a series of conferences in

1971 to discuss the need for increased development of noncommissioned officers as managers of Air Force resources. The conferees recommended the founding of an Air Force community college and on November 9, 1971, General John D. Ryan, air force chief of staff, approved the establishment of the CCAF. The secretary of the Air Force approved the activation plan on January 25, 1972, and the college was established on April 1, 1972, at Randolph AFB, Texas.

http://www.au.af.mil/au/barnes/ccaf/about.asp

The college mailed its first official transcript on November 9, 1972, and issued its first credential, the Career Education Certificate, on August 23, 1973. As the college gained prestige, increasing numbers of enlisted service members registered and more Air Force technical, special and professional schools joined the CCAF system. As a result, 143 such schools have been affiliated (108 with current affiliation) with the college after meeting rigorous standards for participation. The SACS Commission on Occupational Education Institutions accredited the college on December 12, 1973.

By the mid-1970s, many civilian consultants were reporting that the CCAF standards exceeded the minimum requirements of associate degree programs in civilian community colleges and the Air Force sought degree-granting authority for the college from Congress. President Gerald R. Ford signed Public Law 94-361 on July 14, 1976, authorizing the ATC commander to confer the associate degree.

PATHWAY TO GAIN ADMISSIONS AND ENROLL

Admissions and Registration

When assigned to an Air Force career field, enlisted active-duty, Air National Guard (ANG) and Air Force Reserve (AFRC) members are automatically enrolled into the college and registered in the degree program designed for their Air Force specialty. Airmen are enrolled in the degree program free of charge after initial skills training and are considered active students at this point.

Active student status does not change until airmen graduate from their respective program, retrain into a different program or separate from service. Air Force members may also earn subsequent degrees in any other Air Force Specialty Codes (AFSCs) they hold if they complete the associated requirements within specific time frames.

Eligibility for Participation in CCAF Degree Programs

Air Force Instruction 36-2648 governs eligibility to participate in degree programs and certifications sponsored by the CCAF. In support of the spirit and intent of Title 10, U.S. Code, Section 9315, CCAF: Associate Degrees, and the stated purposes of the college as outlined in paragraph one of this instruction, eligibility to participate in CCAF degree programs is restricted to active-duty enlisted Air Force, ANG, Selected Reserve, and other service member CCAF instructors' teaching degree applicable courses. An eligible member of the Selected Reserve or the AFRC is defined as an individual in training pay category A, B, or D, who is a member of a unit and regularly participates in paid inactive duty training and annual training. Individuals must be in pay status. Active-duty ANG individuals must be in training or retention category A and receiving pay.

COMBAT WOUNDED, ILL, AND INJURED AIRMEN (WOUNDED WARRIORS) AND THE CCAF

The 2012 National Defense Authorization Act section 555 provided opportunities for our combat-related wounded warriors to participate in CCAF degree programs after separation or retirement. This legislation change amended Section 9315 of Title 10, United States Code, to expand the CCAF degree program eligibility to include former or retired enlisted members of the armed forces who at the time of the member's separation from active duty are categorized by the Service Secretary concerned as seriously wounded, ill, or injured as that term is defined in section 1602(8) of the Wounded Warrior Act. This change allows the Air Force to extend its commitment to these members into the postseparation period and meet its pledge to care for warriors who have sacrificed so much in the service of our country.

Eligible combat-related injured veterans are authorized to participate in CCAF programs for up to ten years after separation, provided they were enrolled in a CCAF program when they separated. This provision applies to members categorized in this manner after September 11, 2001; for those separated between September 12, 2001, and December 30, 2011, the ten-year commencement date will be December 30, 2011.

The Air Force uses the 9W-series Reporting Identifier to categorize combat-related wounded warriors. Members must have been actively enrolled in a CCAF associate degree program at the time of their separation to participate.

Academic counseling may be provided by local education services counselors, as available, or directly from the CCAF's education services staff.

This legislative change supports the Secretary of the Air Force's priority to ensure that the combat-related wounded warriors receive the services and support they need throughout the recovery process and also provides a transition into additional educational opportunities through the GI Bill or the VA's Vocational Rehabilitation program. In March 2015, the CCAF awarded associate degrees to its ninth wounded warrior.

Students who do not hold a 9W-series RI, but believe they qualify for combat-related wounded warrior status should contact the Air Force Wounded Warrior Program Office at: wounded.warrior@us.af.mil, toll-free 1-800-581-9437, or check the following website for more information: http://www.woundedwarrior.af.mil/. The Air Force Wounded Warrior Program personnel will determine status, effective date of status, if applicable, and update the appropriate personnel data and records.

ACCREDITATION

Accreditation adds validity to degree programs and benefits students by making credit transfer between institutions easier. The CCAF as part of the Air University system is accredited by the Southern Association of Colleges and Schools Commission on Colleges (SACS), meaning it holds regional accreditation. This is the same organization that accredits Vanderbilt University as well as the Universities of Georgia, Florida, and Alabama. As stated in chapter 4, schools that hold regional accreditation, such as SACS, provide the most highly transferable college credits to students. The accrediting process that the CCAF has undergone demonstrates the USAF's commitment to offering its members a highly sought after and valuable education.

The CCAF does accept transfer credit from other regionally accredited schools and on a course-by-course basis from nationally accredited schools. Students who earned college credit prior to entering the service can have their official transcripts evaluated for transfer credit into the CCAF. Students who separate from the service can have peace of mind knowing that the credits they have earned through the CCAF are highly transferable.

CCAF transcripts are free and may be requested by Air Force members (active or retired), civilians, students, and other services' members via written request or through the Air Force Virtual Education Center (AFVEC), or the following web address: http://www.au.af.mil/au/barnes/ccaf/transcripts.asp. (See the CCAF Advisor Handbook or the CCAF General Catalog for details, and the CCAF nonpublic website.) Many students opt to use Credentials Incorporated to deliver their transcripts due to the expedited shipping option they provide.

Civilians, other service personnel, and retirees without computer access may send written requests to the college for their transcripts that includes their full name, or former name as appropriate, social security account number, date of birth, and the address of the location where the transcript is to be sent. A student's signature is the legal authorization for the CCAF to release his or her transcript.

THE CCAF SYSTEM

The massive CCAF system is comprised of administrators, instructors, classrooms, laboratories, record systems, counselors, and students located throughout the world, but the administrative center is currently located on Maxwell AFB, Gunter Annex, Alabama. The CCAF's organization and administration that provides instruction at numerous locations around the world is often perceived as a nontraditional aspect of the college, but is an integral aspect to the program's success due to the geographic dispersion of students pursuing degrees.

Civilian collegiate institutions provide the coursework to satisfy the general education requirements (GER) of the degree programs and also provide coursework to satisfy technical education, and leadership, management and military studies (LMMS) requirements not completed at CCAF affiliated schools. For example, if you are stationed at Maxwell Air Force Base in Alabama, you can chose to attend one of several dozen local schools in residence such as Auburn University's Montgomery campus, Troy University, Faulkner University, Amridge University, or Alabama State University.

There are seventy-eight colleges in Alabama alone and almost four thousand nationwide eligible to receive your tuition assistance (TA). This allows airmen flexibility in completing the general education classes necessary for the degrees from the CCAF. It also allows airmen to test drive a school and determine if he or she wants to continue on to a bachelor's degree with that same institution or chose one that might be a better fit for his or her needs. If students prefer online classes, they can consider the classes offered by local schools or select from thousands of classes offered nationwide.

The AFVEC is designed to connect students to degree programs and classes offered nationwide, both in resident and online. Students can select to query a particular school to examine options or select options within a certain state. The local education office can assist and show students the valuable tools available for their use. The AFVEC, AU/ABC, and GEM sections later in this chapter will provide more detailed information in this regard.

Staff at the CCAF administrative centers track and monitor the progress of all enrolled students and complete the graduation process. The administrative center is comprised of approximately one hundred active-duty, AFRC, ANG, Air Force civil service and civilian contract personnel. The staff brings together all of the elements of the system under the matrix authority of Air Force Instruction 36-2648, CCAF.

Today's CCAF is a colossal organization and a model of efficiency. Over the years, the college has seen tremendous growth both in numbers and recognition. With more than 300,000 registered students, the college is the largest multicampus community college in the world. The CCAF's 108 affiliated schools are located in thirty-seven states and nine foreign locations. About 6,200 CCAF faculty members provide quality instruction at these locations for the personal and professional development of enlisted personnel.

More than a million transcripts have been issued in the last nine years. During a historical and record-breaking 2015 academic year, the CCAF students earned more than two million hours of college credit. This represents a huge tuition savings to the Air Force. Since the CCAF issued its first degree in 1977, the college has awarded more than more than 470,000 associate in applied science degrees. The college has broken the annual graduation records consecutively from 2009 through 2015.

The administrative staff translates AF technical training schools' curricula into semester-hour credit, develops course descriptors, designs and manages degree and certification programs, and maintains nearly three million records of student achievement and progress toward degree completion. The staff also ensures that the system's schools maintain the standards required for accreditation, constructs, prints and distributes official catalogs and other publications, and provides training and guidance to the worldwide network of counselors.

http://www.au.af.mil/au/barnes/ccaf/about.asp

The Academic Operations flight develops and manages guidance in support of the sixty-eight degree programs (listed later in this chapter), while ensuring that the programs maintain accreditation. The flight is the conduit between the students, the CCAF, Air Force Career Field Managers, and collegiate institutions. The major function for the flight is degree program management.

CCAF degree program managers are located in the CCAF administrative center and are experts in program curriculum. They are unique enlisted positions. These airmen are selectively manned and thoroughly screened for their technical ability as well as written and oral communication skills. Effective from July 2014, all CCAF program managers must possess at least an associate degree in the discipline, and professional certification(s) commensurate with their duty position. Program managers are considered functional experts and are selected to their positions for career-field expertise in their AFSC. They routinely communicate with Air Force senior enlisted leaders. Each program manager is responsible for over 9,200 students, processes nearly seven hundred graduate records, and applies for 33,000 semester hours of credit each year. Collectively, they also validate the two thousand technical courses from affiliated schools that award collegiate credit.

CCAF program managers perform the following functions:

1. Develop and maintain degree programs for assigned AFSCs.
2. Monitor career field changes and the need for new degree programs or revision of existing degrees on a continuing basis.
3. Maintain communications with career field functional managers, civilian colleges and universities, and business and industry to ensure state-of-the-art degree programs.
4. Evaluate and translate curriculum content of Air Force technical courses for conversion to civilian collegiate credit.
5. Develop course descriptions and titles commensurate with civilian academic institutions.
6. Advise student academic advisors worldwide on matters concerning CCAF academic programs and policies.
7. Attend and provide briefings at their applicable Specialty Training Requirement Teams (STRT).

CCAF Credentialing Programs Flight

Professional Certifications

The CCAF is the focal point for developing, managing, and administering professional certification programs supporting the enhancement of mission readiness, professional development, and career transitions of Air Force enlisted members. The college assists in aligning degree programs from the CCAF with industry standards that lead to credentialing eligibility upon completion of an applicable degree. They also manage credentialing programs offered through the CCAF, which directly support the mission of the CCAF.

Certification program managers perform the following functions:

1. Develop, manage, and administer professional certification programs that directly broaden an airman's occupational professional development.
2. Develop and maintain specialized courses that support certification programs for airmen pursuing professional certification.
3. Monitor the need for new certification programs or revision of existing programs on a continuing basis.
4. Evaluate curriculum content of Air Force and civilian technical courses for applicability toward certification program requirements.
5. Advise students and academic counselors worldwide on matters concerning professional certification opportunities, requirements, and policies.
6. Maintain communications with certification agencies and industry to ensure program compliance with certification agency rules, policies, and requirements.
7. Research national professional certifications related to Air Force occupational specialties and develop needed programs that guide personnel toward professional certification.
8. If possible, and in the best interest of the Air Force, align degree programs with industry standards that result in, or lead to, eligibility or award of certification upon completion of the applicable degree from the CCAF.
9. Evaluate national professional certifications for award of CCAF collegiate credit. The CCAF may award collegiate credit for national professional certifications applicable to specific degree programs and satisfy specific technical education and program elective requirements. Update certificate completions in Military Personnel Data System.

CCAF student academic advisors, as part of the administrative staff, train and advise education and training section chiefs and leaders, education advisors, guidance counselors, education specialists, education and training technicians, and Air National Guard Base Education training managers and training technicians as well as AFRC education and training technicians.

Student academic advisors advise enlisted members on CCAF associate degree completion using the guidelines set forth in the CCAF Advisor Handbook that can be viewed at: http://www.au.af.mil/au/barnes/ccaf/publications/student_handbook.pdf.

The advisors also use the CCAF General Catalog located at http://www.au.af.mil/au/barnes/ccaf/catalog/2014cat/index.asp.

Community College of the Air Force Action Requests are submitted via the web page 968 Community College of the Air Force Action Request, or electronically through a feature of the Air Force Automated Education

Management System (AFAEMS) to update records, change degree programs, change catalogs, register in a subsequent degree program, and nominate students for degree candidacy.

Air Force installations must conduct at least one graduation ceremony either independently or as part of a consolidated event. This is intended to ensure that graduates are recognized and diplomas are presented at an appropriate ceremony.

The Education and Training Section serves as the liaison between the CCAF and the designated professional organization orchestrating the event. Education centers ensure that a listing of graduates and diplomas are provided. This section also recommends the use of professional organizations such as the installation's Chiefs' Group, First Sergeants' Council, Top Three, Company Grade Officers Association, etc., to conduct the event.

CCAF Affiliated Schools

The affiliated schools of the CCAF are responsible for developing, validating, and delivering CCAF courses. The schools currently manage over two thousand accredited courses of instruction. These Air Force schools provide technical, skill-level awarding instruction to enlisted members after basic military training as well as leadership, management, and military studies education at certain intervals throughout an individual's career. Two prominent affiliated schools are the USAF School of Aerospace Medicine at Wright-Patterson AFB in Ohio and the USAF Special Operations Air Warfare Center at Hurlburt AFB in Florida.

Coursework offered by the affiliated schools may satisfy part or all of the technical education, LMMS, and/or program elective requirements. The courses are subject to increases and decreases in credit-hour value based on revisions and evaluations designed to meet the immediate needs of the Air Force. Credit hours for CCAF courses entered on the student transcript reflect the semester hour value of the courses when they were completed.

The affiliated schools must meet standards established by the Air University's regional accrediting body (SACSCOC) and the CCAF. Details regarding the affiliation of prospective schools and the documentation described in this publication are found in the CCAF Campus Affiliations Policies, Procedures and Guidelines (PPG). The PPG is directive in nature and compliance is mandatory. To become an affiliated school and maintain affiliation, a school must agree to accept certain responsibilities, comply with the requirements in these guidelines, and provide required information. Attending affiliated school gives students regionally accredited collegiate credit. The importance of this type of credit is explained in the accreditation section of chapter 4.

EDUCATION SERVICES AND ACADEMIC POLICIES

The following policies can be viewed online at: http://www.au.af.mil/au/barnes/ccaf/publications/student_handbook.pdf.

The Air Force provides academic advice and offers financial assistance to airmen in planning and pursuing their educational goals. Education services offices are composed of professional educational administrators, guidance counselors, academic advisors, education technicians/specialists, and test examiners.

Education services personnel supporting active Air Force installations, training technicians working with the ANG, and education services coordinators assigned to the AFRC counsel students and serve as the direct link between students and the administrative center. Counselors guide students toward degree completion and work with civilian collegiate institutions to arrange for the course offerings that are needed to satisfy CCAF degree requirements.

Education services personnel also administer the College Level Examination Program (CLEP), Defense Activity for Non-Traditional Education Support (DANTES) Subject Standardized Tests, and Excelsior College Examinations. The point of contact for ANG and AFRC affairs is CCAF/DEAC, 100 South Turner Boulevard, Maxwell AFB, Gunter Annex, Alabama 36114-3011; (334) 649-5023/4 or DSN 749-5023/4. Check with your local base education center for more information on taking CLEP exams and read chapter 8, "Prior Learning Credit," for more information on the benefit of taking these tests while on active duty.

Degree Time Limit

Registration in all degree programs, except for the Instructor of Technology and Military Science (ITMS), is limited to six years from date of registration. A student who is pursuing a first degree and does not complete it in the allotted time will automatically be moved to the primary occupational specialty degree program in the most current catalog.

A student who does not complete degree requirements within six years from the date of enrollment, and whose primary occupational specialty is not assigned to a specific degree program, will not be registered. A student who is pursuing a subsequent CCAF degree will be dis-enrolled at the end of the allotted time.

A student enrolled in the ITMS degree program has two years from the registration date to complete requirements. A student who does not complete the degree in the allotted time will be dis-enrolled. Any student wishing to reenroll may follow the procedures outlined above provided the student is still performing duty as a full-time CCAF instructor and meets all other requirements for registration.

Subsequent Degree

An airman may register in a subsequent degree program in his or her primary, secondary, tertiary, or fourth AFSC (not duty/control) provided the airman has not been awarded a degree in a program designed for that AFSC. A student registered in a subsequent degree program must earn and apply a minimum of twenty-four semester hours of unique (different) technical credit—at least twelve semester hours must be CCAF credit.

Grading Policy

Academic performance is determined and reported by using a pass or fail system. A student successfully completing a course is reported to the registrar who records a grade of "S" (satisfactory) on the transcript. This equates to a grade of C or better.

All courses are taught at the collegiate level. Affiliated schools employ a variety of instructional methods and assessment techniques designed to ensure successful achievement and attainment of desired learning outcomes. Course completion requirements, including grading standards, are provided to the student at the beginning of each course.

Award of Credit

A credit hour is the amount of work represented in intended learning outcomes and verified by evidence of student's achievement. CCAF follows sound practices for determining the amount and level of credit awarded for courses.

Transfer Credit

The college accepts transfer courses that meet specific criteria and the learning outcomes applicable to the degree. Credit earned at accredited colleges and universities may be accepted in transfer. Courses completed at foreign institutions are considered on an individual basis when submitted with a course-by-course evaluation from a National Association of Credential Evaluation Services or American Association of Collegiate Registrars and Admissions Officers member.

The Civilian Course Conversion Tool is a CCAF product and online tool available to assist education counselors with student advisement. This tool lists courses approved for transfer credit toward a degree from the CCAF. In March 2015, the list of approved courses surpassed a staggering 1.17 million courses in the following areas:

General Education Requirement	Number of Courses Accepted
Social Sciences	376,650
Humanities	358,976
Mathematics	229,743
Written Communication	142,759
Oral Communication	71,163

Civilian College Courses

Courses completed with a C or higher at accredited civilian institutions may apply to CCAF degree programs. A letter grade of C or D is not acceptable in transfer and a letter grade of D must be repaid. Courses must be program-applicable and cannot duplicate credit previously applied from other sources.

Department of Defense and Other Service Schools

If the Department of Defense (DoD) and other service schools are accredited and issue a transcript, the college will consider accepting the credit in transfer. See the *Guide to the Evaluation of Educational Experiences in the Armed Services on the American Council on Education* (ACE) website (http://www.acenet.edu/news-room/Pages/Military-Guide-Online.aspx) for credit information on other courses that may apply to a CCAF degree.

Many Air Force enlisted members attend Army, Navy, and/or DoD initial or advanced technical training courses instead of the Air Force technical training courses. The college does not award resident credit for these courses since these schools are not part of the CCAF system; however, the college does award proficiency (P) credit to Air Force enlisted members completing these courses. Proficiency credit is applied to a student's program after attaining the journeyman, five skill level.

Credit by Examination

A maximum of thirty semester hours of degree-applicable examination credit may be applied to satisfy degree requirements. Credit may be applied for examinations offered by DANTES, CLEP, College Board, Excelsior College, and the Defense Language Proficiency Test (DLPT) once CCAF receives the original test score report from the administrating agency.

Official transcripts or score reports must be sent directly from the issuing agency to the CCAF registrar. Examination results documented on other college or university transcripts are not acceptable.

Degree Program and Catalog Change

The college encourages students to complete the program of initial registration; however, students may request a change to another program when eligible. The associate dean of academic programs authorizes degree program changes. Students may also elect to move from the catalog of registration to the current catalog. In either case, the student is obligated to abide by all of the policies and program requirements of the catalog current on the date of the change. One reason a student may opt to use the criteria in the new catalog is that the degree titles sometimes change. For example, in the 2014–2016 catalog there is a degree called practical nursing technology. The same degree was called allied health technology in the 2011–2013 catalog. Some students may find one of the degree titles more appealing, so they must evaluate their options and make a choice.

Advanced Standing

A student attains advanced standing (registration status code 2 or 5) after completing forty-five semester hours of degree-applicable coursework and applying civilian course or test credit. At this point, a counselor should provide special guidance to assist the student in completing the degree requirements.

There is no waiver policy for CCAF-award credentialing programs. All published program requirements must be successfully completed. Waiver requests or exception to policies will not be accepted or approved.

Candidacy Status and Graduation

Education services counselors, advisors, or training technicians notify the student of candidacy status. After a student meets all of the requirements, the college that he is attending notifies the student's current education services office, or nominating training or education service office of degree completion. All degree requirements must be satisfied before separation, retirement, or commissioning and a student must have been enrolled in a degree program before that date. A student has six years from retirement, separation, or commissioning to file for graduation. The college has two graduating classes each year—April and October. Diplomas are mailed to the education services offices about one week before graduation.

Degree Award Date

The student's degree award date is the date the CCAF Administrative Center receives the completed AF Form 968, CCAF Action Request, nominating the student for graduation in a specific CCAF degree program. The CCAF Action Request is submitted by education services counselors or advisors to the CCAF Administration Center via the AFAEMS.

All degree requirements must be completed and recorded to the CCAF student record prior to nomination. Students should consider the time necessary for course and/or examination score reporting and transit time for college or university transcripts needed for credit in transfer decisions.

Students should not assume CCAF degree requirements are automatically completed upon successful completion of required courses via a civilian college or university, or that this is the date that they will become a CCAF graduate. Students must satisfy all requirements, up to and including nomination, for graduation before the completion of the members' Enlisted Performance Report (EPR). CCAF's policy is not to back date any student's graduation date to satisfy requirements for Senior Rater Endorsement, EPR, award packages, etc.

Student Rights and Grievances

Any Air University student has the right to present a program-related grievance or to appeal adverse action taken against him/her to leadership using the channels outlined in AU Policy, Regarding Student Rights and Grievance and those supplemented by CCAF affiliated schools.

Educational Documents

To initiate a record update, students must contact the education services office or ANG/AFRC CCAF advisor. To progress in a CCAF degree program, students must submit educational documentation reflecting course completion, such as a transcript.

The issuing institution or agency must mail these documents directly to:

CCAF/DESS
100 South Turner Boulevard,
Maxwell AFB, Gunter Annex, Alabama 36114-3011

Appropriate documents may include:

- Official transcript of applicable coursework completed at accredited post-secondary institutions.
- Official transcript from the Educational Testing Service reflecting CLEP or DANTES tests taken at a certified DANTES testing site.
- Foreign transcript with an external course-by-course evaluation from American Association of Collegiate Registrars and Admissions Offices or National Association of Credential Evaluation Services member. Foreign transcripts must be official and in English or accompanied by an English translation from the evaluation service.
- Request for verification of course completion of an affiliated school course that was not added to the academic record.
- Official verification of professional certification, licensure, or registry.
- Official verification of successful completion of a course conducted by or for US Government agencies for which the ACE recommends credit.

CCAF Student Feedback

Student participation is integral to the future development and continuous improvement of the college. This feedback is incorporated into every phase of the CCAF's strategic planning process that continually impacts policies and procedures, course and program reviews, affiliated school operations and educational support services.

Students can offer feedback through a number of avenues, to include classroom feedback, follow-up surveys completed by the schools, directly with the college, with the student leaders at each affiliated school, and through the formal waiver review process. There are affiliated school representatives who also address student interests on the Policy Council, the Affiliated Schools Advisory Panel, and the Education Services Advisory Panel.

Student Conduct

CCAF students are required, as a condition of good standing and continued enrollment, to conduct themselves in a manner that does not discredit the CCAF system. Plagiarism, cheating, submitting fraudulent academic documentation, and other forms of academic dishonesty are prohibited. Any action punishable under the Uniform Code of Military Justice involving direct or indirect participation in, or support of, academic misconduct as determined by the Dean of Academic Affairs, may result in suspension and/ or expulsion from the CCAF.

CCAF's disciplinary action process is outlined in CCAF Instruction 33-8, CCAF Review Board and CCAF Instruction 33-9, and Administration of Altered Academic Documentation or Other Acts of Misconduct.

AIR UNIVERSITY ASSOCIATE-TO-BACCALAUREATE COOPERATIVE (AU-ABC) PROGRAM AND GENERAL EDUCATION MOBILE

The AU-ABC program links CCAF associate in applied science (AAS) graduates to online accredited civilian academic institutions that offer baccalaureate-level educational opportunities to Air Force enlisted personnel. The AU-ABC program establishes partnerships between the Air Force and civilian institutions to provide CCAF graduates advanced education opportunities at the baccalaureate level.

This program targets active-duty Air Force, AFRC, and ANG members. Degree requirements may be completed after students retire or separate from the Air Force; this grants students a great degree of flexibility. Students will work directly with the AU-ABC school to complete enrollment and degree requirements.

Other colleges and universities are attracted to graduates of CCAF because of their likely success at the baccalaureate and higher level. Troy University is a prime example. According to an e-mail sent by Mr. Carl Collins, the Director of Enrollment Services at Troy University, on March 5, 2015, "Troy University has been proud to partner with the Community College of the Air Force with both the GEM and AU-ABC programs. Air Force members normally complete graduation requirements and are awarded their degree by accomplishing the additional sixty-hours required above and beyond their degree from the CCAF. Troy University has had a long standing relationship with the military as a whole, dating back to 1965, and values the quality of student the Air Force and the military in general provide to our University."[3]

AU-ABC was launched on June 15, 2007, as a partnership between the Air University and accredited civilian academic institutions.

Key features of and benefits from the partnership include the following:

- It maximizes application of military career education and training.
- It builds on CCAF degree.
- CCAF graduates can earn bachelor's degrees after completing no more than sixty semester hours beyond their associate degree.
- Every participant receives a binding degree completion contract that locks in transfer credit and states remaining degree requirements.
- Air Force-friendly colleges and universities award the bachelor's degrees.
- Many degree choices that meet Air Force needs—for example, as of March 2015, forty-nine AU-ABC graduates became Air Force commissioned officers.

AU-ABC Categories

Category I—Programs designed for airmen with an AAS degree from the CCAF. These CCAF graduates are guaranteed that no more than sixty semester hours of additional credit will be required to complete a bachelor's degree.

Category II—Programs designed primarily for airmen who are currently enrolled in a CCAF AAS degree program. Partnering institutions will identify specific prerequisite coursework the CCAF students need to complete as part of their CCAF general education and program elective requirements.

These courses would simultaneously fill both the CCAF AAS requirements and some of the AU-ABC degree requirements. Upon completion of a degree from the CCAF, students are guaranteed that no more than sixty semester hours of additional credit will be required to complete an AU-ABC degree if the published AU-ABC degree plan is followed.

Category III—Programs that require CCAF AAS graduates to complete more than sixty semester hours of credit beyond the AAS but meet all other AU-ABC specifications. The degrees in this category must still link to one or more CCAF AAS programs and have exceptional value for the Air Force.

CCAF students and graduates can search for degree programs from a list of military-friendly civilian institutions via the AFVEC. After familiarizing yourself with the system's capabilities, you will find the AFVEC provides seamless integration of all academic functions applicable to your degree completion. The following list demonstrates some of the benefits of the integrated system:

- Virtual campus
- Online enrollment and instruction

- Full spectrum of distance learning courses
- Web-based guidance counseling
- Access to academic institutions' programs and services
- Manage TA and other financial services
- No campus residency
- Tracking and program management
- Order CCAF transcripts
- One-stop shopping for service member

AU-ABC Degree Programs

AU-ABC baccalaureate programs cover graduates of all sixty-eight CCAF associates in applied science degrees. Currently, more than 200 baccalaureate degree programs are available in a variety of disciplines to include:

- Accounting
- Applied Management
- Aviation Maintenance
- Business Administration
- Computer Science
- Criminal Justice
- Early Childhood Development
- Electronics Engineering Technology
- Energy Management
- Engineering Technology
- Fire Science
- General Engineering Technology
- General Studies
- Health Sciences
- Human Resources Management
- Industrial Technology
- Intelligence Studies
- Information Technology Management
- Information Systems
- Logistics Management
- Marketing
- Multidisciplinary Studies
- Occupational Education
- Operations Management
- Professional Aeronautics
- Psychology
- Security Management
- Sports Science
- Strategic Leadership
- Technical Management
- Terrorism and Counterterrorism Studies
- World and Strategic Studies

The Air Force Portal/AFVEC is the gateway for participation offering the following options:

- AU-ABC program search
- Links to AU-ABC partner schools web pages
- Generic program degree plans
- TA processing

AU-ABC SCHOOLS AS OF MARCH 2015

Allied American University
American Military University
Amridge University
Angelo State University
Ashford University
Baker College Online
Bellevue University
Bismarck State College
Bowling Green State University
Brandman University
Colorado Technical University
Columbia College
Columbia Southern University
DeVry University Chicago
East Carolina University
ECPI University
Embry-Riddle Aeronautical
  University
Empire State College-SUNY
Excelsior College
Fort Hays State University
Grand Canyon University
Granite State College
Grantham University
Indiana State University
Jones International University
Kaplan University Online
Liberty University
National American University
National Graduate School of Quality
  Management
National Louis University

Northern Arizona University
Northwestern State University of
  Louisiana
Old Dominion University
Park University
Saint Leo University
Southern New Hampshire University
Southwestern College
Strayer University
Thomas Edison State College
Touro University Worldwide
Trident University International
Troy University
United States Sports Academy
University of Arizona
University of Great Falls
University of Management and
  Technology
University of Maryland University
  College
University of Northwestern Ohio
University of Oklahoma
University of Phoenix
University of the Incarnate Word
University of West Alabama
Vaughn College of Aeronautics and
  Technology
Waldorf College
Wayland Baptist University
Webster University
Western Governors University
Wilmington University

General Education Mobile (GEM)

The following information can be found on the Air Force GEM website.

The GEM program links CCAF students to online regionally accredited civilian academic institutions that offer freshman- and sophomore-level general education courses via distance learning. The prevetted courses can be used to fulfill the fifteen semester hours of the CCAF AAS degree GER. The partnering schools must offer at least one, but no more than ten, general education courses in each of the five following disciplines: oral communication, written communication, mathematics, social science, and humanities.

Criteria for participating GEM schools are as follows:

- Schools must sign the Department of Defense Voluntary Education Partnership Memorandum of Understanding (DODMOU) and agree to operate according to the stated rules (Department of Defense Instruction 1322.25, http://www.dodmou.com)
- All institutions must hold regional accreditation
- Schools must deliver all approved coursework and prerequisites, to include placement tests through a distance learning (mobile) format
- A GEM registration application must be completed
- Institutions must ensure that GEM courses are listed and identified in the offering institution's general catalog and satisfy the institution's freshman and sophomore general education graduation requirements designed for transfer
- Develop a GEM landing page that includes a GEM logo/heading, point of contact information, list of approved GEM courses, online academic support, enrollment information, tuition/fees, and current course schedule
- Utilize the AI Portal to register and submit course(s) for review and approval
- Offer only courses that meet the CCAF general education requirements
- Confirm that tuition rates for military students do not exceed rates for civilian students
- Notify GEM designee in writing of all changes in course descriptions, titles, and/or course additions/deletions
- Notify GEM designee in writing of intent to withdraw from the GEM program

Airmen can view GEM schools and approved courses via the AFVEC GEM search tool (https://afvec.langley.af.mil/afvec/Home.aspx). The search tool lists all potential GEM schools and the institutions' approved GEM courses. Airmen are able to view any particular school's GEM plans and landing pages. Airmen will contact their GEM school of choice directly for more school/course information.

GEM SCHOOLS AS OF MARCH 2015

Alamo Community College District
American Intercontinental University
American Military University
Anne Arundel Community College
Argosy University
Armstrong State University
Ashford University
Bismarck State College
Brandman University
Broward College
Burlington County College
Butler Community College
Central Texas College
Clovis Community College
Coastline Community College
Colorado State University—Global
    Campus
Colorado Technical University
Columbia College
Community College Of Aurora
Dakota College At Bottineau
Dallas Colleges Online
Duquesne University
ECPI University
Empire State College—Suny
Faulkner University
Fisher College
Florida State College At Jacksonville
Georgia Military College—All
    Campuses
Georgia Perimeter College
Gulf Coast State College
Harrisburg Area Community College
Jones International University

Kaplan University—Online
Klamath Community College
Lamar University
Louisiana Tech University
Maysville Community & Technical
    College
Miami Dade College
National American University
National University
Niagara University
Nicholls State University
Northern Arizona University
Northwestern State University of
    Louisiana
Park University
Pikes Peak Community College
Pima County Community College
Regent University
Rio Salado College
Southeast Missouri State University
Southern New Hampshire University
Southwestern College—Kansas
State Fair Community College
Strayer University
Thomas Edison State College
Touro University Worldwide
Trident University International
Troy University
University of Arkansas at Little Rock
University Of Maryland University
    College
University Of Phoenix
University Of West Florida
Wiregrass Georgia Technical College

AIR FORCE PROFESIONAL CREDENTIALING
AND CERTIFICATION OPTIONS

Many of the professional credentials awarded by the CCAF complement the academic degrees and are in high demand by large companies. In 2000,

J. R. Breeding, the CCAF Dean of Academic Programs, led a Joint Service Aviation Maintenance Technician Certification Council meeting in Atlanta, Georgia.

According to Breeding, he posed the following question to the human resource manager at Delta Airlines (who was unaware that he was a CCAF employee): "If you had two applicants to fill one position, one was a civilian member holding the Federal Aviation Administration Airframe and Powerplant certification and the other was a military member holding the FAA A&P certification, and the resumes were similar, which one would rack-and-stack higher to be hired for the position?" She replied, "The Air Force has the CCAF. If the military member was also awarded the Aviation Maintenance Technology degree from the CCAF, that person would be hired over the other."

The Air Force recognizes two primary types of academic credentialing: licensure and certification. Licensure is a credential normally issued by federal, state, or local governmental agencies. A license is issued for individuals to practice in a specific occupation, and they are typically mandatory for employment in selected fields. Federal or state laws or regulations define the standards that individuals must meet to become licensed.

A certification is a credential normally issued by nongovernmental agencies, associations, schools, or industry-supported companies. A certification is issued to individuals who meet specific education, experience, and qualification requirements. These requirements are generally established by professional associations, industry, or product-related organizations. Certification is typically an optional credential, although some state licensure boards and some employers may require specific certifications.

The CCAF awards collegiate credit to airmen who possess specific national professional credentials that satisfy applicable degree program requirements. Professional credentialing is important to the Air Force and airmen for several reasons:

1. Helps develop a more diversely skilled workforce
2. Broadens the professional development of airmen
3. Validates an airman's professional knowledge and skills gained through Air Force technical education and training
4. Helps prepare airmen to meet the mission challenges of the future

Some civilian colleges and universities award credit for specific professional credentials. To support documentary evidence of training, skills, and practical experience, airmen are highly encouraged to maintain records of all previous and current education, training, and qualifications. Speak with your school about any credentials you hold, whether you might receive credit for these credentials, and if so, how you can submit for credit evaluation.

Airmen are encouraged to pursue occupation-related credentials while serving in the Air Force to increase their Air Force occupational skills, broaden their professional development, and better prepare for transition back into the civilian sector. Airmen interested in pursuing professional credentials should contact the credentialing agency for information on credentials, eligibility requirements, and testing procedures. Graduates of CCAF degree programs or courses accredited by credentialing agencies should contact the credentialing agency for requirements and processes.

CCAF-SPECIFIC CERTIFICATIONS

Air Force members can gain specific information about the following certification programs by visiting the CCAF portal site in the AF portal (https://www.my.af.mil/gcss-af/USAF/search?text=CCAF). Due to personal identifiable information (PII) protection requirements starting on January 15, 2015, the CCAF will only accept credentialing requests from a government domain (.mil, .gov, etc).

Air Force Airframe and Power Plant (A&P) Certification Program

Most military aircraft maintenance technicians are eligible to pursue the Federal Aviation Administration (FAA) Airframe and power plant (A&P) certification based on documented evidence of thirty months practical aircraft maintenance experience in airframe and power plant systems per Title 14, Code of Federal Regulations (CFR), Part 65-Certification: Airmen Other Than Flight Crew Members; Subpart D-Mechanics.

The Air Force A&P Certification Program was developed to bridge gaps between a technician's Air Force education, training, and experience and FAA eligibility requirements per Title 14, CFR, Part 65.77. This is a rigorous, FAA-approved voluntary program that benefits the technician and the Air Force, with consideration to professional development, recruitment, and retention, and transition. Completing this program as outlined in the program Qualification Training Package (QTP) will assist technicians in meeting FAA eligibility requirements and being better prepared for the FAA exams.

The A&P certification is a four-tier training and experience program. The following elements are required for program completion and important for individual development, knowledge assessment, meeting FAA certification eligibility, and preparation for the FAA exams:

1. On-The-Job Training (OJT).
2. Three Air University Online Specialized Courses.
3. Documented evidence of thirty months practical experience in airframe and power plant systems.
4. Four years of time-in-service already completed.

Program Eligibility

Active-duty, guard and reserve technicians who possess at least a five skill level in one of the following aircraft maintenance AFSCs are eligible to enroll: 2A0X1, 2A090, 2A2X1, 2A2X2, 2A2X3, 2A3X3, 2A3X4, 2A3X5, 2A3X7, 2A3X8, 2A390, 2A300, 2A5X1, 2A5X2, 2A5X3, 2A5X4, 2A590, 2A500, 2A6X1, 2A6X3, 2A6X4, 2A6X5, 2A6X6, 2A690, 2A691, 2A600 (except AGE), 2A7X1, 2A7X2, 2A7X3, 2A7X5, 2A790, 2A8X1, 2A8X2, 2A9X1, 2A9X2, and 2A9X3.

Technicians who previously gained FAA authorization to test for A&P certification are not required to enroll and complete this program. Personnel who retrain out of aircraft maintenance are eligible to enroll provided they were awarded the five-skill level in an AF A&P Program, were eligible in aircraft maintenance AFSC prior to re-training, and have not been out of the aircraft maintenance AFSC for more than two years.

Program Enrollment

Technicians may enroll once they have been awarded the five-skill level via CCAF's secured website using the A&P Enrollment Form (https://www. my.af.mil/gcss-af/USAF/ep/contentView.do?contentType=EDITORIAL&co ntentId=c88B4F00B41D2F51E01420946721B0912&programId=t88B4F00 B41D2F51E01420943DB3F0911&channelPageId=s6925EC13447C0FB5E- 044080020E329A9). Due to security reasons, you must access from a .mil domain or via Common Access card (CAC) access. Once complete, e-mail the form to ccaf.faa@us.af.mil.

Once enrolled, a CCAF program manager will evaluate all program-applicable formal Air Force and civilian coursework reflected on the technician's CCAF academic record. The CCAF program manager will develop the technician's QTP and credit the applicable areas based on the evaluation.

The CCAF program manager will e-mail the program QTP to the technician to begin the program. The QTP includes the CG-G-EAE-2 Form, FAA Certification Performance of Job Tasks, CG-G-EAE-3 Form, Joint Military Services Airframe and Power plant Program, and instructions for completing program requirements.ir Force A&P Certification Program.

CCAF Instructor Certification (CIC) Program

The CIC Program targets qualified instructors who teach CCAF collegiate-level credit awarding courses at a CCAF affiliated school. It is the most popular credential with over 26,000 instructor certifications awarded as of March 2015. The CIC is a professional credential that recognizes the instructor's extensive faculty development training, education, and qualifications that are required to teach a CCAF course, and formally acknowledges the instructor's practical teaching experience. Qualified officer, enlisted, civilian, and other service instructors are eligible for this certification. Although qualified instructors who meet CIC program requirements are eligible, once an instructor leaves CCAF instructor duty, he or she is no longer eligible for the CIC.

The CIC Program consists of three specific levels of achievement.

- CIC-I: formally recognizes an instructor's qualification as a CCAF instructor and his professional accomplishment.
- CIC-II: formally recognizes an instructor's advanced level of professional accomplishments beyond the CIC-I.
- CIC-III: formally recognizes an instructor's advanced level of professional accomplishments beyond the CIC-II or OIC.

A qualified instructor is a CCAF instructor who has completed the CCAF faculty development program and is assigned to a CCAF-affiliated school teaching a CCAF credit-awarding course. The instructor may be an officer, enlisted, civil service, contractor, other-service, or foreign-service member.

Instructor assistants, student instructors, guest lecturers, subject-matter experts, speakers of opportunity, approved EQILD instructors, and instructors who do not teach a CCAF credit-awarding course are not eligible. Instructors must meet the specific requirements of the certification level which they are being nominated for. Applicants must comply with the following:

a. CCAF Instructor Certification—Level I (CIC-I) qualification requirements:
   - Currently teaching a CCAF credit-awarding course(s) at an affiliated school at the time of nomination.
   - Must be assigned to a CCAF course(s) in the CCAF Faculty Database (STARS-FD). And complete at least three semester hours of CCAF-approved Instructor Methodology coursework.
   - Completed the twelve semester-hour CCAF teaching internship.
   - Subject-matter qualified in the CCAF course assigned to teach.
   - Hold an associate's or higher-level degree from an accredited college.

- Have at least one year of teaching experience as a CCAF instructor from the date assigned instructor duties (DAID).
- Have at least 1,000 hours of documented practical experience teaching a CCAF course.
- Be recommended for certification by the affiliated school commander or commandant.

b. CCAF Instructor Certification—Level II (CIC-II) qualification requirements:
- Currently teaching a CCAF credit-awarding course at an affiliated school at the time of nomination.
- Assigned to a CCAF course in the CCAF STARS-FD.
- Awarded the CIC-I.
- Subject-matter qualified in the CCAF course assigned to teach.
- Have at least two years of teaching experience as a CCAF instructor from the DAID.
- Have at least 2,000 hours of documented practical experience teaching a CCAF course.
- Be recommended for certification by the affiliated school commander or commandant.

c. CCAF Instructor Certification—Level III (CIC-III) qualification requirements:
- Currently teaching a CCAF credit-awarding course at an affiliated school at the time of nomination.
- Assigned to a CCAF course in the CCAF STARS-FD.
- Awarded the CIC-II or OIC.
- Subject-matter qualified in the CCAF course assigned to teach.
- Hold a bachelor or higher-level degree from an accredited college.
- Have at least three years teaching experience as a CCAF instructor from the DAID.
- Have at least 3,000 hours of documented practical experience teaching a CCAF course.
- Have at least twenty-four semester hours of CCAF-approved teacher/instructor education coursework in one or more of the following subject areas (may be CCAF or civilian):
  - Instructional methodology
  - Educational counseling or psychology
  - Academic and performance measurement
  - Curriculum or instructional development
  - Communication skills
  - Instructional technology
  - Be recommended for certification by the affiliated school commander or commandant

CCAF Instructional Systems Development (ISD) Certification Program

The CCAF offers the ISD Certification Program for qualified curriculum writers and managers who are formally assigned to affiliated schools to develop and manage CCAF collegiate-level credit awarding courses. The ISD Certification is a professional credential that recognizes the writer's or manager's extensive training, education, qualifications, and experience required to develop and manage CCAF courses. The certification also recognizes the individual's ISD qualifications and experience in planning, developing, implementing, and managing instructional systems. The program is designed to broaden faculty and professional development.

Qualified officer, enlisted, civilian and other service curriculum writers, and managers are eligible. Once an individual leaves curriculum writer or manager duty, he is no longer eligible for the ISD certification.

ISD Certification Program Requirements for airmen are as follows for potential participants:

- Must be currently assigned to a CCAF affiliated school performing CCAF curriculum development duties at the time of nomination.
- Must possess an associate's or higher degree from an accredited college.
- Must have completed at least three semester hours of CCAF-approved ISD coursework.
- Must have completed at least three semester hours of CCAF-approved instructor methodology coursework.
- Must have completed a twelve semester-hour CCAF ISD internship.
- Must have at least one-year curriculum development experience from the CCAF ISD internship completion date.
- Must be recommended for certification by the affiliated school commander, commandant, or faculty development chief.

CCAF Instructional Systems Development (ISD) Internship

The CCAF ISD internship is a vital element of the CCAF ISD Certification Program. CCAF ISD internship completion is reported per standard CCAF business practices referenced in the CCAF Campus Affiliations PPG.

The CCAF ISD internship provides newly assigned curriculum writers with knowledge and practical experience above that received in formal ISD coursework. During the CCAF ISD internship, students receive additional training and experience while under the direct supervision of a fully qualified subject matter expert responsible for developing CCAF collegiate-level curriculum.

The CCAF ISD internship consists of two measured areas:

1. Knowledge: The student should know, understand, and be able to perform all phases of the current Air Force ISD model.
2. Supervised Instructional Development: A minimum of 180 contact hours of supervised, field-oriented, experience in which the student designs and implements a system of instruction, analysis technique, and evaluation design consistent with the current Air Force ISD model. The student will work with qualified subject matter experts and perform research to plan, analyze, design, develop, implement, and evaluate learning programs.

Individuals must document CCAF ISD internship and experience on the CCAF ISD internship and certification worksheet. Procedures for documenting the worksheet can be found in the CCAF Campus Affiliations PPG.

Professional Manager Certification (PMC) Program

The PMC is a popular program for enlisted members. Over 16,600 PMCs have been awarded. This professional credential formally recognizes an individual's advanced level of education and experience in leadership and management, as well as professional accomplishments. The PMC is a culmination of a military member's Enlisted Professional Military Education (EPME), military experience, and continued dedication to education. Certification for the PMC must be made directly by the unit commander or commandant.

The PMC is primarily designed for Air Force SNCO's. However, any enlisted airmen who meet all program requirements may be nominated and awarded the PMC. Once an individual retires, separates, or is commissioned, he or she is no longer eligible for the PMC. All program requirements must be completed prior to retirement, separation, or commissioning.

PMC Program Requirements demand that individuals have:

- Received the seven skill level or higher
- Completed the Airman Leadership School (in-residence or correspondence)
- Completed the Non-Commissioned Officer Academy (in-residence or correspondence)
- Completed the Senior Non-Commissioned Officer Academy (in-residence or correspondence course)
- Completed thirty semester hours of leadership/management coursework

At least six semester hours of the leadership/management coursework must be completed from an accredited civilian college or by testing credit such as CLEP, DSST, or Excelsior exams.

Civilian courses must emphasize the fundamentals of leadership and/ or management of human resources. The following are a few examples of potential courses:

- Principles of Management
- Personnel Management
- Human Resource Management
- Principles of Supervision
- Organizational Behavior

A copy of the civilian college transcript reflecting completion of acceptable leadership or management courses is required. College transcripts do not have to be official copies, but must include the members name, the course taken, credits, and grade received. All civilian management courses will be evaluated by CCAF/DEAL staff. A copy of the CCAF transcript is not required.

Credit earned by completion of EPME is applied toward the following, which require thirty semester hours:

- A degree award from the CCAF.
- A recommendation for certification by the unit commander or commandant.

Nomination Procedures

The PMC program requires a formal application process, with recommendation by the individual's unit commander or commandant. If you believe you qualify for the PMC, please follow the directions below. CCAF/DEAL will evaluate your education record and submitted documents.

Note: Due to the high level of interest in the PMC program, CCAF cannot provide an initial review of each member's record, or provide an initial evaluation of status, prior to the member submitting their PMC nomination package. Often, courses on the member's civilian college transcript will require an evaluation for acceptability. Therefore, interested members must submit all required documents and follow the guidance below.

Note: The PMC nomination package must include a copy of civilian college transcripts, applicable CLEP/DSST exam score reports, and a signed letter of recommendation by the member's commander.

The following are instructions for making an application:

1. Complete the letter of recommendation and coordinate for the unit commander's or commandant's signature.

2. Collect civilian college transcripts and/or applicable CLEP/DSST exam score reports.
3. Scan and e-mail the required documents to ccaf.deal@us.af.mil. This is the preferred method for submitting nomination packages.
4. If you are unable to scan and e-mail your nomination package, the required documents may be mailed to:
   Community College of the Air Force Credentialing Programs
   100 South Turner Blvd
   Maxwell-Gunter AFB, AL 36114-3011
5. Upon receipt of PMC nomination package, CCAF/DEAL will complete an evaluation and validate all program requirements are met.
6. If a member is denied award of the PMC, he may reapply upon completion of all program requirements.

Individuals who are awarded the PMC will receive a certificate, and the PMC will be officially recorded on the member's CCAF student record and CCAF transcript. Contact the base education center for updating MilPDS record.

CCAF Collegiate Credit for Professional Certification, Licensure and Registry

CCAF awards collegiate credit for approved national professional credentials. This credit may be applied toward applicable CCAF degree program requirements. A registered student desiring credit for degree-applicable credentials must request the credential issuing agency to provide a written memorandum of verification that includes full name, SSN, date of birth, type of credential awarded and current standing, and award date.

Airmen should consider pursuing occupational-related credentials while serving in the Air Force to increase their Air Force occupational skills, broaden their professional development, and be better prepared for transition. Airmen interested in pursuing professional credentials should contact the credentialing agency for information on credentials, eligibility requirements, and testing procedures. Graduates of CCAF degree programs or courses accredited by credentialing agencies should contact the credentialing agency for requirements and processes.

To support documentary evidence of training, skills, and practical experience, airmen are highly encouraged to maintain records of all previous and current education, training, and qualifications. The following national professional credentials are recognized by CCAF and approved to fulfill technical education requirements of applicable degree programs.[4]

Table 5.1 Air Force Professional Credentialing and Certification Options

Credential Title	Credential Issuing Agency	CCAF Credit	CCAF Degree Program
Certified Executive Chef (CEC)	American Culinary Federation (ACF)	4 SH	Restaurant, Hotel & Fitness Management (1FRS)
Registered Health Information Technician	American Health Information Management Association (AHIMA)	3 SH	Health Care Management (7GCY)
Certified Paraoptometric (CPO)	American Optometric Association, Commission on Paraoptometric Certification (CPC)	4 SH	Ophthalmic Technician (7GDI)
Certified Paraoptometric Assistant (CPOA)	American Optometric Association, Commission on Paraoptometric Certification (CPC)	8 SH	Ophthalmic Technician (7GDI)
Certified Paraoptometric Technician (CPOT)	American Optometric Association, Commission on Paraoptometric Certification (CPC)	10 SH	Ophthalmic Technician (7GDI)
Magnetic Resonance Imaging	American Registry of Radiologic Technologists (ARRT)	13 SH	Diagnostic Imaging Technology (7GDH) Diagnostic Medical Sonography (7GDK) Nuclear Medicine Technology (7ABJ)
Nuclear Medicine Technology	American Registry of Radiologic Technologists (ARRT)	15 SH	Diagnostic Imaging Technology (7GDH) Diagnostic Medical
Radiography	American Registry of Radiologic Technologists (ARRT)	15 SH	Diagnostic Imaging Technology (7GDH) Diagnostic Medical Sonography (7GDK) Nuclear Medicine Technology (7ABJ)
Sonography	American Registry of Radiologic Technologists (ARRT)	16 SH	Diagnostic Imaging Technology (7GDH) Diagnostic Medical Sonography (7GDK) Nuclear Medicine Technology (7ABJ)
Histotechnician (HT)	American Society for Clinical Pathology (ASCP)	20 SH	Histologic Technology (7GAE) Medical Laboratory Technology (7GAF)

(Cont.)

Medical Laboratory Technician (MLT)	American Society for Clinical Pathology (ASCP)	13 SH	Medical Laboratory Technology (7GAF)
Level II—Liquid Penetrant Testing (PT)	American Society for Nondestructive Testing (ASNT)	4 SH	Nondestructive Testing Technology (4VXR)
Level II—Magnetic Particle Testing (MT)	American Society for Nondestructive Testing (ASNT)	3 SH	Nondestructive Testing Technology (4VXR)
Level II— Radiography Testing (RT)	American Society for Nondestructive Testing (ASNT)	9 SH	Nondestructive Testing Technology (4VXR)
Level II— Ultrasonic Testing (UT)	American Society for Nondestructive Testing (ASNT)	9 SH	Nondestructive Testing Technology (4VXR)
Level II—Visual Testing (VT)	American Society for Nondestructive Testing (ASNT)	3 SH	Nondestructive Testing Technology (4VXR)
Certified Calibration Technician (CCT)	American Society for Quality (ASQ)	10 SH	Electronic Systems Technology (4VHP)
Certified Defense Financial Manager (CDFM)	American Society of Military Comptrollers (ASMC)	6 SH	Financial Management (9GEC)
Certified Biomedical Equipment Technician (CBET)	Association for the Advancement of Medical Instrumentation (AAMI)	8 SH	Biomedical Equipment Technology (7GAA)
Certified Radiology Equipment Specialists (CRES)	Association for the Advancement of Medical Instrumentation (AAMI)	8 SH	Biomedical Equipment Technology (7GAA)
A+	Computing Technology Industry Association (CompTIA)	4 SH	Computer Science Technology (0CYY) Electronic Systems Technology (4VHP) Information Management (1AUY) Information Systems Technology (0IYY) CyberSecurity (0CYC)
A+ IT Technician	Computing Technology Industry Association (CompTIA)	4 SH	Computer Science Technology (0CYY) Electronic Systems Technology (4VHP) Information Management (1AUY) Information Systems

(Cont.)

Security+ (SY0-301)	Computing Technology Industry Association (CompTIA)	3 SH	Computer Science Technology (0CYY) Electronic Systems Technology (4VHP) Information Management (1AUY) Information Systems Technology (0IYY) CyberSecurity (0CYC)
Occupational Health and Safety Technologist (OHST)	Council on Certification of Health, Environmental and Safety Technologists (CCHEST)	12 SH	Bioenvironmental Engineering Technology (7GAM)
ProChef Certification Level I— Certified Culinarian	Culinary Institute of America (CIA)	3 SH	Restaurant, Hotel & Fitness Management (1FRS)
Certified Dental Assistant (CDA)	Dental Assisting National Board (DANB)	10 SH	Dental Assisting (7GBC)
Certified Dietary Manager	Dietary Managers Association (DMA)	6 SH	Dietetics and Nutrition (7GAD)
Aircraft Dispatcher	Federal Aviation Administration (FAA)	11 SH	Aviation Management (1AVY)
Aviation Mechanic— Airframe	Federal Aviation Administration (FAA)	18 SH	Aviation Maintenance Technology (4VAD) Aviation Operations (4VCB) Avionic Systems Technology (4VHS) Metals Technology (4VLB) Nondestructive Testing Technology (4VXR)
Aviation Mechanic— Airframe & Power Plant	Federal Aviation Administration (FAA)	30 SH	Aviation Maintenance Technology (4VAD) Aviation Operations (4VCB) Avionic Systems Technology (4VHS) Metals Technology (4VLB) Nondestructive Testing Technology (4VXR)

(Cont.)

Aviation Mechanic— Power Plant	Federal Aviation Administration (FAA)	18 SH	Aviation Maintenance Technology (4VAD) Aviation Operations (4VCB) Avionic Systems Technology (4VHS) Metals Technology (4VLB) Nondestructive Testing Technology (4VXR)
Commercial Pilot—Airplane	Federal Aviation Administration (FAA)	10 SH	Air Traffic Management (4VEN) Aviation Management (1AVY) Aviation Operations (4VCB)
Flight Engineer— Turbojet/ Turboprop	Federal Aviation Administration (FAA)	17 SH	Aviation Operations (4VCB)
Parachute Rigger—Senior	Federal Aviation Administration (FAA)	3 SH	Aircrew Safety Systems Technology (4VAT) Survival Equipment (4VPF)
Private Pilot— Airplane	Federal Aviation Administration (FAA)	5 SH	Air Traffic Management (4VEN) Aviation Management (1AVY) Aviation Operations (4VCB)
General Radiotelephone Operator (GROL)	Federal Communication Commission (FCC)	9 SH	Air Traffic Management (4VEN) Aviation Management (1AVY) Avionic Systems Technology (4VHS) Electronic Systems Technology (4VHP) Information Systems Technology (0IYY)
Security Essentials Certification (GSEC)	Global Information Assurance Certification (GIAC)	6 SH	Computer Science Technology (0CYY) Electronic Systems Technology (4VHP) Information Management (1AUY) Information Systems Technology (0IYY) CyberSecurity (0CYC)

(Cont.)

Certified Alcohol & Other Drug Abuse Counselor (AODA)	International Certification Reciprocity Consortium (IC&RC)	6 SH	Mental Health Services (7GAP)
Certified Food Executive (CFE)	International Food Service Executives Association (IFSEA)	2 SH	Restaurant, Hotel & Fitness Management (1FRS)
Certified Food Manager (CFM)	International Food Service Executives Association (IFSEA)	2 SH	Restaurant, Hotel & Fitness Management (1FRS)
Master Certified Food Executive (MCFE)	International Food Service Executives Association (IFSEA)	3 SH	Restaurant, Hotel & Fitness Management (1FRS)
Certified Information Systems Security Professional (CISSP)	International Information Systems Security Certification Consortium, Inc. (ISC)²	4 SH	Computer Science Technology (0CYY) Electronic Systems Technology (4VHP) Information Management (1AUY) Information Systems Technology (0IYY) CyberSecurity (0CYC)
Systems Security Certified Practitioner (SSCP)	International Information Systems Security Certification Consortium, Inc. (ISC)²	3 SH	Computer Science Technology (0CYY) Electronic Systems Technology (4VHP) Information Management (1AUY) Information Systems Technology (0IYY) CyberSecurity (0CYC)
Microsoft Solutions Expert (MCSE) Server Infrastructure Certification	Microsoft Corporation	5 SH	Computer Science Technology (0CYY) Electronic Systems Technology (4VHP) Information Management
Microsoft Solutions Expert (MCSE) Private Cloud Certification	Microsoft Corporation	5 SH	Computer Science Technology (0CYY) Electronic Systems Technology (4VHP) Information Management (1AUY) Information Systems

(Cont.)

Microsoft Solutions Expert (MCSE) Messaging Certification	Microsoft Corporation	5 SH	Computer Science Technology (0CYY) Electronic Systems Technology (4VHP) Information Management (1AUY) Information Systems Technology (0IYY)
Microsoft Solutions Expert (MCSE) Communication Certification	Microsoft Corporation	5 SH	Computer Science Technology (0CYY) Electronic Systems Technology (4VHP) Information Management (1AUY) Information Systems Technology (0IYY)
Microsoft Solutions Expert (MCSE) SharePoint Certification	Microsoft Corporation	5 SH	Computer Science Technology (0CYY) Electronic Systems Technology (4VHP) Information Management (1AUY) Information Systems Technology (0IYY)
SpaceTEC Certified Aerospace Technician	National Aerospace Technical Education Center (SpaceTEC)	25 SH	Aviation Maintenance Technology (4VAD) Avionic Systems Technology (4VHS) Metals Technology (4VLB) Missile & Space Systems Maintenance (4VAK) Nondestructive Testing Technology (4VXR)
Certified Automotive Fleet Manager (CAFM)	National Association of Fleet Administrators (NAFA)	3 SH	Maintenance Production Management (4VJG)
Certified Automotive Fleet Supervisor (CAFS)	National Association of Fleet Administrators (NAFA)	3 SH	Maintenance Production Management (4VJG)
Certified Dental Technician (CDT)	National Board for Certification in Dental Laboratory Technology (NBCDLT)	18 SH	Dental Laboratory Technology (7GBB)

(Cont.)

Aircraft Electronics Technician (AET)	National Center for Aerospace & Transportation Technologies (NCATT)	5 SH	Avionic Systems Technology (4VHS)
Emergency Medical Technician— Basic/ Intermediate	National Registry for Emergency Medical Technicians (NREMT)	4 SH	Fire Science (9IFY) Survival Instructor (2IBS)
Certified Pharmacy Technician (CPhT)	Pharmacy Technician Certification Board (PTCB)	17 SH	Pharmacy Technology (7GAH)
Professional Household Manager (PHM)	Front Range Training & Consulting	6 SH	Restaurant, Hotel & Fitness Management (1FRS)
Certified Ethical Hacker (CEH)	International Council of E-Commerce Consultants (EC-Council)	3 SH	CyberSecurity (0CYC)

"Welcome to the CCAF Credentialing Programs Flight." The Air University. Accessed March 18, 2015. http:www.au.af.mil/au/barnes/ccaf/certifications.asp.

AIR FORCE CREDENTIALING OPPORTUNITIES ONLINE (AFCOOL)

With an extensive credentialing program in place, why provide additional Air Force credentialing? Credentialing has two purposes. First, it continues to professionalize the enlisted force by providing up-to-date industry-recognized credentials in an Airman's Air Force job. Second, it provides a way for airmen to prepare for civilian life by ensuring that they are qualified and ready for work in the civilian sector.

There are many aspects to credentialing including certifications and licenses. In addition, there are a variety of agencies that provide credentialing. Some are at the national level while others are state or industry driven. As of March 2015, AFCOOL added 642 additional credentials offered to airmen. According to the website (https://afvec.langley.af.mil/afvec/Public/COOL/HowDoesAfCoolWork.aspx), AFCOOL provides information about credentialing and licensing and can be an indispensable tool for the following:

- Background information about civilian licensure/certification in general and specific information about individual credentials, including eligibility requirements and resources to prepare for the exam.

- Identifying licenses and certifications relevant to Air Force specialties.
- Learning how to fill gaps between Air Force training, experience, and civilian credentialing requirements.
- Learning about resources available to airmen that can help them gain civilian job credentials.

AFCOOL will take the place of the military TA certification program for enlisted and total-force airmen seeking certifications. The CCAF-specific certifications such as the Professional Manger Certification, the ISD, and the Instructor Certifications will not be affected by AFCOOL. The program allows active-duty enlisted members to complete one credential aligned with their primary AFSC. Senior noncommissioned officers are also eligible for leadership and management credentialing programs within the lifetime cap. Funding for the program began in January 2015 with full functionality in March. Eligible students are encouraged to meet with education advisors and review the updated Air Force instruction to ensure that they are familiar with all the changes to the program.

Senior noncommissioned officers are also eligible for leadership and management credentialing programs within the lifetime cap. Funding for the program began in January 2015, with full functionality expected by the year's end. Eligible students are encouraged to meet with education advisors and review the updated Air Force instruction to ensure that they are familiar with all the changes to the program.

The AFCOOL website is located at the following link: https://afvec.langley.af.mil/afvec/Public/COOL/HowDoesAfCoolWork.aspx.

This website allows airmen to view a wide array of credentials for all enlisted AFSCs. While airmen can only receive TA on approved credentials, they can view other occupations they may have an interest in for future planning. Search results will include the certifications and licenses related to those AFSCS and other information such as related civilian occupations. Airmen can also search by civilian career area, credential name, and credentialing agency name.

When an airman acquires one or more of these credentials and earns a degree from the CCAF, the qualifications can be appealing to prospective employers. Combine these qualifications with an Air Force high-level security clearance and on-the-job experience and it's easy to see why airmen are so highly regarded for the skills they obtain while in the Air Force. Examine the degree requirements from the CCAF below followed by information found on the AFCOOL website:

CYBERSECURITY Occupational Specialty 1B4X1

Degree Requirements The five-skill level must be held at the time of program completion.

Technical Education (Twenty-four semester hours)
A minimum of twelve SHs of technical core subjects or courses must be applied and the remaining semester hours applied from technical core or technical elective subjects or courses. Requests to substitute comparable courses or to exceed specified semester hour values in any subject or course must be approved in advance.

Technical Core	*Maximum Semester Hours*
CCAF Internship	18
Cyber Defense & Countermeasures	18
Cyber Laws & Ethics	3
Industrial Control Systems	3
Networking Principles	12
Principles of Communication Networks	6
Principles of Telephony Networks	3
Systems Analysis	6

Technical Electives	*Maximum Semester Hours*
Certified Ethical Hacker	3
College Algebra or higher-level Mathematics	6
Computer Science	6
CompTIA Certification	3
Global Information Assurance Certification	6
Information Security	6
(ISC)² Certification	3
Network Security	6
Physics	3

Leadership, Management and Military Studies

(Six semester hours) Professional military education, civilian management courses accepted in transfer and/or by testing credit.

Physical Education (Four semester hours)

General Education (Fifteen semester hours) Applicable courses must meet the criteria for application of courses to the general education requirement and agree with the definitions of applicable courses.

Subjects/Courses	*Semester Hours*
Oral Communication (Speech)	3
Written Communication (English composition)	3
Mathematics (Intermediate algebra or a college-level mathematics course satisfying delivering institution's mathematics graduation requirement—if an acceptable mathematics course applies as technical or program elective, you may substitute a natural science course for mathematics)	3
Social Science (Anthropology, archaeology, economics, geography, government, history, political science, psychology, sociology)	3
Humanities (Fine arts (criticism, appreciation, historical significance), foreign language, literature, philosophy, religion)	3

Program Elective (Fifteen semester hours) Courses applying to technical education, LMMS, or GER; natural science courses meeting general education requirement application criteria; foreign language credit earned at Defense Language Institute; maximum nine SHs of CCAF degree-applicable technical course credit otherwise not applicable to program of enrollment.

Navigating the AFCOOL website reveals an abundance of useful job-specific information. Airmen can select a specific specialty and uncover related credentials, AFSC information, civilian equivalent jobs, as well as federal occupations and state licenses applicable to the job.

For Cybersecurity, the following certificates demonstrate just a few of those that are available to airmen on the Air Force COOL website.

Certified Information Systems Security Professional

The Certified Information Systems Security Professional (CISSP) is an advanced skill-level certification for experienced professionals in the computer security field who are responsible for developing the information security policies, standards, and procedures and managing their implementation across an organization. To be eligible for CISSP, candidates must have five years of information security experience in at least two of the following areas:

Access Control; Application Security; Business Continuity and Disaster Recovery Planning; Cryptography; Information Security and Risk Management; Legal, Regulations, Compliance and Investigations; Operations Security; Physical (Environmental) Security; Security Architecture and Design; and Telecommunications and Network Security.

Certified Wireless Network Administrator

The Certified Wireless Network Administrator (CWNA) is an administrator-level certification for networkers who are in the field and need to thoroughly understand RF behavior, site surveying, installation, and basic enterprise Wi-Fi security. CWNA is where you learn how RF and IP come together as a Wi-Fi network. The CWNA certification is valid for three years.

Certified Wireless Network Expert

The Certified Wireless Network Expert (CWNE) is an expert-level Wi-Fi certification for the most elite Wi-Fi professionals. By successfully completing the CWNE requirements, candidates will have demonstrated that they have the most advanced skills available in today's enterprise Wi-Fi market. The CWNE certification assures that candidates have mastered all relevant skills to administer, install, configure, troubleshoot, and design wireless network systems. Protocol analysis, intrusion detection and prevention, performance and QoS analysis, spectrum analysis and management, and advanced design are some of the areas of expertise candidates will need to know.

Certified Wireless Security Professional

The Certified Wireless Security Professional (CWSP) is a professional-level certification for network engineers who seek to establish their expertise in enterprise Wi-Fi security. The CWSP certification will advance a candidate's career by ensuring they have the skills to successfully secure enterprise Wi-Fi networks from hackers, no matter which brand of Wi-Fi gear an organization deploys. Candidates must have a current CWNA credential to take the CWSP exam. The CWSP certification is valid for three years.

Cisco Certified Design Associate

Cisco Certified Design Associate (CCDA) validates knowledge required to design a Cisco converged network. Cisco Associate–level certifications are the apprentice or foundation level of networking certification. With a CCDA certification, a network professional demonstrates the skills required to design routed and switched network infrastructures and services involving LAN, WAN, and broadband access for businesses and organizations.

This includes designing basic campus, data center, security, voice, and wireless networks. The CCDA certification is appropriate for Information Technology occupations such as network and computer systems designers, operators, and administrators. There are no experience or education requirements that must be met prior to taking the exam. However, beginning October 1, 2013, the CCENT certification will become a prerequisite prior to achieving the CCDA certification.

The website will also list some comparable civilian jobs such as Computer and Information Systems Managers, Information Security Analysts, Computer Systems Engineers/Architects, and Command and Control Center Specialists.

Applicable federal occupations include the Information Technology Management series, Computer Operation series, Computer Clerk and Assistant series, Cryptography series, Cryptanalysis series, and the Computer Science series.

Two state licenses include the following:

- Computer and Information Systems Managers found at: http://www.career-infonet.org/LicensedOccupations/lois_agency.asp?stfips=99&by=occ&onetcode=11-3021.00
- Information Security Analysts found at: http://www.careerinfonet.org/LicensedOccupations/lois_agency.asp?stfips=99&by=occ&onetcode=15-1122.00

To apply for a voucher to have a credential paid for, follow the steps under the link titled "How Do I Apply?" There are six steps to requesting payment. Command must verify that you are eligible to take the exam based on the listed parameters, and you must ensure that you possess the knowledge required to successfully complete the exam(s) during your review of the certification and the approval process.

As you can see, a degree from the CCAF coupled with at least one of the certifications tailored to a specific job gives your resume the potential to stand out from others competing for the same position. The AFCOOL tools allow airmen to channel their efforts quickly and more concisely than those who do not have access to this valuable program.

Chapter 6

Air Force Commissioning and Professional Continued Education Programs

Wouldn't it be nice if you didn't have to worry about how you were going to pay for college or find a job after graduation? The Air Force seeks service from the nation's best and brightest men and women and offers an array of attractive collegiate alternatives for qualified applicants. There are many opportunities to attend numerous colleges and gain access to a variety of scholarships that can help to relieve the financial burden of a college education. In addition to getting financial assistance for attending college, appointment by the president of the United States and service as an Air Force officer await those who successfully graduate.

The following topics will be covered in this chapter:

- Air Force Reserve Officer Training Corps (ROTC)
  – Airman Scholarship and Commissioning Program (ASCP)
  – Nurse Enlisted Commissioning Program (NECP)
  – Scholarships for Outstanding Airmen to ROTC (SOAR)
- Air Force Physician Assistance Training Program
- Leaders Encouraging Airman Development (LEAD)
- The Air Force Academy and Prep School

AIR FORCE COMMISSIONING AND PROFESSIONAL CONTINUED EDUCATION PROGRAMS

Air Force Reserve Officer Training Corps (ROTC)

The Air Force ROTC scholarship can help relieve the financial burden that a college education can create and assist you in securing a job after graduation. The

Air Force ROTC program is available at more than 1,100 colleges and universities across the country. ROTC offers scholarships to high-school students, college students, and enlisted airmen with outstanding academic and leadership qualities.

Air Force ROTC offers one- to four-year scholarships on a competitive basis to both high-school and college students. Individuals accepted into the program receive partial or full tuition, as well as a nontaxable monthly stipend. In 2015, the monthly stipend was set at $300 for freshmen, $350 for sophomores, $450 for juniors, and $500 for seniors. Many colleges also offer ROTC cadets an additional subsidy for tuition, fees, and books.

To be eligible for scholarship consideration, you must achieve a SAT composite of at least 1180 (math and critical reading portions only) or an ACT composite of 26, as well as attain a cumulative GPA of at least 3.0 or higher. Applications for scholarships are due on specific cutoff dates each year. Visit the following link for current information: https://www.afrotc.com/scholarships/application.

According to the U.S. Air Force's ROTC website (https://www.afrotc.com/scholarships/types), the application process follows the same format for each of the three available scholarships:

- Type 1 pays full college tuition, most fees, and a book allowance. Approximately 5 percent of four-year scholarships are Type 1—mostly in technical fields as deemed needed by the Air Force (careers with a scientific basis such as engineering, chemistry and meteorology).
- Type 2 pays college tuition and most fees up to $18,000 per year (currently) and offers a book allowance. Approximately 15 percent of four-year scholarship winners will be offered a Type 2 scholarship (again, mostly in technical fields). If a student attends an institution where the tuition exceeds $18,000 per year (currently), he or she is responsible for the difference.
- Type 7 pays college tuition up to the equivalent of a public school's in-state rate and offers a book allowance. If a student receives a Type 7 offer but wishes to attend a college/university where they do not qualify under the guidelines, the student can convert the four-year Type 7 scholarship to a three-year Type 2 scholarship. Students cannot activate a Type 7 scholarship at a nonqualifying school and pay the difference.

To obtain current information on scholarships, visit the following site: https://www.afrotc.com/scholarships/types

Scholarships are decided by a selection board made up of senior Air Force officers who evaluate each applicant's record and interview to determine if he or she will be offered a scholarship. Consideration is given to overall potential and the "whole person" concept, specifically evaluating academic scores, leadership/work experience, extracurricular activities, results from your personal interview, and questionnaire results. Qualitative factors, such as grade point average, aptitude test scores, and unit commander evaluation determine if a candidate has officer potential.

AF ROTC allows students to have a normal college experience for the most part. Program-specific courses include Profession of Arms, Communication Skills, Leadership Studies, and Military Studies/International Security Studies. Other ROTC unique requirements for students to complete include the Air Force ROTC General Military Course (GMC), the freshman and sophomore years. After students complete the GMC requirements and want to be considered for entry into the last two years of the program, certain requirements must be met. Qualified students committed to completing their degree and becoming a commissioned officer must attend the Professional Officer Course (POC) their junior and senior years.

Once enrolled in POC, students attend class three hours a week and participate in a one- to two-hour weekly Leadership Laboratory. Students must also complete a twenty-four-day summer field training course at Maxwell AFB, Alabama, usually between their sophomore and junior years. More specific information on each course can be found at: https://www.afrotc.com/college-life/courses.

Upon successful degree and program completion, cadets accept commissions as second lieutenants in the Air Force and are appointed by the president of the United States.

Professional Officer Course Early Release Program (POC-ERP) offers active duty enlisted airmen who can complete all bachelor's degree and commissioning requirements within a two-year timeframe an opportunity for an early release from the active duty Air Force to enter the Air Force ROTC. This program is open to students in all majors. If selected, candidates separate from the active duty Air Force, join ROTC at a participating college and become a full-time student. Candidates must pursue a bachelor's degree and will be commissioned as a second lieutenant upon graduation and completion of the two-year program. Typically within sixty days of commissioning, they will then be returned to active duty for at least four years. Applicants must commission by age thirty or up to age thirty-five with a waiver that must be approved by headquarters AFROTC.

The length of the initial service commitment depends on the career pathway chosen. Most cadets will have a four-year, active-duty service commitment. Pilots have a ten-year, active-duty service commitment and both the combat system officers and the air battle managers' career fields have a six-year service commitment.

ROTC programs are designed to meet the shifting needs of the Air Force and can frequently change. To get the most up-to-date information on how the Air Force can help with your college education, contact an adviser or visit the official Air Force ROTC website at https://www.afrotc.com/.

Airmen Scholarship and Commissioning Program (ASCP)

The Airman Scholarship and Commissioning Program offers active-duty enlisted personnel the opportunity to earn a commission while completing their bachelor's degree as an Air Force ROTC cadet. Applicants must have at least twenty-four hours of graded college coursework, expect to have a minimum of a 3.0 cumulative GPA and have a minimum ACT composite score of 26, an SAT combined reading and math score of 1180, or an AFOQT academic aptitude score of 57. Applicants who apply for ASCP must be under the age of thirty-one on December 31st of their graduation year in order to earn a commission. This provision cannot be waived. A selection board is held once a year, typically focusing on the commander's recommendation, the airman's duty performance, and their academic performance. The selection criteria and process is subject to change from year to year. Visit the following website for current information: http://www.au.af.mil/au/holmcenter/afrotc/EnlistedComm/ASCP.asp.

Those selected separate from the active-duty Air Force, join ROTC at a participating college, and become a full-time student. This scholarship is awarded for two to four years, depending on how many years you have remaining in your bachelor's degree program. Upon graduation and completion of the program, you will be commissioned as a second lieutenant and will then be returned to duty with a military obligation of four years on active duty and four years in the Air Force Reserves.

Participants receive a tuition and fees scholarship for (currently) up to $18,000 per year, as well as a textbook allowance and a monthly nontaxable stipend. The scholarships are awarded in a variety of fields to include topics such as engineering, meteorology, architecture, nursing, prehealth, and foreign language areas.

Nurse Enlisted Commissioning Program (NECP)

AFROTC also encompasses the NECP which enables eligible students to pursue careers in nursing. Active duty airmen gain the opportunity to earn a bachelor's degree in nursing, an in-demand career field in the Air Force. NECP students will complete their degree at a college or university that participates in ROTC. Students commission after passing the National Council Licensure Examination (https://www.ncsbn.org/nclex.htm) and then attend Commissioned Officer Training and the Nurse Transition Program. NECP allows airmen to remain on active duty and continue to receive an income while going to school full time. Airmen selected for NECP receive a tuition and scholarship fees for up to $15,000 per year (2015), as well as a textbook allowance of $600 per year. This is subject to change each year, so always check the website for current information (http://www.airforce.com/healthcare/).

Those selected may participate for up to three years, depending upon their degree programs and previous academics. Nurse applicants must be commissioned prior to their forty-second birthday, pending the needs of the Air Force. Applicants commissioning over the age of thirty-five will need to submit a waiver request to the headquarters AFROTC.

For complete eligibility criteria and application instructions, airmen with a current computer access card can logon to myPers at: https://myPers.af.mil and enter "Nurse Enlisted Commissioning Program" in the search window, or visit the Air Force Medical Service Knowledge Exchange at https://kx2.afms.mil/kj/kx1/AFNurseEducation.

If you want to learn more about Air Force nursing along with other medical career fields, visit the following site: http://www.airforce.com/healthcare/.

Scholarships for Outstanding Airmen to ROTC (SOAR)

SOAR scholarships are offered to active-duty enlisted airmen who would like to attend college and become commissioned officers in the Air Force. Up to fifty airmen are nominated yearly for ROTC scholarships, which pay most tuition and all fees.

SOAR candidates separate from the Air Force to earn their degree. Scholarships are awarded for two to four years and are currently set at up to $18,000 per year, depending on how many years candidates have remaining in their bachelor's degree program. Airmen with some or no college credit may apply for the program. Scholarships are awarded in a variety of fields, including technical (engineering, meteorology, architecture, etc.), nontechnical, nursing, prehealth, and foreign language areas. Applicants who apply for SOAR must be under age thirty-one on December 31st of their graduation year to earn a commission.

AIR FORCE PHYSICIAN ASSISTANCE TRAINING PROGRAM

The Physician Assistance (PA) Training Program offers qualified airmen the advanced education and training they need in order to provide expert medical care to military personnel and their families. Only active-duty airmen are eligible to apply for this program. The scholarship covers all tuition, books, small equipment items and supplies needed for study, and lab fees. You also receive a monthly allowance for living expenses. Once you graduate, you will be commissioned as a lieutenant and serve a three-year active-duty commitment.

To join the team of Air Force Physician Assistants you must be a U.S. citizen, at least eighteen years of age, and able to receive a commission by age forty-one. You must also be a graduate of, or enrolled in, a nationally accredited physician assistant program at an AF ROTC institution, already be nationally certified (PA-C), and able to meet the Air Force physical and moral requirements. The minimum education requirements to perform as an Air Force Physician Assistant is a master of science (MS) in physician assistant studies from an accredited institution or associate degree in physician assistant studies with any bachelor's degree.

To learn more about the Air Force Physician Assistant program, call 1-800-588-5260 or visit the following sites: www.airforce.com/pdf/219_physician_assistant.pdf, http://www.airforce.com/careers/detail/physician-assistant/.

THE LEADERS ENCOURAGING AIRMAN DEVELOPMENT (LEAD)

The LEAD program allows commanders to seek out outstanding, deserving, and qualified airmen to compete for appointments to the Air Force Academy and the Air Force Academy Preparatory School. The LEAD program is an ongoing effort to give the best and brightest airmen an opportunity to become commissioned officers by relying on unit and wing commanders to nominate those that they believe are highly qualified and possess the potential to excel.

The LEAD program is available to airmen who are at least seventeen years old but not older than twenty-three on July 1 of their academy entry year. To be competitive, applicants must be of high moral character, unmarried with no dependents, a U.S. citizen prior to preparatory school graduation, and cannot have a legal obligation to support a child or another individual.

Typically, there are 170 appointments available for the Air Force Academy and the Academy Preparatory School for regular and reserve enlisted airmen every year; although, this is subject to change based on the needs of the Air Force. Those who wish to apply for the LEAD program are required to submit an Air Force form 1786 and a completed package that is due by specific cutoff dates. Updated information on the program and the Air Force form 1786 is available at: http://www.academyadmissions.com/admissions/advice-to-applicants/enlisted-airmen/.

THE AIR FORCE ACADEMY

Of all the Air Force scholarship opportunities available, appointment to the Air Force Academy is clearly the most stringent and respected. The prestigious Air Force Academy gives students (cadets) a high-quality, cost-free education in exchange for their commitment to be appointed by the president of the United States to serve as a commissioned officer in the Air Force. One of the big scholarship benefits to this program is that there are no tuition charges. Room, meals, medical and dental care, and a salary equal to the military rank held when admitted are all provided.

The academic program at the Air Force Academy has traditionally focused most heavily on science and engineering, since many graduates will be expected to manage complex air, space, and information technology systems. As a result, the Academy's engineering programs have traditionally been ranked very highly. Regardless of major, all graduates receive a bachelor of science degree because of the technical content of the core requirements. Cadets may choose from a variety of majors, including engineering, the basic sciences, social sciences, humanities, as well as in a variety of divisional or interdisciplinary subjects.

The academic program has an extensive core curriculum, in which all cadets take required courses in the sciences, engineering, social sciences, humanities, military studies, and physical education.

The mission of the Air Force Academy is to, "educate, train, and inspire men and women to become officers of character, motivated to lead the U.S. Air Force in service to our nation."[1] The Academy's goal is to produce Air Force officers who have the knowledge, character, motivation essential to leadership, pride in all they do, and commitment to an Air Force career. Each year eighty-five active-duty airmen and eighty-five airmen serving in the Air Force Reserve and Air National Guard may receive appointments to the Air Force Academy.

Applicants considering appointment to the Air Force Academy must obtain a nomination. A nomination does not guarantee appointment, but appointments cannot be offered without one. Securing nominations is a competitive process. The majority of applicants to the Academy obtain nominations in the Congressional and Vice Presidential categories. The Academy also reserves a select number of cadet appointments for nominees in the Military-Affiliated, U.S. Territory, and International categories. To seek nominations, applicants must first determine the categories for which you are eligible and follow the guidance on the following link: http://www.academyadmissions.com/admissions/the-application-process/nominations/.

Vacancies are available for enlisted members of the regular and reserve components of the Air Force. Applicants must complete Air Force Form 1786 to compete for appointment. Active-duty, Guard and Reserve applicants must submit the form through the unit commander and Military Personnel Flight. For more specific instructions on nominations in this category, visit this link: http://www.academyadmissions.com/admissions/advice-to-applicants/enlisted-airmen/.

The basic eligibility requirements include being at least seventeen but not past your twenty-third birthday by July 1 of the year you enter the Academy, having U.S. citizenship, and being unmarried with no dependents. Selection criteria are very strict for admission into the Academy. Applicants must take either the Scholastic Aptitude Test (SAT) or the American College Testing Program (ACT). Scores for nonstandard tests are not considered. Applicants must take a thorough medical exam scheduled by the Department of Defense Medical Examination Review Board (DODMERB). Healthy individuals with normal vision usually experience little difficulty in passing the exam.

Applicants must also pass a fitness test, which measures coordination, strength, and endurance. Preparation for the exam should include participation in organized athletics and vigorous physical activities, such as distance running and sustained exercises, to prepare for the fitness test. The Academy's elevation of more than seven thousand feet affects physical performance. The Academy will evaluate cadet's leadership potential through their record of participation in athletic activities, including team or individual sports, and nonathletic activities, such as class offices, public speaking, Civil Air Patrol, and scouting. Applicant's grades from high-school transcripts and from any preparatory school or college attended after high school will be the basis for determining academic potential. The Academy will also consider accomplishments on active duty and recommendations from supervisors if applicable.

A selection panel that is composed of senior Academy staff reviews each application and makes selections based on the "whole person concept" based on the criteria mentioned above.

The following statistics demonstrate the competitiveness of the areas of focus. A typical Academy freshman profile includes qualifications of high-school students:

- 10 percent were valedictorian/salutatorian
- 16 percent were class president or vice president
- 51 percent were in the top 10 percent of their high-school class
- 82 percent held athletic letter awards
- 64 percent were in the National Honor Society
- 29 percent participated in scouting
- Average SAT scores ranged from 590 to 660 verbal, 630 to 690 mathematics
- Average ACT scores ranged from 27 to 31 in English, 28 to 32 reading, 28 to 32 mathematics, 27 to 31 science reasoning

For detailed current information visit the following link: http://www.academyadmissions.com/admissions/the-application-process/selection-criteria/.

To obtain current information on the application steps, visit: http://www.academyadmissions.com/admissions/the-application-process/application-steps/#checkeligibility.

THE ACADEMY PREPARATORY SCHOOL (PREP SCHOOL)

More candidates seek admission to the Academy every year than there are available appointments (http://www.academyadmissions.com/the-experience/prep-school/prep-school-admissions/). Applicants with promising potential not offered appointment to the Academy may be selected to attend the Academy Prep School. Completion does improve your chances to be offered appointment to the Academy, but does not guarantee it. Admission is limited to enlisted members of the Air Force Regular and Reserve components and to selected civilian students. Prep School candidates do not need a nomination in order to attend, but they will need nominations in order to gain an appointment to the Academy. Prep school is considered active service, so if an airman doesn't complete it, they revert to their previous active or Reserve status.

Instruction in English, Science, Math, Military Training, and Athletic Development prepares students to be competitive for the limited number of appointments to the Academy.

For more information visit the following link: http://www.academyadmissions.com/the-experience/prep-school/prep-school-program/.

What to Expect

Basic Cadet Training (BCT) is a strenuous thirty-eight-day program that begins the applicant's transition to cadet life. Participants develop leadership qualities through participation in vigorous physical conditioning programs and military activities. Students learn teamwork as they solve problems working with other cadets. The highly competitive and rapidly paced training teaches cadets how to perform effectively in a short time. Cadets learn to face stress with confidence through meeting the challenges of BCT. The prep school has a similar two-week basic training program.

The Academy trains students to become professional career officers. During the fall and spring semesters, cadets learn about the armed forces and Air Force operations. Students gain first-hand knowledge of these studies when they undertake summer training programs at the Academy and other military installations worldwide. Cadets gradually develop leadership skills as they progress from follower to leader in the Cadet Wing. Flying is introduced through orientation flights and aviation instruction. All cadets may pursue interests in aviation, soaring, parachuting, or navigation. Qualified cadets who are selected to enter either pilot or navigator training after graduation take a specialized program in flight.

Military training is also part of everyday life at the prep school. It provides leadership opportunities to prepare for the military programs of the Academy. Cadets must also live by principles of professional ethics that extend beyond the code's minimum standards. Some of the principles include responsibility, confidence, respect for others, selflessness, courage, honesty, fairness, self-discipline, loyalty, and a keen sense of duty.

Academic Instruction

The academic curriculum develops innovative, analytical, and resourceful Air Force officers. Cadets complete a balanced sequence of prescribed courses in the basic and engineering sciences, social sciences, and humanities. Demanding academic workloads are carried from the time students enter the institution until graduation. In the fall of the first year, cadets enter academic classes and begin working toward a degree.

The Academy offers thirty-two majors, which relate to the Air Force career fields. Students may choose a major in a subject area suited to their interests.

If cadets have the talents and interests to pursue further study, they may take elective enrichment courses.

The honors version of core courses offers more in-depth study of course material. Prep school courses begin on the high-school level and proceed rapidly to college-level material. Intensive instruction in English, math, and science prepares participants for the SAT and ACT tests required for entrance into the Academy and the Academy's challenging academic programs.

Physical Education and Athletics

The athletic program helps build physical fitness and develop leadership attributes such as confidence and the will to win. Cadets learn skills for many sports in the physical education classes and compete in a variety of intramural contests. If cadets have an aptitude for a particular sport, they can join one of the Academy's twenty-seven intercollegiate teams.

Known as the Falcons, the teams compete in the Mountain West Conference (MWC) along with Brigham Young University, Colorado State University, University of Nevada Las Vegas, San Diego State University, Texas Christian University, and universities in New Mexico, Utah, and Wyoming.

The men's and women's teams participate in Division I of the NCAA. The teams also compete against the other service academies. The prep school athletic program includes physical conditioning classes, intramural sports, and varsity athletics. The four varsity athletic teams are known as Huskies.

Extracurricular Activities

The Community Center Chapel, the Cadet Chapel, and local area churches provide many opportunities for religious worship. Chaplains of all major faiths are available to counsel students. To further cadet's own hobbies and interests, they can join cadet clubs and professional groups. Cadets can entertain guests in the cadet social center on weekends. Cadet dances and concerts by popular entertainers are held there frequently.

The prep school also has several clubs and activities throughout the year. On-campus recreation facilities include swimming pools, outdoor courts, and golf courses. Cadets can also hike, backpack, and fish right in the area or at other nearby places. Many Colorado ski resorts are less than a three-hour drive from the Academy. The most obvious benefit of the scholarship is paid tuition. Room and board, medical and dental care, and an $845 monthly cash allowance are provided so students can often afford to partake in events such as ski trips.

The school calendar reflects fall and spring semesters, plus two-month summer terms. The total semester hours equals approximately 160 hours with graduates earning a bachelor of science degree and an Air Force commission. All graduates are career assigned and there is a wide variety of career areas available to choose from in the Air Force. For those interested in flying, selected graduates may enter pilot or navigator training. Airmen have the opportunity to retire between the twenty- and thirty-year point of their active service.

All Air Force Academy graduates must serve at least five years on active duty. Pilots and navigators must serve for a longer commitment. The length of commitment is determined by Air Force policy in effect at the time of graduation from flight training.

Chapter 7

Cost and Payment Resources

Funding for school can be an easy and painless process if airmen plan accordingly. If on active duty, choose a school within the available Tuition Assistance (TA) funding limits. If transitioning off active duty, choose a school that is within GI Bill coverage parameters. Conducting quality research according to the methods outlined in this book will enable airmen to pursue a debt-free, quality education. Why pay for school if you have access to funding options?

The following topics will be covered in this section:

- Financial Goals
- Air Force Tuition Assistance
- MGIB
- Post-9/11
- GI Bill Top-Up
- GI Bill Activation
- Transferability
- Yellow Ribbon Program
- VA GI Bill Feedback System
- Federal Student Aid
- State-Based Veteran Education Benefits
- Scholarships (Including Dependents)
- Textbook Buying Options
- Free Subject Matter Study Support

FINANCIAL GOALS

Transitioning from the service is a difficult process. Veterans who prepare for it in advance will find the experience to be less stressful, which will enable them to focus on their studies more effectively. Forming a plan in advance will help to minimize potential distractions. Veteran students that minimize their risk of distraction during the school year will achieve a higher degree of academic success. Successfully educated or trained veterans will be more productive in their future endeavors and better able to enrich their surrounding civilian communities.

Bypassing the work option, veterans have three main sources of income while attending school, not including any potential scholarships that veteran students might apply for and receive. These sources include:

- GI Bill housing stipend
- Federal Student Aid (Pell Grant)
- Unemployment

If a veteran is able to maximize benefits under each of these three options, he or she will have a good base from which to start and hopefully not have to worry about daily stressors, such as making rent, gas, and food.

The housing stipend on the Post-9/11 GI Bill typically is not enough to take care of one individual's personal needs, especially because "break pay" money is not paid while the student is not physically in school. The section titled "Post-9/11" in this chapter explains that the housing allowance is prorated, and veterans will most likely not be receiving as much money as they expect.

Federal Student Aid (FSA) Pell Grant money can be a great benefit for veterans attending school. Think about having upwards of an extra $5,775 (2015–2016) per academic year to help with education-related expenses above and beyond the GI Bill. How much better off would you be for spending thirty minutes to fill out the FAFSA? The time will be well spent, especially if you are awarded assistance.

Your previous year's tax information is required to fill out the FAFSA, so you need to pay attention upon your initial separation from active duty. If you have recently separated from the military, your tax information may not reflect your current financial situation. For example, if Staff Sergeant Kirk separates in July of 2015 and plans on beginning college in August 2015, he will submit his 2014 taxes on the FAFSA that reflect his military pay. The main problem is that he will no longer be working and receiving this level

of pay. In most cases, a veteran's pay is drastically reduced upon separation. If Staff Sergeant Kirk does not receive an award or does not receive the full amount, he needs to visit the financial aid office at his school, explain that he has a special circumstance, and request to have his listed income level readjusted. Hopefully, upon readjustment of his income, he will be eligible for the maximum amount of Pell Grant award. Be aware that Pell Grant money is based on your tax information, so it will fluctuate from person to person depending upon household finances.

The Unemployment Compensation for Ex-Servicemembers (UCX) program may help eligible separating service members rate some level of unemployment. Unemployment will vary state by state because the law of the state determines how much money an individual can receive, the length of time to remain eligible, and any other eligibility conditions. Veterans must have been honorably separated in order to be eligible. Information on unemployment can be located on the Department of Labor's website (http://workforcesecurity.doleta.gov/unemploy/uifactsheet.asp).

Contact your local State Workforce Agency (http://www.servicelocator.org/OWSLinks.asp) upon separation to determine eligibility and apply. Make sure to have a copy of your DD-214.

Some military members may receive a service-connected disability percentage; others may not. When you separate from the military, you will be screened by the VA to determine whether you sustained any injuries or diseases while on active duty, or if any previous health-related issues were made worse by active military service. If you receive a minimum rating of 10 percent or higher, you may be eligible to receive a tax-free stipend from the VA every month. Zero percent ratings do not have a monetary stipend attached; however, in the "State-Based Benefit" section of this chapter, you will see that many states offer benefits that are tied to these disability ratings. For example, in California a zero percent rating equals free tuition for your children at state-supported institutions of higher learning. If you receive a percentage rating, this may help with your expenses. Be aware that ratings can take as long as twelve months to be determined, and there is such a thing as no rating.

Make sure to be screened prior to exiting the military. If you are not sure where to find your local VA office, it might even be on the base where you are stationed. The Disabled American Veterans (DAV) and the Veterans of Foreign Wars (VFW) maintain offices at several military bases and may assist you as well. Many academic institutions have visiting representatives from these organizations. They will help you with your initial claim if you did not make it while still on active duty. They can also help you submit for a claims adjustment if your medical situation has changed. Speaking with an individual from a service organization may help you complete a more thoroughly organized claim and assist you in eliminating any further complications.

TUITION ASSISTANCE

Interested in attending school while on active duty? The Air Force offers TA to those serving within its ranks. Pursuing classes while on active duty will help airmen expedite their schooling upon separation, and maybe even help to save GI Bill benefits for a master's degree at a later date.

TA is only available to cover the tuition; books and supplies are out of pocket. These costs can sometimes become expensive. Prepare in advance for all potential funding possibilities by checking out a few other options. FSA money is a great source of funding, if you are eligible. Many airmen are eligible for the Pell Grant portion of FSA. Pell Grant awards do not need to be repaid, but must be used for educational expenses only. These students are often able to continue their educations throughout the year even if they reach their TA fiscal year funding caps. More information on this topic can be found later in this chapter.

The Air Force military TA program is currently governed by Air Force Instruction (AFI) 36-2649 dated October 1, 2014. The Air Force provides TA for the cost of tuition, not to exceed $250.00 per semester hour (SH) credit, $166.66 per quarter hour (QH) credit, and a fiscal year TA cap of $4,500.00, applicable to all eligible airmen. Any combined use for reservists of active-duty TA and Reserve TA also has an annual cap of $4,500.00. The two funds cannot be used to pay for the same course. For example, TA for activated Guard and the TA benefit offered by the state Air National Guard cannot be used to pay for the same course.

The Air Force provides TA when term dates fall within an airman's dates of activation, for active-duty and activated/mobilized Air Reserve Component (ARC) personnel with an approved e-Degree in the Air Force Automated Education Management System (AFAEMS) and an education record. Enlisted members must be on active duty for the length of the term. If duty dates do not correspond with term dates, they must be eligible to reenlist and show written intent.

Regular Air Force on active-duty (RegAF) officers must have a date of separation (DOS) or deactivation date that is two years or more after the end of the term date listed on the application for TA for the requested class. Officers unable to meet this requirement will not be authorized TA. Officers eligible to receive TA will incur a two-year Active Duty Service Commitment (ADSC). ADSCs are computed based on the term end date reflected on the AF Form 1227. Officers are subject to recoupment action on remaining ADSC if they should separate or retire before the ADSC is completed.

Activated Reserve and Guard Airmen on Title 10 or Title 32 orders must supply a copy of orders and meet all eligibility requirements for receiving TA. All documents must be uploaded to the AFAEMS file to include airman's home unit address. Activated/mobilized officers must agree to remain a member of the AF Reserve or Individual Ready Reserve (IRR) for at least four years after completing a course funded by TA. Officers unable to meet this commitment will not be authorized TA.

Activated/mobilized reserve officers must agree to remain a member of the Selected Reserve (SELRES) or IRR for four years after completion of any courses for which TA was assigned. A signed Reserve Commitment (RSC) contract reflecting the four-year ADSC will be uploaded into AFAEMS prior to issuing TA. The request for activated reserve officers will be routed first to Air Reserve Personnel Center (ARPC) for validation of the ADSC before going to the active-duty supervisor for final approval.

Airmen using TA must use the electronic degree plan (E-Degree) on the Air Force Virtual Education Center (AFVEC). Degree plans must be officially evaluated by the degree granting institution and include all transfer credit accepted toward degree completion. Transfer work includes, but is not limited to, academic tests, Community College of the Air Force credit, other Air Force training, and courses taken at other academic institutions. The e-Degree must include all courses required for completion of the degree and include the original plan supplied by the institution to the airman for a single degree. Airmen must provide an evaluated degree plan from the academic institution no later than completion of the first six SHs (or equivalent) with the institution. TA will be denied until an evaluated degree plan is received and approved by the education center. Courses taken after the completion of six SHs but before the approval of the e-Degree for which airmen use any other funding source will not be eligible for retroactive TA.

Any changes to the education plan after approval may result in the denial of TA until a new plan is submitted and approved. Courses taken during the denial period using other funding sources will not be eligible for retroactive TA. TA must be reimbursed by the student for unsatisfactory or missing grades. Unsatisfactory grades are a D and below for undergraduate courses and a C or below for graduate courses. Missing grades are grades not received and updated in official student education records by the sixtieth day after the end of the term on the approved TA request (AF Form 1227, Authority for TA).

Airmen receiving incomplete or "I" grades must attain a satisfactory grade within the time limit stipulated by the institution or 120 calendar days after the end of the term as listed on the AF Form 1227, whichever comes first. At the end of this period, refund action will be initiated if a satisfactory grade has not been received. Should an airman present a grade after the deadline, TA money will not be returned to the airman since he or she failed to meet the completion requirements. Recoupment action cannot be stopped or suspended.

Airmen must maintain a cumulative undergraduate GPA of 2.0 or higher at the undergraduate level upon completion of fifteen SHs or the equivalent or they will not be eligible to have TA authorized for future classes until they raise their GPA to the required level. This means paying out of pocket in most cases. For graduate-level courses, a GPA of 3.0 or higher on a 4.0 grading scale after the completion of six SHs or the equivalent must be maintained. The Air Force will not reimburse a student for course(s) taken at a student's own expense or for courses taken while using any other funding source to raise his or her GPA. If a student falls below the minimum GPA, then takes courses paid for using other funding sources in order to meet minimum GPA requirement, these grades will be used to compute the new GPA.

Airmen who have an Unfavorable Information File (UIF), are on a control roster, have failed their most recent physical fitness test or are overdue, and/ or have a current referral EPR/OPR at the time of application for TA are not eligible, and no waivers are given. Airmen who are denied TA and use other means to fund courses are not eligible for retroactive TA for those courses after the removal of the above-listed barriers. All other eligibility requirements apply in order for airmen to resume receiving TA.

Supervisors must approve or disapprove all TA requests and can deny based on certain criteria if they believe any of the below circumstances will impede successful completion of the requested courses. Situations include but are not limited to times when airmen:

- Are in Upgrade Training.
- Will be Temporary Duty (TDY) during any portion of the course.
- Will be PCSing during any portion of the course.
- Are scheduled to attend or are enrolled in Professional Military Education (PME).

Other factors can be deemed by the supervisor to be impediments to successful course completion, including excessive course load (two or more courses in an accelerated term). Airmen assigned overseas must meet eligibility criteria outlined in DoD Instruction 1322.19, Voluntary Education Programs in Overseas Areas.

The Air Force can assign TA for courses provided by institutions that sign the DoD Partnership MOU (http://dodmou.com/), AF Addendum, and an Installation MOU if the institution conducts business on a base. Institutions must be accredited by a regional, national, or specialized accrediting body recognized by the U.S. Department of Education (DoEd).

Air Force TA funds may be authorized for off-duty courses leading to the completion of a high-school diploma, up to 124 SH (186 QH) for a bachelor's degree and 42 SH (70 QH) for a graduate degree. Airmen may pursue more than one major within the same degree as long as the total number of semester hours for the degree outlined above is not exceeded. Those enrolled in a degree program that exceeds the semester hour limit before the date of AFI 36-2649 dated the first of October, 2014, will be allowed to continue in their program; however, if airmen change their program of study they will be subject to the guidelines outlined in this publication.

TA is not authorized to be used toward an educational goal at a lower or equal level of one attained either before or after entering the service. Airmen who have a degree from the CCAF are not eligible to use TA to fund a civilian associate's degree, but may pursue a subsequent degree from the CCAF. Airmen can have multiple degrees from CCAF because many retrain into different jobs that often have an aligned CCAF degree.

Officers who have completed an AF-sponsored master's degree, such as the Air Force Institute of Technology (AFIT), Air War College (AWC), and Air Command and Space College (ACSC), are ineligible to pursue a degree using TA. TA may be approved for an officer who already possesses a master's degree and who has received Secretary of the Air Force International Attaché Program (SAF/IAPA) approval to pursue a master's degree in a designated program for a foreign language or international political-military studies with a foreign area concentration. Officers holding a doctorate (or equivalent) are ineligible. In addition, TA is not authorized for post-master's courses or doctoral degrees and their equivalents.

Airmen are required to reimburse the government for missing grades, non-completions, withdrawals, or unsatisfactory grades (a grade of D or below at undergraduate level and a grade of C or below at the graduate level) of a TA funded course. Airmen and their supervisors will receive notification of the student's indebtedness via e-mail. The e-mail will direct the student to log on to the AFVEC for guidance and initiation of reimbursement action. It is imperative that students maintain an updated official Air Force e-mail in AFVEC in order to facilitate the delivery of up-to-date information.

Airmen must complete TA training annually. This can be done by logging on to the AFVEC and navigating to the "Annual TA Benefits Training" link on the "My Education Record" Menu. For more information about how to get started accessing your TA, contact your local education center. The counselors can assist you in finding a school that will meet your needs and walk you through the process of using the benefit. The new TA DECIDE website (http://www.dodmou.com/TADECIDE/) can help you find reputable schools that fit your search parameters as well as detail any complaints that have been made and verified within the DODMOU-approved school systems.

MONTGOMERY GI BILL (MGIB)

Not all service members have MGIB. When you entered the service, if you elected to opt into MGIB and paid $100 per month for your first year of service to total $1,200, you might rate MGIB. You must be separated with an honorable discharge as well; that goes for most benefits. Double-check your eligibility on the GI Bill website (http://www.benefits.va.gov/gibill/).

As of October 1, 2015, MGIB will pay $1,789 per month for up to thirty-six months for school. MGIB does not have a separate housing and book stipend like the Post-9/11. It is a flat payment amount. MGIB can be used for academic degrees, certificate programs, on-the-job training (OJT), correspondence classes, apprenticeship programs, and flight training. Benefits are good for ten years after separation from the military.

Some service members participated in the $600 Buy-Up Program under MGIB. For those who did, an extra $150 per month will be added to their MGIB payments. That amount per month pays you back the $600 investment within the first four months. Every month after that point is money you are profiting from the program. If you cannot remember if you paid the optional Buy-Up Program, check with DFAS. You must pay the $600 at DFAS and it is important you keep your receipts and provide them to the VA because you must prove that you took part in the program. For those who did not pay the money, check with the veterans' representatives at the school you are interested in attending before running off to pay it now. If you select Post-9/11, you forfeit the $600 that it takes to fully fund the Buy-Up. Smaller Buy-Up packages can be bought for prorated amounts. If you rate it and decide to stay under MGIB, you will most likely want to pay the Buy-Up for increased monthly payments.

Currently, if you have paid into MGIB, remain under MGIB, and have exhausted all thirty-six months of the benefit, you may be able to extend out an extra twelve months on Post-9/11. Contact the VA for final eligibility determination on this pathway. Typically, this requires that you have one period of qualifying service between August 1, 2009 and July 31, 2011, or completed two periods of qualifying service active duty after August 1, 2011. Multiple periods of active duty before August 1, 2009, will also make you eligible. See the following website for more information: https://gibill.custhelp.com/app/answers/detail/a_id/1475/kw/12%20month%20extension%20after%20MGIB/session/L3RpbWUvMTQ0MDc5MzA5OC9zaWQva1RFMzM0dm0%3D. This may enable you to save some benefit for a master's degree or a certificate program after completing a bachelor's degree. The problem is that in most cases, MGIB will not cover all of your bills.

You must decide whether you want less money consistently over forty-eight months or more money over thirty-six months using the Post-9/11. Graduate programs tend to be considerably more expensive than undergraduate programs and if you use all thirty-six months of the Post-9/11 getting your bachelors you may need to use loans to get a graduate degree. Think wisely and be as creative as possible with the combination of benefits that are at your disposal.

POST-9/11

The Post-9/11 GI Bill is truly an amazing educational benefit available to eligible veterans. To determine your eligibility, visit the website (http://www.benefits.va.gov/gibill/). Basically, to rate 100 percent of the Post-9/11, you need to meet these criteria:

• Served thirty-six consecutive months after September 11, 2001
• Received an honorable discharge

There are other categories for approval, but, like I have stressed at other points in this book, always check to determine your specific eligibility. In this case, contact the VA at 1-888-GIBILL-1.

The Post-9/11 GI Bill has three financial components built into the program: books and supplies, housing, and tuition.

Books and Supplies

Post-9/11 has a books and supplies stipend. The stipend is prorated at $41.67 per credit hour for a maximum of $1,000 per academic year. A regular full-time student, who enrolls in a minimum of twelve credits per semester, would receive the full $1,000. The stipend is broken into two payments per academic year and paid at the beginning of each semester.

You should take note that $1,000 is not actually a great amount for books. Oftentimes books can run over $200 per class. Many universities list the approximate costs of textbooks for the school year on their website. For example, California State University, Long Beach (CSULB), estimates their books at $1,860 for the 2015–2016 academic year. According to their calculations, $1,000 won't cut it for books. You definitely need to check into other options. The "Textbook-Buying Options" section in this chapter is dedicated to helping you find used or rental books.

Housing

The housing stipend gets slightly more complicated. Referred to as the Monthly Housing Allowance (MHA), it is equivalent to the salary for an E-5 with dependents and applies for everyone. That is great if you separated anywhere near E-5, but if you separated as a general, you will need to do some adjusting with your budget (sorry—that is my bad sense of humor!). You can use the GI Bill Comparison Tool (http://department-of-veterans-affairs. github.io/gi-bill-comparison-tool/) to determine the amount of MHA attached to the institution you would like to attend. That is right; the MHA is based on the zip code of your school, not your abode. So, all veterans attending the institution will be set at the same rate for their stipends.

If attending school strictly online, the Post-9/11 housing rate was set at $783.00 as of August 1, 2015. This amount can vary each year. Check the website, http://www.benefits.va.gov/GIBILL/resources/benefits_resources/ rates/ch33/ch33rates080115.asp, for current rates.

Tuition

Tuition under the Post-9/11 GI Bill can get complicated to explain. I am going to keep it simple. If you follow the most basic of parameters, you will not pay a dime for your school. Go outside of these parameters and you run into technical billing questions; in this case, you should contact the school you are interested in attending for further information. If you are pursuing an undergraduate or graduate degree, plan on attending a state school and using your Post-9/11 GI Bill, and finish your degree within the thirty-six months of benefit that you have allotted, your schooling should be covered. The thirty-six months is enough for most bachelor's degrees if you stay on track because it equates to nine months of school per year over the course of four years. Traditionally, we do not usually attend school in the summer, although you may if you are interested. If one of these factors changes, so might your bill. Veterans who choose to attend private school will receive a maximum of 21,084.89 for the academic year 2015–2016 (http://www.benefits. va.gov/GIBILL/resources/benefits_resources/rates/ch33/ch33rates080114. asp). Anything above that amount and you run the risk of having to pay out of pocket. I state it this way because many schools participate in the Yellow Ribbon Program (http://www.benefits.va.gov/gibill/yellow_ribbon.asp), and it may help cover private school costs that come in above the maximum VA allotted threshold.

What about out-of-state tuition, you ask? Out-of-state tuition is what non-residents must pay a public school when enrolled. Tuition can be much higher for nonresidents because they have not contributed to the tax pool of that state, hence they have not earned the resident rate of tuition. The Veterans Access, Choice, and Accountability Act of 2014 (https://veterans.house.gov/ the-veterans-access-choice-and-accountability-act-of-2014-highlights) was passed in July 2014 and as of the academic year 2015–2016, schools that take Post-9/11 dollars will need to list veterans as instate residents for tuition purposes. If you attend a public college within three years of your separation date and use a GI Bill for payment, out-of-state tuition charges should not be a problem as of the start of the Fall 2015 semester. If you decide to remain off your GI Bill in the beginning, schools do not have to extend the honorary in-state residency benefit to you.

If you elect to stay off of your GI Bill until a later date and intend to pay out of pocket, double-check to see if the state has passed state-based legislation offering veterans honorary instate residency. Approximately half of the states in the country have some type of legislation that will assist with this matter.

As stated above, the VA will pay you the full-time housing allowance if you pursue school at the full-time rate. The VA considers twelve credit hours to be full-time. However, if you have no previous college credit and intend on pursuing a bachelor's degree, twelve credits per semester will not suffice. Most bachelor's degrees require students to complete 120 semester credit hours of specific subject matter in order to have the degree conferred on them. This equates to fifteen credit hours each semester, or five classes.

The college year runs similar to the high-school year, two semesters each year over the course of four years. So, 120 semester hours breaks down to fifteen semester hours each semester to total thirty credits each year (freshman year: 30; sophomore year: 30; junior year: 30; senior year: 30—total: 120). If you follow the VA's minimum guidelines of twelve credits each semester, or four classes, you will run out of benefits at the end of your senior year, but only have earned ninety-six semester credit hours, which will make you twenty-four credits shy of the 120 required. You will be out of benefit but will not have obtained your degree. The academic counselors at the school you attend will help you with your degree plans. If you need to make changes or have questions, contact them for further advice.

The Comparison Tool on the main GI BILL website (http://department-of-veterans-affairs.github.io/gi-bill-comparison-tool/) will allow you to complete a quick comparison between schools that you might be interested in attending. You can determine factors such as what you will receive based upon the federal benefit you elect to use, the amount of money you will receive for the housing stipend under Post-9/11, graduation rates, how many veterans attend the school, and the institution's Yellow Ribbon status which can be important if you elect to attend a private school. In most cases, you will use the site to help determine whether MGIB or Post-9/11 will be a better choice. Since the current MGIB rate is set at $1789 a month, you can make solid comparisons between the two bills. Remember that this site will not account for any state-based education benefit that you might also have available for use.

After inputting the required information, you can view the "Total GI Bill Benefits" number given by the tool which is worth nine months of schooling (one academic year). On the drop-down menu select any GI Bill to see what it is worth at that institution, and compare this number for each school. Since the MGIB is currently worth $1,789 a month, every nine-month period will equal $16,101, so compare this number to the housing stipend under Post-9/11 for nine months to determine what each bill is worth for a particular school to determine proper usage.

MGIB VERSUS POST-9/11

I have only found a few situations in which it makes more sense for the veteran to remain under MGIB instead of opting for Post-9/11. There are three big ones. The first is if your MHA is low. This may occur in areas where the cost of living is not that high, such as large rural areas where the MHA rarely breaks the $800 or $900 mark. Be aware that you still need to calculate the cost of your tuition and fees into the total overall money being spent. You might make more initially but after paying your school and book bills you may find yourself a little short of money. Typically, the cost of the school needs to be very low in order for this tactic to be beneficial.

The second situation occurs if a veteran determines that an online program is the best fit. Students pursuing online-only school under the Post-9/11 GI Bill currently receive $783.00 per month (2015–2016 school year) for a housing stipend. The amount is half of the national average of the housing stipend paid for the face-to-face rate. Student veterans should do careful cost comparisons in this situation and enlist the assistance of someone from the local education center who thoroughly understands the GI Bills. The overall costs of the classes compared to the amount received under MGIB for the time span must be considered as well as the difference of what the student would have received under Post-9/11, to include the book stipend. Calculations can get tricky, so reach out for help.

The third situation occurs when veterans attend school in a state with a full state-based benefit. The "State-Based Veteran Education Benefits" section of this chapter will review these circumstances and demonstrate why a veteran might elect to remain under MGIB. States can also offer nonmilitary specific programs that may pay tuition. California, for example, has the Board of Governors Waiver (BOG) which pays tuition at any community college in the state if you are eligible. The Post-9/11 will not pay tuition twice, so the benefit is effectively worth less in this situation, thereby potentially increasing the overall worth of the MGIB in comparison. Be careful in this situation though. Oftentimes, even though the BOG might pay the school, in most areas of California the housing stipend under Post-9/11 is significantly higher than the $1,789 that MGIB currently pays out per month.

Prior to choosing either GI Bill, it is best to discuss all available options. Contact your state VA to determine your available state benefits and learn how to use them. Contact the veterans' department at the institution you would like to attend and request guidance. Typically, the veterans' representatives can offer great advice pertaining to the best benefit pathway. They have already blazed the trail and learned the ropes for themselves. If you are eligible, you might be able to use the MGIB if it is going to be worth more at your initial school, and then switch to the Post-9/11 if you decide to go to a more expensive school or a school with a higher MHA at a later date. Be careful to check your eligibility with this option as it does not pertain to everyone (https://gibill.custhelp.com/app/answers/detail/a_id/1475). You will simply have the remaining months left out of the total thirty-six months. The VA also offers guidance and can be reached at 1-888-GIBILL-1.

You must also verify your enrollment at your school, using the WAVE system, or Web Automated Verification of Enrollment, to receive your $1,789 per month. This system can be found here: https://www.gibill.va.gov/wave/index.do. Many veterans are concerned that they must pay the full cost of tuition up front when using the MGIB, and this might be the case for you.

If you determine that the MGIB will net you more money than the Post-9/11 at your particular school, it might make a bit more work for you. Many schools prefer the Post-9/11 because tuition is paid up front; however, schools have been using the MGIB for many years and are familiar with the system. Many schools have also offered to delay tuition payments until the veteran receives enough money from the MGIB to pay tuition or may place veterans on an interest-free payment plan. This might not be relevant if you are double-dipping from a state-based benefit that is covering your tuition. Be your own best advocate and research all possible options, including discussing your situation with the school, before committing to any one pathway. If you need more guidance on the process, visit your local education center for advice.

GI BILL TOP-UP

If an airman is attending school while on active duty and chooses a school that costs more than the amount allotted under TA, GI Bill Top-Up can be used to top off the TA. The airman would activate his or her GI Bill and tap into it as a funding resource for the portion of the class that was not covered by TA. This would affect the airmen's overall remaining benefit amount upon separation from the military.

TA only covers up to $250 per credit hour. If an airman chooses a school that costs $350 per semester hour and is taking a three-semester hour class, he or she will be $300 out of pocket for the entire class after using TA. The remaining amount of money will be his or her responsibility to pay out of pocket. In this case, Top-Up could be used to cover the amount.

Using Top-Up may be necessary in some cases, but typically using the GI Bill while on active duty should be avoided. Tapping into Top Up will pull on the airman's available GI Bill months, thereby reducing the amount of benefits remaining after separation from the military.

GI Bill benefits are calculated differently if used while on active duty, and it is not to your advantage. Top Up avoids this problem because you will only lose the amount above what is covered by TA, but Top Up does not function correctly under the Post-9/11 GI Bill. Under Post-9/11 Top Up users lose benefits based on time; under MGIB users lose benefits based on cost amount. Under MGIB, if the cost of the class is $250 above the allotted TA amount, then you only lose $250 of your benefit. If MGIB is worth $1,789 for thirty days, then $300 is about five days of benefits used. Under the Post-9/11, it is your status as a student multiplied by the number of days in class that is used. If you are a 50 percent time student enrolled in a class that is two months long then that is one whole month of the Post-9/11 spent. Talk to an education counselor, a GI Bill counselor (1-888-GIBILL-1), and the VA certifying official at your school before making a decision about which benefit to use in this case. Remember that once you elect to use the Post-9/11 GI Bill you cannot go back to MGIB. In some cases, but not all, if you opt to use MGIB while on active duty you can switch to Post-9/11 at a later date.

Many institutions across the country cost less than or equal to the amount covered under TA. If the institution you are planning on attending is over the $250 threshold and recommending GI Bill Top Up, please speak to an academic counselor for advice prior to making any final decisions.

Three situations come to mind when I discuss using Top-Up for service members.

1. If the individual is about to run out of TA money, is at the end of his or her degree, and is separating from active duty soon. In this case, it is important to note that the individual will obtain the degree prior to separating, and will be able to list the accomplishment on his or her résumé. This enables the veteran to get into the workforce faster.
2. In most master's degree programs, the cost is above and beyond the $250 per credit hour that TA can cover. Completing an advanced degree while still on active duty will be an enormous benefit to separating service members.
3. If the service member is looking to attend a prestigious university and cannot cover the costs out of pocket. In this case, I would typically recommend attending a local community college (many have fully online, fast-paced programs available) for as long as possible prior to transferring into the university. At least this way, the individual would not be drawing from his or her GI Bill for such an extended period of time.

For the undergraduate rate of study, try all possibilities prior to looking into Top-Up. Oftentimes, the Pell Grant is a viable option (check the "Federal Student Aid" section). Ultimately, the decision to use Top-Up must be the service member's, but the guidelines above offer solid advice and should be considered prior to making a move.

GI BILL APPLICATION AND CONVERSION PROCESS

The application process for the GI Bill is not complicated; however, it does currently take approximately four to six weeks to receive the Certificate of Eligibility (COE) statement. Make sure to allot time for the wait prior to starting school. If you find yourself in a time crunch, check with your school to see if the institution will defer payment, based on your veteran status, until you receive the COE.

If you have MGIB and you are positive you want to convert to Post-9/11, the process can be done at the same time you activate the benefit for a specific school. This process can occur before or after you separate from the military, so it would be wise to be absolutely certain of what school you will be attending before deciding which GI Bill to use. If you choose to switch to the Post-9/11, but you decide to attend a different school at a later, you will not be able to switch back if the MGIB is the more advantageous benefit to use at your new school.

To activate the GI Bill, you will need to access the Veterans Online Application (VONAPP) (http://www.vabenefits.vba.va.gov/vonapp/default.asp). You can also access it by going to the main GI Bill website (http://www.benefits.va.gov/gibill/): select the "Post-9/11" link on the right-hand side, select "Get Started" on the left-hand side, select "Apply for Benefits," and lastly select "Apply Online." You will need three pieces of information before you proceed:

- Your school's name and address
- A bank account and routing number (VA is direct deposit)
- An address you will be at in the next four to eight weeks

The easiest way to prepare for the application process is to be accepted to your intended institution prior to applying to activate your benefit, but you can change the required information at a later date by contacting the VA at 1-888-GIBILL-1.

The VA does not send hard checks anymore. Inputting your bank account and routing numbers enables them to directly deposit your MHA and book stipend money. If you later change the bank with which you have an account, you may change the bank account information using the VA's Direct Deposit form.

The address you list will be where your COE is delivered. Airmen living in the barracks might want to send their COEs to their parents or another reliable family member's address. Just make sure that the individuals located at the listed address keep an eye out for the document and inform you when it arrives. You will need to take that document to the veterans' representative at your school as soon as you receive it, because it is the school's ticket to receive payment from the VA. This is part of the process for you to receive the housing allowance if you are using the Post-9/11.

Process of Applying

On entering the VONAPP website (http://www.vabenefits.vba.va.gov/vonapp/default.asp), you will be asked if you are a first-time VONAAP user; answer accordingly. Next, you will be asked if you possess an eBenefits Account. I find this to be a difficult way to enter the site. If you answer that you do not have an eBenefits account, you will need to create a VONAPP account (this seems to be a much easier pathway!). Be aware that you will need an eBenefits account for all other VA-related concerns. Once settled, select the "22-1990 Education Benefits" form to proceed. The first question on the form will ask you which GI Bill you wish to use, and if you elect to receive a benefit you do not currently have, it will also ask you which GI Bill you will be giving up, which will be MGIB in most cases. The VONAPP website will also ask you information pertaining to your active-duty tours, prior education and training, upcoming start date for your school and training (input a date later than the actual start date and you will not have benefits until that time!), pursuit of study (associate degree, bachelor's degree, graduate degree, or apprenticeship or on-the-job training), and so on. The form is not overly complicated, so do not overthink the answers to the questions.

If you are concerned about the questions on the 22-1990 or whether you are making the correct choices, contact the VA at 1-888-GIBILL-1. The veterans' representatives at your intended school are usually good sources of information as well. Check with your base's education center to see if they keep paper copies of the 22-1990s if you would like to see the required information in advance or request advice.

Once you receive the COE, you need to take it (a copy!) to the veterans' representatives at your school. You will also need a copy of your DD Form 214. When you finish filling out and submitting the 22-1990, the main page on the VONAPP will maintain two links (side by side) with required, printable information; one is your submitted application, and the other is your local processing center, which is oftentimes not in the same state. Most institutions will also want a copy of your DD-214 for verification purposes.

If you have used the VA benefit before and are transferring to a new school, you will need to fill out the 22-1995 form, but only if you are not changing the GI Bill chapters. The 22-1995 form can be found on the VONAPP website.

POST-9/11 TRANSFERABILITY TO DEPENDENTS

Active-duty service and some reserve members may be eligible to transfer their Post-9/11 GI Bill benefits to dependents. The transfer process requires a four-year commitment to stay in the military. If benefits are successfully transferred, certain rules apply while the service member remains on active duty.

To be eligible to transfer benefits, service members must be eligible for Post-9/11 and:

- have completed six years of active-duty service to transfer
- have four years remaining on contract (enlisted) or commit four more years (officer)

OR is precluded by standard policy or statute from serving an additional four years (must agree to serve maximum time allowed by such policy). These exceptions commonly include Mandatory Retirement Dates, Retention Control Points, or a medical separation. Transfer must be approved the while service member is still in the Armed Forces.

In a nutshell, airmen need to have completed the required time in service, depending upon transferring to a spouse or a child, and have four years left on their enlistment. The best time to complete the process is at the same time as a re-enlistment or extension package that gives the individual the required amount of payback time. Check the "How to Transfer Benefits" site on the following milConnect link: https://www.dmdc.osd.mil/milconnect/faces/faqs?ct=fSu&_adf.ctrl-state=44golmy6o_4&_afrLoop=3106517153964458, or following the following steps:

1. Use your Common Access Card (CAC), DoD Self-Service Logon (DS Logon), or DFAS Account (MyPay) to sign in to the milConnect portal application: http://milconnect.dmdc.mil

- When the milConnect Home page displays, select "Education → Transfer of Education Benefits" (TEB) from the menu bar.
- When the TEB portal page displays, your family members are listed in the table under the "List of Family Members" section.

Note: If a family member is not eligible for DEERS benefits, and thus is not eligible to receive transferred benefits, the word "ineligible" will display in the "Relation" column to the right of your relationship to that family member.

2. To transfer benefit months to a family member, do the following:
   - Locate the name of the appropriate family member in the table.
   - From the "months" drop-down list, select the number of months (0 to 36) to transfer.
   - Optionally, enter an end date in YYYY-MM-DD format.
   - Repeat this process for each family member.
3. Once transfer months have been assigned to your family members, you must submit your transfer request for approval by doing the following:
   - Select the "Post-9/11 GI Bill Chapter 33" button in the select the educational program from which to transfer benefits section.
   - Select all the boxes in the "Transferability of Education Benefits Acknowledgements" section to indicate that you have read and understood each statement.
   - Click the "Submit Request" button.

   If the submission is successful, a confirmation message displays. After you have submitted your transfer request, the sponsor information section at the top of the TEB page updates to show that the status is now submitted. The "status date" is blank and will remain blank until a service representative approves, rejects, or sets your request to a pending status.

   To track the status of your request, you will need to return to the TEB page to check the "Status" in the Sponsor information section. Once your transfer request is approved, the status will be updated to "Request Approved" and the approval status date will be set to the date the service representative approved the request.
4. Once your transfer request is approved, your request data is sent to the Department of Veterans Affairs (DVA). Each family member must first apply for a COE from the DVA before they can use their transferred benefits. Once the DVA receives the request data and VA Form 22-1990E, they will be able to process your family members' requests to use their benefits. The application for the COE (VA Form 22-1990E) can be found through the Department of Veterans Affairs' VONAPP Web Site http://

vabenefits.vba.va.gov/vonapp/main.asp. A paper form is also available at http://www.vba.va.gov/pubs/forms/VBA-22-1990e-ARE.pdf. Or you can call the DVA for Education Benefits information at 1-888-GIBILL1.

5. After receiving their certificates of eligibility from the DVA, your family members must provide the certificates to the school.
6. If your family members do not receive their certificates of eligibility from the DVA before they enroll in school, they should ask the veterans' certifying official at the school to submit to the DVA an enrollment certification for the academic term.

Tuition funds will be sent directly from the DVA to the school. Children are eligible for the monthly living stipend and/or the books and supplies stipend while you are serving on active duty. Your spouse is eligible for the books and supplies stipend, but not the monthly living stipend, while you are on active duty, because both you and your spouse are already receiving the Basic Allowance for Housing (BAH). If you are not currently serving on active duty, then both your spouse and children are eligible for the monthly living stipend and/or the books and supplies stipend.

Note: If you are an active-duty service member, you and your spouse can continue to use the benefit for up to fifteen years after you are last released (discharged or retired) from active duty. If you are a Selected Reserve member, you and your spouse can continue to use the benefit for up to fifteen years after you are last released from your last active-duty period of at least ninety consecutive days. Children can use their benefits until their twenty-sixth birthdays.

Service members may revoke transferred benefits at any given time. Designated months may also be changed or eliminated through the website while on active duty or through a written request to the VA once separated.

Eligible dependents:

- Spouse
- Service member's children
- Combination of spouse and children

Dependents must be in the Defense Enrollment Eligibility Reporting System (DEERS).

Spouses

- May use the benefit immediately
- Are not entitled to the MHA while the service member remains on active duty, but are entitled once the service member separates

- Are entitled to the book stipend
- May use the benefit for up to fifteen years from the service member's EAS date, just like the service member

Children

- May use the benefit only after the service member has attained ten years on active duty
- May use the benefit while the parent is on active duty or after separation
- Must have obtained a high-school diploma or equivalency certificate, or have turned eighteen
- May receive the MHA while a parent remains on active-duty status
- Are entitled to the book stipend
- Do not fall under the fifteen-year delimiting date; however, benefits must be used prior to turning twenty-six years old.
- Must have been given the benefit before the age of twenty-one. An extension can be granted by DEERS to transfer benefit before the age of twenty-three if you are still on active duty.

Airmen can commit the required payback time of four years after separating from active duty and dropping into the reserves.

The current website and e-mails:

http://www.benefits.va.gov/gibill/post911_transfer.asp

The DOD Fact Sheet on Post-9/11 GI Bill Transferability:

http://www.benefits.va.gov/gibill/docs/factsheets/Transferability_Factsheet.pdf

YELLOWRIBBON PROGRAM (YRP)

http://www.benefits.va.gov/gibill/yellow_ribbon.asp

YRP was initially designed to cover tuition above and beyond the maximum allowable rate for a private school or tuition above and tuition above and beyond the in-state rate at a state school. The Veterans Access, Choice, and Accountability Act of 2014 (https://veterans.house.gov/the-veterans-access-choice-and-accountability-act-of-2014-highlights), has mostly made the use of the Yellow Ribbon Program at state schools no longer necessary, since it demands that students using a GI Bill benefit receive the in-state tuition rate. Always double-check your eligibility with the school as some states have been granted waivers (http://www.benefits.va.gov/GIBILL/702.asp). YRP is still relevant to help cover private school tuition that is more than the maximum allotted rate of the Post-9/11 GI Bill.

YRP is not automatic, and there are many stipulations to watch out for prior to determining if the benefit will work for your particular purpose. YRP does not pay the student any money.

Eligibility

- Must rate 100 percent of the Post-9/11 GI Bill
- Active-duty members of the military are not eligible, nor are their spouses; however, children of active-duty service members may qualify (if the active-duty parent is eligible for 100 percent of 9/11).

YRP potentially enables veterans to cover costs above and beyond the Post-9/11 GI Bill parameters. Not all schools participate, and a school's participation for one year does not guarantee participation in subsequent years. You do not need to maintain full-time status in order to be eligible for YRP. Summer terms may be eligible as well, but check with your particular institution.

Schools must re-establish their YRP program with the VA every year. This means, and I have seen it happen, that a school may participate one year but not the next. You could get left hanging. For example, a technical sergeant attended a well-known private school in Georgia. The school participated during her first year, but not the following years. She was out of pocket roughly $22,000 per year for her school at that point—ouch!

Schools may participate on different levels by limiting the amount of YRP spots available and the amount of money they offer. This can restrict veterans from considering certain institutions based on financial constraints. The following is a hypothetical breakdown:

- School A participates in YRP with unlimited spots and unlimited money. Therefore, you shouldn't pay out of pocket. But you still run the risk of the school choosing not to participate in upcoming years.
- School B participates with twenty spots and $4,000 per student. Therefore, you may or may not get one of those twenty spots (remember that it is first come, first serve!), and the VA will match the $4,000, effectively giving you an extra $8,000 toward tuition (this is a rough explanation of how it actually works).

You must also check to see how the program at your school is participating. Consider the following hypothetical situation:

- School C: The graduate-level school of business participates with seventeen spots and $11,000 per student.

- School C: The graduate-level school of education participates with four spots and $6,000 per student.

Notice that different programs within the same school may participate with different amounts of money and available spots.

Last, a school may participate differently at the graduate level than it does at the undergraduate level. See the following example:

- School D participates at the undergraduate level with five spots and $8,000 per student.
- School D participates at the graduate level with three spots and $1,000 per student.

While it can become complicated to determine the benefit you may be eligible for, the vet reps at the school can usually offer sound advice. You can search YRP participating schools by state (at http://www.benefits.va.gov/GIBILL/yellow_ribbon/yrp_list_2015.asp). However, I always recommend contacting the VA directly for solid confirmation that the school you are applying for does participate and to what degree.

Do not make the mistake of thinking that a small, off-the-beaten-path school might not fill their YRP seats. I spoke with a small college in Washington State that participates in the YRP, wondering if they often fill their openings. Prior to speaking to the veterans' representative, I thought to myself that it was nice they had allotted so many spots even though they probably do not need them. I mean, how many veterans are relocating to this rural area? I was so wrong! The school had a waiting list for its YRP spots that was in the double digits. Apparently, while the school was located in a rural area, it was also the closest school to one of the state's main snowboarding mountains and maintained a fairly large veteran population. On the flip side, I was happy to hear that our veterans were getting some much-needed R&R after their military service along with a good education.

If you intend on transferring, you must speak with your new school regarding YRP eligibility at their institution. Eligibility at one does not guarantee eligibility at another. If you take a hiatus from your school and were enrolled in YRP, you may get dropped for subsequent semesters. Before you make any decisions, talk with your academic advisor and/or veteran department. The more informed you are, the better you can plan.

VA GI BILL FEEDBACK SYSTEM

http://www.benefits.va.gov/GIBILL/Feedback.asp

The VA has recently implemented a new system to handle complaints pertaining to issues involving the Principles of Excellence. Educational institutions that have agreed to abide by the specific guidelines of the program are agreeing to do the following:

- Inform students in writing of the costs associated with education at that institution.
- Produce educational plans for military and veteran beneficiaries.
- Cease all misleading recruiting techniques.
- Accommodate those who are absent due to military requirements.
- Appoint a point of contact (POC) that offers education-related and financial advice.
- Confirm that all new programs are accredited before enrolling students.
- Align refund policies with Title IV policies (FSA).

Schools that participate in the Principles of Excellence program can be found on the VA website (http://www.benefits.va.gov/gibill/principles_of_excellence.asp).

Complaints should be submitted when institutions participating in the program fall below the above-listed set of standards. Complaints are filed on subjects such as recruiting practices, education quality, accreditation issues, grade policies, failure to release transcripts, credit transfer, financial topics, student loan concerns, refund problems, job opportunities after degree completion, and degree plan changes and subsequent requirements. To file a complaint, visit the website and follow the directions.

FEDERAL STUDENT AID (FSA)

Airmen have other sources of funding to pursue above and beyond TA and the GI Bills. Student aid money is offered by the U.S. federal government, states, schools, and nonprofit organizations. FSA money is the most actively sought-after money and is available through the U.S. Department of Education. Active duty and veteran service members can apply for FSA and should be encouraged to do so, in order to cover any extra costs they are unable to get funded. For example, TA cannot cover books or supplies. Under the Post-9/11 GI-Bill, if a student attends school full-time he or she will receive a $1,000 per academic year toward books and supplies. In most cases, this is not enough to cover book expenses. FSA might be a viable option to help in these circumstances if an airman qualifies. Since this benefit is not specific to the military, military spouses are encouraged to apply to help fund their educations as well.

Prior to choosing a school, it is important to consider the costs associated with attending a particular institution. Although you have different types of educational benefits available to use because of your military status, these benefits do not cover all expenses in most cases. School expenses can vary significantly from institution to institution. Prospective students should consider expenses above and beyond the tuition and fees. Books, travel, and equipment costs can add up and create a substantial financial burden for service members.

The U.S. Department of Education recommends that if attending a particular school is going to require you to pay money above and beyond the amounts covered under your available benefits,

> you'll want to make sure that the cost of your school is reasonable compared to your earning potential in your future career. In other words, you want to make sure that you can earn enough money to cover any student loan payments you may need to make, along with living expenses, after you graduate.[1]

Schools that participate in FSA programs are required to provide potential students information pertaining to the cost of attending and to provide a net price calculator on their websites. Students can also access the College Score-Card (http://collegecost.ed.gov/scorecard/index.aspx), provided by the U.S. Department of Education's College Affordability and Transparency Center (http://collegecost.ed.gov/catc/), to help in making more informed decisions regarding an institution's value and affordability.

Prior to applying for FSA, it is important to understand what it is, how it works, and what you would want to accept. FSA, or Title IV Programs as they are categorized, come in three forms: work-study, loans, and grants. For active duty and veteran students using their GI Bills, loans are usually not necessary. In fact, it is best to avoid them at all costs. In most cases, active-duty service members have access to TA money and veterans typically have access to their GI Bills. Loans have to be repaid with interest and you should think carefully before accepting them. VA Work-Study is discussed in depth in chapter 11.

Pell Grant money should be the goal for most service members. Pell Grant money does not need to be repaid and is awarded for first-time bachelor's or associate's degree-seeking students only. In certain instances, students might receive a Pell Grant award if they are attending a postbaccalaureate teacher certification program. The maximum Pell Grant award is currently set at $5,775 for the 2015–2016 academic year. That amount is based upon maximum financial need and a full-time rate of pursuit.

In order to be eligible to apply for FSA students must meet the following parameters:

- Most programs require demonstrating financial need
- Must be a U.S. citizen or eligible noncitizen
- Have a valid social security number (exceptions apply)
- Be registered with the Selective Service
- Be enrolled or accepted at minimum of half-time as a regular student into an eligible degree or certificate program
- Maintain satisfactory progress

FSA applicants will also need to sign statements stating:

- Student is not defaulting on any federal student loans.
- Student does not owe money on any federal grants.
- Student will only use aid money for educational related expenses.
- Student must demonstrate evidence of eligibility by having a high-school diploma, GED, or completed homeschool program approved by state law.

Financial need eligibility is based upon "your Expected Family Contribution, your year in school, your enrollment status, and the cost of attendance (COA) at the school you will be attending."[2]

The Expected Family Contribution (EFC) is a number that the financial aid department employees use to help determine the amount of financial aid you would potentially need to attend that particular school. The information that you file when completing the Free Application for Federal Student Aid (FAFSA) is used within a special formula that was established by law to determine your EFC. Financial information pertaining to your taxed and untaxed income, benefits, and assets can all be taken into account, as well as your family size. More detailed information on how the EFC is calculated can be found on the following DoEd website: http://ifap.ed.gov/efcformulaguide/attachments/090214EFCFormulaGuide1516.pdf.

Your enrollment status is simply your rate of pursuit. Award amounts are based upon the degree to which you pursue school and are reported by your school to the DoEd. Full-time school is usually difficult for active-duty airmen to maintain considering mission demands. Veterans must attend school at the full-time rate in order to rate full-time Post-9/11 GI Bill benefits.

The COA is the actual amount of money it will cost in order for you to attend an institution. Typically, for traditional educational programs the COA is calculated on a yearly basis. The estimate includes:

- tuition and fees;
- the cost of room and board (or living expenses for students who do not contract with the school for room and board);
- the cost of books, supplies, transportation, loan fees, and miscellaneous expenses (including a reasonable amount for the documented cost of a personal computer);
- an allowance for child care or other dependent care;
- costs related to a disability; and/or
- reasonable costs for eligible study-abroad programs.[3]

After determining the COA, your EFC is subtracted from your COA to determine your financial need.

Service members need to reapply for FSA every year even if they were not awarded Pell Grant money the previous year. Economic circumstances for military members can change drastically from year to year, thereby changing financial need determination. For example, certain billets have different pay attached to them or you might have been in a combat zone. Also, you might get married, divorced, separate from the military, or have a child, all of which can affect your financial situation. I often work with higher ranking service members that tell me they make too much money and will not be eligible for a Pell Grant award. I have worked with E-9s that have received the full award and E-2s that have been denied, so let the DoEd tell you what might be available to assist with your educational expenses.

If you are separating from the Air Force, filled out your FAFSA, and did not receive an award, or received very little, visit with the financial aid department at your school. They have the ability to fix your FAFSA based upon your new income levels (considered a special circumstance). In many instances, this can drive the previous number up, helping you cover your expenses.

If a student is awarded Pell Grant money, the amount is sent to the school, and the school pays the student. If any money is owed toward tuition and fees, schools remove that amount from the award prior to turning the remainder of the money over to the student. Award money is typically turned over to students in check, cash, or bank deposit. Federal Pell Grant money is paid out in at least two disbursements. Most schools pay students at least once per semester. Since most veteran students' tuition is covered by the GI Bill, most veterans should get to keep the full amount of the award. Remember this prior to choosing an institution that may not be fully covered under Post-9/11 or MGIB.

If you have depleted your military-based educational benefits and are considering taking out student loans, be sure to research and understand where a student loan is coming from prior to accepting any money. Student loans can be federal or private depending on the source. Federally backed loans and private loans have many differences. Here are just a few of the reasons that federally backed loans can offer greater flexibility than loans from private sources.

- Federal loans can offer borrowers fixed interest rates that are typically lower than private sources of loans.
- Borrowers are given a six-month grace period upon completion of the degree to begin repayments. Often, private school loans will require payments to be made while the student is still attending school.
- Only federally backed loans are subsidized, meaning the government pays the interest for a period of time.
- Interest may be deductible, not an option for private loans.
- Federal loans can be consolidated into a Direct Consolidation Loan, private loans cannot.
- Private loans may require that the borrower already has an established credit record. Most federal student loans do not require a credit check.
- Federal loans tend to have greater offer forbearance or deferment options.
- Private loans may demand that repayments begin immediately.

(Information taken from the following site, http://studentaid.ed.gov/types/loans/federal-vs-private)

Federal student loans come in three shapes and sizes. Federal student loans can be Direct Subsidized Loans or Direct Unsubsidized Loans, Direct PLUS Loans (for advanced education), or Federal Perkins Loans.

According to the DoEd, Direct Subsidized Loans have slightly better parameters for students with financial need. Direct Subsidized loans are only available for undergraduate students, and the amount awarded cannot exceed the financial need. Interest on this type of loan is covered by the U.S. Department of Education while students remain in school at minimum of half-time and for the first six months after graduation (grace period).

Direct Unsubsidized Loans demand a demonstration of financial need and are available for undergraduate and graduate school. The amount borrowed is regulated by the school and is based upon the school's costs. Interest is the responsibility of the borrower at all times. If the borrower chooses not to pay interest while in school, the amount accrues and is added into the overall loan and will be reflected in payments when they come due.

Federal PLUS loans are available for graduate or professional degree seeking students and parents of dependent undergraduate students. Schools must participate in the program for students to be eligible. Loans are fixed at a specific rate, and borrowers must not have an adverse credit history. For information regarding the current rates for loans, visit the DoEd website (https://studentaid.ed.gov/types/loans/interest-rates#what-are-the-interest-rates-of-federal-student-loans).

The National Student Loan Data System (NSLDS) is the DoEd's central database for student aid and maintains information regarding Title IV loans and grants. If you have already received loans or grants and need information regarding your awards, you can access the information on the website (https://www.nslds.ed.gov/).

Federal Student Aid has many resources available to assist service members. A review of the following chart, which can also be found on the DoEd website (https://studentaid.ed.gov/sites/default/files/military-student-loan-benefits.pdf), will give you a brief overview of the available benefits.

The DoEd also offers military students readmissions assistance if their schooling was interrupted due to military duty. More information regarding the assistance and the point of contact can be found on the DoEd website (http://www2.ed.gov/policy/highered/guid/readmission.html).

If you plan on applying for Federal Student Aid, you will need access to your taxes from the previous year. For example, if applying for student aid for the 2015–2016 school year you will need your 2014 IRS 1040 tax document. The FAFSA application opens in January of each year and must be reapplied for each year. In 2015, the DoEd changed the time frame within which a student can apply for federal student aid.

If you are not eligible for any money one year, do not let it deter you from applying in subsequent years. You may be eligible at another time. If you are under the age of twenty-four, but have already served on active duty, you will not need to enter your parents' tax information on the FAFSA. You will enter your personal tax information.

If you are interested in applying for Federal Student Aid, but are unsure how to proceed, contact your local education center or the financial aid office of your school for further guidance.

Table 7.1   DoEd and DoD Student Loan Repayment Options for Service Members[4]

Benefit	Description
Servicemembers Civil Relief Act (SCRA) Interest Rate Cap	Interest on federal student loans obtained prior to your military service is limited to 6 percent during periods of active duty. The interest rate limitation also applies to any private education loans you may have.
Military Service Deferment	You can postpone federal student loan repayment during certain periods of active duty, such as during war, other military operation, or national emergency, and immediately following active duty.
Public Service Loan Forgiveness	You may qualify for forgiveness of the remaining balance of your direct loans when you've made 120 qualifying payments after October 1, 2007, while employed in public service, including military service.
Deferments After Active Duty	You can postpone repayment while you prepare to return to school following your active duty.
Zero Percent Interest	While you are serving in a hostile area that qualifies you for special pay, you do not have to pay interest on direct loans made on or after October 1, 2008, for up to sixty months.
Repayment Based on Income	Repayment plans that base your monthly payment on your income are available. Under these plans, you may qualify for a low or zero payment amount with the possibility of forgiveness of the remaining balance in the future.
HEROES Act Waiver	While you are on active duty, the Department of Education waives many of the documentation requirements attached to program benefits. For example, if you are on a payment plan based on your income and military service prevents you from providing updated information on your family size and income, you can request to have your monthly payment amount maintained.
Department of Defense (DOD) Repayment of Your Loans	In certain circumstances, as determined by the DOD, all or a portion of your loans may be repaid by the DOD.
Veterans Total and Permanent Disability Discharge	If you have a service-connected disability, you may qualify for discharge of your federal student loans.

"For Members of the U.S. Armed Forces." Federal Student Aid. Accessed July 27, 2015. https://studentaid.ed.gov/sites/default/files/military-student-loan-benefits.pdf.

Here is a quick checklist for applying for federal financial aid:

1. Have your tax information from the previous year on hand.
2. Apply on https://fsaid.ed.gov/npas/index.htm for your FSA ID.
3. Apply for Federal Student Aid through FAFSA (http://www.fafsa.ed.gov; you will need to list your school).

4. Verify your submission with your school's financial aid office.
5. Keep an eye out for your financial aid award letter, and monitor your student account on your school's website.
6. Hopefully receive a payment!
7. The http://www.fafsa.ed.gov website offers many helpful hints if you get stuck while filling out the FAFSA. The application will take twenty to thirty minutes to complete online.

A thorough financial aid checklist of all information needed for students to pursue federal student aid can be found on the following website: http://www.financialaidtoolkit.ed.gov/resources/nt4cm/NT4CM-financial-aid-application-checklist.pdf.

More information on Federal Student Aid can be found through the following resources:

- The Federal Student Aid Information Center (FSAIC): 1-800-4-FED-AID (1-800-433-3243)
- Federal Student Aid: https://studentaid.ed.gov/
- Free Application for Federal Student Aid: https://fafsa.ed.gov/
- Veterans Total and Permanent Disability (TPD) Discharge: http://disabilitydischarge.com/home/
- Servicemembers Civil Relief Act (SCRA): Dmdc.osd.mil/appj/scra/
- YouTube: http://www.youtube.com/user/FederalStudentAid

STATE-BASED VETERANS EDUCATION BENEFITS

Many states offer veterans state-based education benefits. These benefits would be above and beyond available federal benefits. Some of these benefits can be used quite liberally and others have very tight restrictions. In a few instances, it is possible to double-dip from MGIB and a state-based benefit to maximize benefits. This can potentially mean more money in the student's pocket or longer lasting education benefits.

Prior to electing to use the Post-9/11 GI Bill, you need to determine if you have a state-based benefit available to use and how it works. Sometimes, veterans can bring in more money by staying under MGIB as opposed to Post-9/11. Electing Chapter 33 (Post-9/11) is an irrevocable choice and all available options should be considered prior to electing the benefit.

While your school's veterans' department might have information regarding your state-based benefits, it is best to make contact with your state's

Department of Veterans' Affairs Office (http://www.va.gov/statedva.htm). The state VA can explain all or your available benefits, not just the education-related options, as well as verify your eligibility. Usually, a quick visit to the website can give you a general understanding of the state-offered benefits, but connecting with a benefit specialist is the best way to gain in-depth knowledge. Sometimes, there are programs available that are not listed on the website because they are location specific. A benefit specialist will be able to assist you with any information that might be available in your location or might be more specific to your needs.

I (Jillian) list and describe many of the state-based benefits later in this chapter. Remember that states may cancel, change, or add benefits throughout time. While I strive to be as accurate as possible, this book was compiled and written in 2015, and things change. Since you are the veteran, you need to double-check what you have available at any specific time.

I have found three situations where MGIB might be a better choice than Post-9/11, and I explain them below. Remember that you can always visit with an education counselor on your base for further advice, and a quick phone call to the veterans' representatives at the school can usually tell you which GI Bill veterans are opting for in the same situation.

Three examples that I have encountered with veterans who sometimes prefer to remain under MGIB are veterans who come from a state that has a full state-based education benefit, veterans who attend school in rural areas where the MHA is low (tuition must be too), and in a few rare cases veterans who choose to attend school fully online. I do not recommend fully online school, because it usually means missing out on a good chunk of housing stipend money. You must take at least one credit hour face to face at the school in order to rate the full housing stipend under Post-9/11.

Here is an example of a veteran who did better by staying under MGIB instead of electing Post-9/11:

Senior Airman Jackson enlisted in Illinois. In 2015, after serving four years of honorable service in the Army, he is about to separate and return home. Senior Airman Jackson is interested in attending University of Illinois in Champaign and needs to determine his available education options.

Senior Airman Jackson learns about the two federal GI Bills and the Illinois Veteran Grant (IVG) after reading this book. Senior Airman Jackson needs to determine if he paid into MGIB, which would have been $100 per month for the first year of his enlistment to total $1,200. He believes he did but cannot remember for sure. He will double-check a Leave and Earnings Statement

(LES) from his first year of service to look for a $100 per month deduction in pay, but continues planning as if he did pay the $1,200 into MGIB.

Senior Airman Jackson might also be eligible for IVG. Only the Illinois state VA can ultimately determine his eligibility, and he will need to verify with them if he will be able to use the benefit prior to following through with the details.

IVG will cover the cost of tuition and certain fees for eligible veterans at state-supported universities and community colleges within the state of Illinois. If Senior Airman Jackson does rate IVG, he might do better financially by using it in tandem with MGIB, as opposed to opting for Post-9/11.

Here is the IVG eligibility list from the Illinois State VA (also at https://www.illinois.gov/veterans/benefits/Pages/education.aspx) that I reviewed with Senior Airman Jackson (remember, things change!):

- Veteran must have received an honorable discharge.
- Veteran must have resided in Illinois six months prior to entering the service.
- Veteran must have completed a minimum of one full year of active duty in the U.S. armed Forces (this includes veterans who were assigned to active duty in a foreign country in a time of hostilities in that country, regardless of length of service).
- Veteran must return to Illinois within six months of separation from the service.

Senior Airman Jackson falls within the above-mentioned parameters, feels confident that he will rate the IVG and proceeds accordingly.

Looking up the MHA stipend for the Post-9/11 GI Bill on the Comparison Tool website (at http://department-of-veterans-affairs.github.io/gi-bill-comparison-tool/), Senior Airman Jackson finds the MHA stipend for the academic year 2015 is $1,102. This tool can also be found by visiting the main Post-9/11 GI Bill webpage (http://www.benefits.va.gov/gibill/).

Champaign, Illinois, is located in a rural, southern portion of the state; hence, the housing allowance under Post-9/11 is on the low side. Senior Airman Jackson feels that he could do better if he elects to stay under MGIB, instead of choosing Post-9/11.

Here are his calculations:

- Post-9/11 MHA: $1,102
- MGIB payments (as of October 1, 2015): $1,789

- Senior Airman Jackson will rate IVG, which will pay most of his public university's tuition and fees.
- If Senior Airman Jackson pays the $600 buy-up to MGIB prior to separation, it will increase his monthly MGIB payments by an extra $150 per month, so his monthly take-home amount would be $1,939, or $837 more than the $1,102 he would receive under Post-9/11. If none of the amounts change over the thirty-six months that Senior Airman Jackson has allotted, he would take home $26,132 more under MGIB than he would under Post-9/11 even after including the $1,000 per year book stipend allotted under Post-9/11 (four years = $4,000).
- One drawback is that IVG can be used for a master's degree as well. If Senior Airman Jackson double-dips on his federal and state-based benefit at the same time, he may not retain any benefits that could have been used for graduate school. That is a personal decision.

Senior Airman Jackson reviews his calculations and realizes that he still needs to verify his IVG with the Illinois state VA and his GI Bill eligibility with the federal VA. He also needs to contact the veterans' representatives (vet reps) at University of Illinois to discuss which GI Bill the veterans already attending the school have chosen and any recommendations that the vet reps may have for him. Senior Airman Jackson must decide whether he minds depleting both of his benefits at the same time, since tapping into them simultaneously will result in that outcome.

In the case of Illinois veterans who meet IVG requirements, they must decide if the extra payoff they obtain by depleting both benefits at the same time is worth it. Many veterans may want to pursue a graduate degree with that benefit at a later date, and others may be more interested in maximizing their benefits immediately. Also remember that Senior Airman Jackson is going to attend a school in a rural area. If you are from Illinois and elect an institution closer to Chicago, your MHA amount will be much higher than the listed amount for University of Illinois in Champaign. For example, the MHA at University of Illinois at Chicago is currently set at $2065 (2015–2016 academic year) per month. Since the cost of living is much higher in the city, the housing stipend is significantly higher as well. In this case, double dipping is not necessary because the housing stipend received under Post-9/11 is greater than the flat monthly amount under MGIB.

The second instance in which some veterans have opted for MGIB is for online-only school. Under the Post-9/11 GI Bill, veterans only receive $783.00 in MHA (as of academic year 2015–2016) for strictly online school, because you must attend a minimum of one face-to-face credit hour every semester in order to rate the full MHA assigned to the zip code of the school. In a few cases, veterans who decide that they can only attend online school may do better by remaining under MGIB and paying the $600 buy-up prior to separation.

In the case of strictly online school, it is difficult to run numbers in this book because there are too many unknown factors. Examples of this include tuition charges, MHA attached to the school's zip code, and fluctuations in GI Bill payouts.

Here is a hypothetical example:

Senior Airman Jackson decides to attend a fully online academic program. The cost of the school per credit hour is $250. He is taking two classes over an eight-week semester. The total cost for his two classes will be $1,500. The MHA for strictly online school at this point in time is $783.00 per month. Senior Airman Jackson paid the $600 buy-up program at DFAS before separating. His combined monthly payout under MGIB and the Buy-Up program for academic year 2015–2016 is $1,939. In the span of his eight-week classes, he will take in $3,878. After paying his $1,500 bill for his two classes (two classes on an eight-week-semester schedule is considered fulltime), he is left with $2,387. That is roughly $812 more than what he would take home if he had elected Post-9/11 and only received the $783.00 that is allotted for strictly online school ($2,387–$1,566 = $812). MGIB, in this case, looks like the better choice. But this also does not account for the prorated amount of book stipend that he would receive under the Post-9/11 GI Bill.

If considering online-only school, make sure to verify all tuition and fee charges prior to making a decision. The above-listed example only worked out to the students benefit because the tuition charges were capped at $250 per credit hour. If your tuition and fee charges amount to a larger sum MGIB might not be the best choice for payment.

The Veterans Access, Choice, and Accountability Act of 2014 (https://veterans.house.gov/the-veterans-access-choice-and-accountability-act-of-2014-highlights), was passed in July, 2014, and as of the academic year 2015–2016, schools that take GI Bill dollars will need to list veterans as in-state residents for tuition purposes. If you attend school within three years of your separation date and use a GI Bill for payment out-of-state tuition charges, there should not be a problem (at least this is how things are at the start of the fall 2015 semester).

If you decide to remain off your GI Bill in the beginning, schools do not have to extend the honorary in-state residency benefit to you. State-based benefits might be of help, but they can be a bit tricky. As of right now, only some states offer in-state tuition to out-of-state residents. Some university systems will also grant in-state tuition for veterans. There are always qualifying criteria you must abide by, so, like I keep stating throughout this book, always check with the state VA or with the vet reps at the school to verify your eligibility.

Lastly, some veterans attending school in rural areas might find staying under MGIB more beneficial than converting to Post-9/11. For example, Staff Sergeant Nelson will attend Coahoma Community College in Clarksdale, Mississippi. The MHA for the school under Post-9/11 is $1,054 per month. After nine months of school for her first year she would have received $9,486. Under MGIB with the $150 Buy-Up paid, she would take in $17,451, but she may need to pay her school up front both semesters. The current cost of Coahoma CC per semester is $1,150 (http://www.coahomacc.edu/admissions-financial-aid/admissions/tuition-fees/index), make note that this does not include some of the extra fees the institution will charge per semester or per year or book expenses. So for one academic year, Staff Sergeant Nelson will pay $2,300 for her tuition charges, but she will still take in more money under MGIB than had she elected Post-9/11. Here are the calculations:

Post-9/11 MHA for nine months = $9,486
MGIB with the Buy-Up for nine months = $17,451
Minus tuition charges for the academic year $17,451–$2,300 = $15,151
Difference between Post-9/11 and MGIB $15,151-$9,486 = $5,665 (this does
    not calculate the $1,000 annual books and supplies stipend under Post-9/11
    into the equation)

As a veteran, it is important that you follow through with your own research on state and federal benefits. States are often updating and adding benefits for veterans. The monetary amounts attached to the federal GI Bills change as well. The only way to stay current with the information is to become fluent with the websites and check back regularly.

STATES THAT OFFER IN-STATE TUITION TO VETERANS

Veterans beginning school on or after fall of 2015 will receive honorary in-state residency at any state school across the country as long as they are entering the institution under their GI Bill and are within three years of their date of separation from the service. Some veterans prefer to stay off their GI

Bill for the first year or two of college. Potential reasons to take this pathway might include a student pursuing a degree that requires more than the typical load of 120 semester hours, or students trying to save benefits for graduate degrees at a later date.

If a student intends to pursue education without using their GI Bill benefits, he should check to see if the state where the school is located offers honorary in-state tuition to all veterans and if he qualifies for the benefit. If so, the tuition rates will be significantly less expensive.

Here are the websites for the states that currently offer in-state residency to veterans. Some of these states offer other veterans' benefits as well. There are specific steps (like registering to vote or getting a driver's license) tied into eligibility for the in-state tuition, and sometimes it is up to the school to participate. Check with the veterans' representatives at the institution you wish to attend to determine how to get going with the process for that particular state.

- Alabama (http://alisondb.legislature.state.al.us/ALISON/SearchableInstruments/2013RS/PrintFiles/HB424-enr.pdf): In-state tuition for veterans who reside in Alabama and were honorably discharged within the five years immediately preceding their enrollment into a state institution of higher learning. Reservists and service-connected disabled veterans are eligible as well.
- Arizona (https://dvs.az.gov/services/education, (602) 255-3373): In-state tuition for veterans who registered to vote in the state and meet at least one of the following parameters: an Arizona driver license, an Arizona motor vehicle registration, demonstrate employment history in Arizona, transfer their banking services to Arizona, change their permanent address on all pertinent records, or demonstrate other materials of whatever kind or source relevant to domicile or residency status.
- California (https://www.calvet.ca.gov/veteran-services-benefits/education, 800-952-5626): Currently, the state of California offers honorary residency to veterans who were stationed in California for one year prior to separation from the military, separate, and stay in the state to attend an institution of higher education.
- Colorado (http://www.colorado.edu/registrar/state-tuition/exceptions-1-year-domicile, (303) 862-3001): In-state tuition for qualifying veterans. Veterans must be honorably discharged and maintain a permanent home in Colorado. Enlisted service members who are stationed in Colorado and receiving the resident student rate (themselves or their dependents) will be able to maintain that rate upon separation from the military if they continue to reside in the state.

- Florida (www.flsenate.gov/Session/Bill/2014/7015/BillText/er/PDF): Instate tuition for honorably discharged veterans at state community colleges, state colleges, and universities.
- Idaho (http://www.legislature.idaho.gov/legislation/2010/S1367.pdf, (208) 577-2310): In-state tuition for qualified veterans and qualifying dependents. Veterans must have served at least two years on active duty, have received an honorable discharge, and enter a public school within one year of separating from the service. Dependents must receive at least 50 percent of their support from the qualifying veteran.
- Illinois (http://www.ilga.gov/legislation/fulltext.asp?DocName=&Session Id=85&GA=98&DocTypeId=HB&DocNum=2353&GAID=12&LegID=7 4133&SpecSess=&Session=): Any individual using the Post-9/11 GI Bill will receive the in-state tuition rate.
- Indiana (www.in.gov/legislative/bills/2013/SE/SE0177.1.html): Veterans enrolled in undergraduate classes no more than twelve months after honorably separating from the armed forces or Indiana National Guard are eligible for in-state tuition.
- Kentucky (http://cpe.ky.gov/policies/academicpolicies/residency.htm, (502) 573-1555): In-state tuition for qualifying veterans.
- Louisiana (http://legiscan.com/LA/text/HB435/id/649958): In-state tuition for veterans who served a minimum of two years on active duty and received an honorable discharge. Veterans who have been assigned service-connected disability ratings and are either already enrolled or applying for enrollment in a state institution are eligible as well.
- Maine (http://www.mainelegislature.org/legis/bills/getDoc.asp?id=39934): Honorably discharged veterans enrolled in a program of education within the University of Maine system, the Maine community college system, or the Maritime Academy are eligible for in-state tuition.
- Maryland (www.in.gov/legislative/bills/2013/SE/SE0177.1.html): In-state tuition for honorably discharged veterans of the armed forces. Veteran must reside in Maryland and attend a state institution of higher learning.
- Minnesota (https://www.revisor.mn.gov/statutes/?id=197.775&format= pdf): In-state tuition at the undergraduate rate for veterans. If the veteran was a resident of the state upon entering the service and begins a state college/university graduate school program within two years of separating from the service, he or she will receive the in-state tuition rate.
- Missouri (http://mvc.dps.mo.gov/docs/veterans-benefits-guide.pdf): In-state tuition for veterans who received honorable or general discharges from the service. Benefit can be utilized at the state two-year or four-year institutions. Two-year institutions also offer the in-district rate.
- Nevada (http://leg.state.nv.us/Session/77th2013/Bills/AB/AB260_EN.pdf): In-state tuition for veterans who were honorably discharged and matriculated no more than two years after their date of separation from the armed forces.

- New Mexico (http://www.dvs.state.nm.us/benefits.html, (505) 827-6374): In-state tuition for qualified veterans.
- North Dakota (http://www.legis.nd.gov/cencode/t15c10.pdf?2013110615 2541): In-state tuition for veterans who served 180 days or more on active duty and separated under other than dishonorable conditions. Dependents who received transferred Post-9/11 benefits may also be eligible.
- Ohio (https://www.ohiohighered.org/veterans): In-state tuition for qualified veterans.
- Oregon (https://olis.leg.state.or.us/liz/2013R1/Measures/Text/HB2158/ Enrolled): Honorably discharged veterans who establish a physical presence in Oregon within twelve months of enrolling in school may be eligible for in-state tuition and fees.
- South Dakota (http://legis.sd.gov/Statutes/Codified_Laws/DisplayStatute. aspx?Type=Statute&Statute=13-53-29.1&cookieCheck=true): Bill 13-53-19.1 exempts veterans from having to meet the twelve-month residency requirement for in-state tuition.
- Tennessee (http://www.capitol.tn.gov/Bills/108/Bill/SB1433.pdf): In-state tuition for veterans discharged within two years and did not receive a dishonorable separation.
- Texas (http://www.statutes.legis.state.tx.us/Docs/ED/htm/ED.54.htm#54. 241): In-state tuition for veterans who qualify for federal education benefits. Dependents may qualify as well.
- Utah (http://veterans.utah.gov/state-benefits/, (801) 326-2372): In-state tuition for qualifying veterans at certain schools. Veterans must demonstrate that they are taking the required steps to gain residency.
- Virginia (http://lis.virginia.gov/cgi-bin/legp604.exe?000+cod+23-7.4): Veterans released or discharged under conditions other than dishonorable are eligible for in-state tuition.
- Washington (http://apps.leg.wa.gov/documents/billdocs/2013-14/Pdf/Bills/ Senate%20Passed%20Legislature/5318.PL.pdf): Veterans (and their dependents) who served a minimum of two years in the military and received an honorable discharge will be granted in-state tuition as long as they enroll in school within one year of their date of separation from the service.

A few state-based university systems across the country may also offer veterans in-state tuition without a state-based benefit in place. The following is a current list:

- University of Alaska school system: http://www.alaska.edu/alaska/about-ua/
- Mississippi Institutions of Higher Learning: http://www.ihl.state.ms.us/ board/downloads/policiesandbylaws.pdf
- University of Wisconsin school system: https://docs.legis.wisconsin.gov/ statutes/statutes/36/27/2/b/4

- Kentucky Public Universities: http://www.lrc.ky.gov/record/11rs/HB425.htm
- University of Iowa school system: http://registrar.uiowa.edu/gi-bill
- University System of Georgia: http://www.usg.edu/policymanual/section7/C453/
- University of Rhode Island: http://www.uri.edu/prov/veterans/VAbenefitsprograms.html
- University of Delaware: http://www.udel.edu/registrar/students/residency.html#section6

Many institutions of higher learning have adopted scholarships for disabled veterans. For example, the University of Idaho has the Operation Education scholarship that may provide financial assistance for eligible service connected disabled veterans and their spouses (http://www.uidaho.edu/operationeducation). Check with the institutions you are interested in attending to obtain information regarding policies or programs that may benefit you.

The following are states with state-based education benefits at this time. Most of the information is taken directly from the state VA websites.

ALABAMA

http://www.va.state.al.us/otherbenefits.aspx
http://www.va.state.al.us/gi_dep_scholarship.aspx

Benefit

Purple Heart recipients may be eligible to have tuition and fees waived for undergraduate studies.

State residents with service-connected disability ratings of 20 percent or higher may qualify for his or her:

- Spouse: three standard academic years without payment of tuition, mandatory textbooks, or instructional fees at a state institution of higher learning, or for a prescribed technical course not to exceed twenty-seven months of training at a state institution.
- Dependent children: five standard academic years or part-time equivalent at any Alabama state-supported institution of higher learning or a state-supported technical school without payment of any tuition, mandatory textbooks, or instructional fees. Dependent children must start school prior to age twenty-six.

Eligibility and residency requirements for veteran:

- Must have honorably served at least ninety days of continuous active federal military service during wartime, or be honorably discharged by reason of service-connected disability after serving less than ninety days of continuous active federal military service during wartime.
- Permanent civilian resident of the state of Alabama for at least one year immediately prior to (1) the initial entry into active military service or (2) any subsequent period of military service in which a break (one year or more) in service occurred and the Alabama civilian residency was established.
- Permanently service-connected veterans rated at 100 percent who did not enter service from Alabama may qualify but must first establish at least five years of permanent residency in Alabama prior to application.

Note: If you are a veteran with a PH and MGIB, you may want to stay on MGIB instead of electing Post-9/11.

The following subsection is a breakdown of current payout under MGIB versus Post-9/11 with a veteran using his or her Alabama state benefit under MGIB at a community college.

Northeast Alabama Community College
MGIB currently pays out $1,789/month + $600 (buy-up) = $1,939/month
Total for 4 months = $7,756
MHA under Post-9/11 $1,168 × 4 months = $4,672

Veterans who qualify for the state-based PH waiver earn $3,084 more in four months under MGIB than if they opted for Post-9/11 ($7,756–$4,672 = $3,084). Remember that the state pays the school tuition in this case.

CALIFORNIA

https://www.calvet.ca.gov/VetServices/Pages/College-Fee-Waiver.aspx

Benefit

- Dependent children tuition waiver at state-supported schools for service-connected disabled veterans.

The California State benefit has four different pathways for eligibility. They can be confusing. Mainly, they are Medal of Honor recipients and their children, National Guard, children of veterans with service-connected disabilities (the most common category), and spouses (veteran is totally disabled, or whose death was service connected). Let's discuss the most common category: children. California veterans who rate a 0 percent disability rating or higher may qualify for their children to receive waivers of tuition at state community colleges and universities. Please note that a 0 percent disability rating is an actual rating. Fees for books, housing, parking, and so on are not included in the waiver. The state of California does not care where you enlisted. If you separate, have a service-connected disability, and become a California resident, you may be eligible.

This is a great way to have your children's college covered. Many veterans use the benefit to send their children to state schools to pursue higher education and not worry about the bills. The universities in the state are used to children using this benefit, and the veterans' representatives at the institutions know how to facilitate it for dependent children.

To read a more thorough breakdown of eligibility, check at https://www.calvet.ca.gov/VetServices/Pages/College-Fee-Waiver.aspx.

Eligibility and residency requirements for child for most common pathway:

- Make less than the annual income limit (changes yearly to reflect cost of living).
- Meet in-state residency requirements determined by school.
- Provide proof of relationship to the veteran.

Benefit

- In-state tuition for veterans. Must be stationed in California for one year prior to separation, separate in the state, and remain in California for school.
- https://www.calvet.ca.gov/VetServices/Pages/Non-Resident-College-Fee-Waiver.aspx.

CONNECTICUT

http://www.ct.gov/ctva/cwp/view.asp?A=2014&Q=290874

Benefit

- Tuition waivers at Connecticut state community colleges and state colleges/universities for eligible veterans.

Only the cost of tuition is waived. Other charges such as books, student fees, and parking are not waived. Students must be matriculated into a degree program.

Eligibility and residency requirements for veterans:

- Be honorably discharged
- Have served at least ninety days of active military duty during war
- Be a resident of Connecticut at least one year prior to enrolling in college
- Be a resident of Connecticut at the time he or she applies for the state benefit

FLORIDA

http://floridavets.org/?page_id=60

Benefit

- Waiver of undergraduate-level tuition at state universities and community colleges for recipients of the PH and other combat-related decorations superior in precedence to the PH. Waiver covers 110 percent of the required credit hours for the degree or certificate.
- Veteran must be admitted as a part- or full-time student in a course of study leading to a degree or certificate.
- Must have been a Florida state resident at the time the military action that resulted in the awarding of the PH (or other award) took place and must currently be a Florida state resident.
- Must submit DD-214 documenting PH to school.

ILLINOIS

http://www2.illinois.gov/veterans/benefits/Pages/education.aspx

Benefit

- The Illinois Veterans' Grant (IVG): IVG is a tuition (and certain fees) waiver for undergraduate and graduate studies at state-supported institutions for veterans who served during a time of hostilities.

Eligibility and residency requirements for veterans:

- Received an honorable discharge.
- Have resided in Illinois six months prior to entering the military.
- Have served a minimum of one year on active duty with the Armed Forces, or was assigned to active duty in a foreign country in a time of hostilities in that country, regardless of length of service.
- Returned to Illinois within six months of separation from the military.

Many Illinois veterans choose to stay under MGIB as opposed to Post-9/11 to fully maximize dollar amounts under their available benefits. If you plan to attend school in a rural area—for example, University of Illinois in Champaign—double-dipping on MGIB and IVG can produce more money on a monthly basis. If the veteran does this, be aware that the veteran will be depleting both state and federal benefits at the same time. This means that the veteran may not have any benefit left for a master's degree later.

If the school the veteran chooses is located in a rural area, and the MHA on Post-9/11 is significantly less than the maxed-out MGIB amount (currently $1,789 per month), then double-dipping will be more beneficial.

Here is an example:

Recently Staff Sergeant Stevens went to the University of Illinois in Champaign. The MHA for the 2015–2016 school year was $1,102. (Check the GI Bill Comparison Tool for current information.) Staff Sergeant Stevens was an Illinois state resident at enlistment and qualified for the IVG. He elected to stay under MGIB, and went to pay the Buy-Up at DFAS prior to his EAS date.

The Buy-Up option under MGIB increases the monthly payments and must be paid while still on active duty. Buy-up can be paid in different increments, but I recommend the maximum of $600 be paid in order to get the maximum monthly increase of $150. After paying the full buy-up amount, the MGIB monthly payments increase to $1,939. Remember these amounts will change yearly as the cost of living (COLA) increases.

Staff Sergeant Stevens will double-dip off IVG and MGIB. IVG will pay the school tuition, and he will collect $1,939 per month under MGIB as opposed to $1,102 per month under the MHA on Post-9/11. That is a difference of $837 per month. Over the course of a nine-month school year, the veteran earns an extra $6,533, even after adding in the book stipend under Post-9/11—a much better deal all around! But, remember, once you select Post-9/11 you can never return to MGIB, so make an educated decision.

Benefit

- Children of Veterans Scholarship: https://secure.osfa.illinois.edu/scholarship-database/detail.aspx?id=1522

Each county in the state is authorized one scholarship yearly at the University of Illinois for children of veterans of World War I, World War II, the Korean War, the Vietnam Conflict, Operation Enduring Freedom, or Operation Iraqi Freedom. Children of deceased and disabled veterans are given priority. These children can receive four consecutive years tuition-free (undergraduate, graduate, or professional studies) at the University of Illinois (Urbana-Champaign, Chicago Health Sciences Center, or Springfield Campus).

INDIANA

http://www.in.gov/dva/2378.htm

Benefit

- Indiana Purple Heart Recipients receive free tuition at the resident tuition rate for 124 semester credit hours at state-supported postsecondary schools for undergraduate study only.

Eligibility and residency requirements:

- Entered service from a permanent home address in Indiana
- Received the PH
- Honorably discharged
- Veteran entered service prior to June 30, 2011 (*Note*: Be aware that the law changed in 2011; see the text that follows for more information.)

Benefit

Be aware that the law changed in 2011. Here is the different between the old and new laws:

- Free resident tuition for the children of disabled veterans or PH recipients.
- Benefit includes 124 semester hours of tuition and mandatory fees at the undergraduate rate.
- Benefit can be used for graduate school, but the difference between the undergraduate and graduate rate is the responsibility of the student.

Eligibility and residency requirements:

- Biological (adopted by age twenty-four) and legally adopted children of eligible disabled Indiana veterans.

- Child must produce a copy of birth certificate or adoption papers.
- Veteran must have served during a period of wartime.
- Veteran must have been a resident of Indiana for a minimum of three consecutive years at some point in his or her lifetime.
- Must rate a service-connected disability (or have died a service-connected death), or received the PH (demonstration of proof is necessary for either).

Under the new law, for a veteran who entered service *on or after* July 1, 2011:

- Free resident tuition for the children of disabled veterans or PH recipients.
- Benefit includes 124 semester hours of tuition and mandatory fees for undergraduate study only.
- Benefit is based on the level of disability the veteran rates (see below).
- Student must maintain a mandatory minimum GPA (see below).
- The program limits the student to eight years.

   Eligibility and residency requirements:

- Biological (adopted by age eighteen) and legally adopted children of eligible disabled Indiana veterans.
- Child must produce a copy of birth certificate or adoption papers.
- Veteran must have served during a period of wartime.
- Must rate a service-connected disability (or have died a service-connected death) or have received the PH (demonstration of proof is necessary for either).
- Student must apply prior to turning thirty-two years old.

Disability rating pro-rated schedule for tuition-taken directly from the website:

- Children of veterans rated 80 percent service-connected disabled or higher by the VA or whose veteran parent is/was a recipient of the Purple Heart Medal will receive 100 percent fee remission.
- Children of veterans rated less than 80 percent service-connected disabled will receive 20 percent fee remission plus the disability rating of the veteran.
- If the disability rating of the veteran changes after the beginning of the academic semester, quarter, or other period, the change in the disability rating shall be applied beginning with the immediately following academic semester, quarter, or other period.

GPA requirements:

- First-year student must maintain satisfactory academic progress.
- Second-, third-, and fourth-year students must maintain a minimum cumulative GPA of 2.5.

MARYLAND

http://www.mdva.state.md.us/state/scholarships.html

Benefit

- Edward T. Conroy Memorial Scholarship

Aid for qualifying veterans or children of veterans to attend part-time or full-time Maryland state school (community college, university, or private career school). Benefit works for undergraduate and graduate school. Award is not based on economic need. The award is for tuition and fees. Award works for five years at the full-time attendance rate or eight years at part-time. More detailed information can be found on the website (http://www. mhec.state.md.us/financialAid/COARenewal/2013-2014/2013-2014%20 conroy%20conditions%20of%20award%20renewal.pdf).

Eligibility and residency requirements:

- Children of veterans who have died or are 100 percent disabled as a result of military service
- Veterans who have a 25 percent or greater disability rating with the VA and have exhausted federal veterans' education benefits
- Be a Maryland resident

Benefit

- Veterans of the Afghanistan and Iraq Conflicts (VAIC) Scholarship Program Award is 50 percent of tuition and fees and room and board at the in-state undergraduate rate at a school within the University of Maryland system (UMUC and University of Maryland, Baltimore, are exempt from this award). The award shall not exceed $10,655 for students residing on-campus for the 2014–2015 school year. All undergraduate majors are eligible. Award works for five years at the full-time attendance rate or eight years at part-time. Students must maintain a minimum 2.5 GPA.

Eligibility and residency requirements:

- Have served in Afghanistan (minimum sixty days) on or after October 24, 2001, or in Iraq on or after March 19, 2003 (minimum sixty days).
- Be on active duty, or a veteran (honorable discharge), or the son, daughter, or spouse of the aforementioned group.
- Must attend school part- or full-time and be degree seeking.
- Supporting documentation of relationship to veteran is necessary (birth certificate or marriage certificate).
- Supporting documentation of active-duty status (orders) or DD-214 is necessary.
- Applicant must be a resident of Maryland (active-duty military stationed in the state at the time of application qualify).

MASSACHUSETTS

http://www.mass.gov/veterans/education/financial-assistance/tuition-waivers.html

Benefit

- Waiver of full or partial tuition at state institutions of higher education on a space available basis for undergraduate study (fees are not included and can be very high). Graduate school waivers are dependent upon each university. Waivers are for degree or certificate programs.

Eligibility and residency requirements:

- Be a resident of the state for at least one year prior to the start of the school year.
- Not be in default of any federal or state loans or financial aid.
- Served a minimum of ninety days and received an honorable discharge.
- Maintain a minimum of three undergraduate credits per semester and make satisfactory academic progress.

MINNESOTA

http://mn.gov/mdva/resources/education/minnesotagibill.jsp
(800) 657-3866

Benefit

- A maximum payment of $1,000 per semester for full-time students and $500 per semester for part-time students. No more than $10,000 per lifetime. Eligible veterans pursuing OJT or apprenticeship programs can receive up to $2,000 per fiscal year.

Eligibility and residency requirements:

- Veteran must be a Minnesota resident, under the age of sixty-two, and enrolled in a Minnesota institution.
- Have received an honorable discharge.
- Spouse of a disabled veteran (total and permanent) or surviving spouse or child of a veteran who died as a result of his or her service (must be eligible to receive benefits under Chapter 33/35).
- OJT and apprenticeships must be completed with eligible employers (http://www.doli.state.mn.us/Appr.asp).
- Training must be documented, be reported, and last for at least six months.
- Veterans must reapply every year. More information and important links can be found on the website.

MISSOURI

http://www.dhe.mo.gov/files/moretheroesact.pdf

Benefit

- Missouri Returning Heroes' Education Act limits Missouri institutions of higher education from charging eligible veterans more than $50 per credit hour.

Eligibility and residency requirements:

- Received an honorable discharge.
- Served in an armed combat zone for more than thirty days after September 11, 2001.
- Veteran was a Missouri resident when he or she entered the service.
- Enroll in an undergraduate degree-seeking program.
- Maintain a minimum 2.5 GPA every semester.

Note: Missouri residents who qualify for this benefit and MGIB should run the numbers before electing Post-9/11. Many of the veterans I (Jillian) counsel choose to stay under MGIB as opposed to Post-9/11 to fully maximize their dollars under their available benefits.

Speak to a counselor at your closest education center on the base, or contact the veterans' representatives at your chosen school for advice. Remember, once you select Post-9/11 you can never return to MGIB, so make an educated decision.

Example: Private First Class Carlson meets the eligibility requirements as listed above. He will attend Three Rivers Community College in Poplar Bluff, Missouri. The housing allowance under Post-9/11 is $1015 per month. The tuition per semester will be $750 (for fifteen credit hours) under his state-based benefit. If he elects to stay under MGIB, he needs to pay the buy-up at DFAS prior to his separation, and then he will receive $1,939 per month (as of October 1, 2015). Check the website for update MGIB amounts around October 1 of each year: http://www.benefits.va.gov/GIBILL/resources/benefits_resources/rates/ch30/ch30rates100115.asp. After paying his tuition the first month, he will have $1189 remaining, but every month past that point he will receive $1,939 for the rest of the semester. That means $924 more per month than if he elected Post-9/11. The process would repeat itself every semester. Veterans who elect this option must remember that the book stipend is only received under Post-9/11.

Let's run the numbers:

- Tuition per semester: $750 (verify that you will not need to pay any other large fees)
- MGIB with Buy-Up: $7,756 (based on a four-month semester)
- Minus the tuition for the semester: $7,006
- Minus the book stipend that would be received under Post-9/11: $6,506
- Post-9/11 MHA for the school $1015 per month: $4,060
- Including the books and supplies stipend under 9/11 for the semester: $4,560

This amounts to more per semester if the veteran decides to remain under MGIB and also qualifies for the state-based benefit. Remember that under MGIB, you must verify that you are attending school each month.

Private First Class Carlson elected to stay under MGIB, and he paid the buy-up at DFAS prior to separation.

Explanation of the MGIB Buy-Up: The buy-up option under MGIB increases the monthly payments and must be paid while still on active duty. Buy-up can be paid in different increments, but I recommend the maximum of $600 be paid in order to get the maximum monthly increase of $150. After paying the full buy-up amount, the MGIB monthly payments are increased to $1,939. Remember that these amounts will change yearly as the COLA increases.

Always remember to verify eligibility for the state-based benefits and call the veterans' representatives at the school before making any final decisions.

MONTANA

http://wsd.dli.mt.gov/veterans/vetstatebenefits.asp

Benefit

• Tuition waivers for eligible wartime veterans who have exhausted all federal education benefits. Award works for undergraduate programs of study for a maximum of twelve semesters. Veteran must make satisfactory academic progress.

Eligibility and residency requirements:

• Be a state resident.
• Have received an honorable discharge.
• Veteran has not already received a bachelor's degree.
• Served in a combat theater in Afghanistan or Iraq after September 11, 2001 (must have received one of the following: Global War on Terrorism Expeditionary Medal, Afghanistan Campaign Medal, or Iraq Campaign Medal).

NEW YORK

http://www.hesc.ny.gov/pay-for-college/financial-aid/types-of-financial-aid/
    nys-grants-scholarships-awards/veterans-tuition-awards.html
http://www.hesc.ny.gov/pay-for-college/financial-aid/types-of-financial-aid/
    nys-grants-scholarships-awards/msrs-scholarship.html

Benefit

• Veterans' tuition awards are available for students attending undergraduate or graduate degree-granting schools, or vocational training programs at the part- or full-time rate.

Award covers the full cost of the undergraduate tuition for New York residents at the State University of New York (SUNY) or the actual amount of the tuition (whatever is the lesser charge).

"Full-time" is defined as twelve or more credits per semester (a maximum of eight semesters for undergraduate study and six for graduate study). "Part-time" is at least three but fewer than twelve credits per semester (within the same time frames).

The benefit was set at a maximum of $6,370 for the 2015–2016 school year. Veterans who qualify for the state benefit and MGIB may be able to double-dip (there is no double-dipping under Post-9/11, unless the veteran is not eligible for 100 percent).

Vocational programs need to be approved by the state of New York and must be at least 320 clock hours in duration.

Eligibility and residency requirements:

- New York State resident.
- Certain eligible periods of service pertain (mainly, if you served in hostilities after February 28, 1961, as evidenced by receipt of an Armed Forces Expeditionary Medal, Navy Expeditionary Medal, or Marine Corps Expeditionary Medal).
- Matriculated in an undergraduate or graduate degree-granting institution in New York State or in an approved vocational training program in New York State.

Benefit

- Military Enhanced Recognition Incentive and Tribute (MERIT) Scholarship: Financial aid for qualifying veterans and dependents of veterans. Award is a maximum of four years (five for approved five-year programs) of full-time study at the undergraduate level. Award works at SUNY or City University of New York (CUNY) schools for the actual tuition and mandatory fees, plus room and board (on campus) and books and supplies. Those who attend school off-campus will receive an allowance. Private school attendees will receive a sum equal to the public school costs.

Eligibility and residency requirements:

- New York residents who died or became severely and permanently disabled (verify degree with the state) while participating in hostilities, or in training for duty in a combat theater.
- Must have occurred on or after August 2, 1990.

NORTH CAROLINA

http://www.nc4vets.com/nc-programs

Benefit

- Scholarships for dependent children of veterans who rate a minimum of 20 percent disability and served during wartime or received the Purple Heart. Maximum of one hundred awards per year. Award is for eight semesters completed within eight years. It covers tuition, an allowance for room and board, and exemption from certain mandatory fees at public, community, and technical colleges and institutions, or $4,500 per academic year at private schools.

Eligibility and residency requirements:

- Natural and adopted (prior to age fifteen) children of qualifying veterans.
- Be under the age of twenty-five.
- Upon submission of application, student must be a resident of North Carolina.
- Veteran must have entered service in North Carolina, or the applicant must have been born in North Carolina and maintained continuous residency in the state.

OREGON

http://www.oregon.gov/odva/BENEFITS/Pages/OregonEducationBenefit.aspx

Benefit

- The Oregon Veteran Educational Aid Program

Financial aid for veterans who have exhausted all federal education benefits. The maximum award is thirty-six months (award months equal months of service) of $150 per month for full-time students or $100 per month for part-time students. Face-to-face classes, home study, vocational training, licenses, and certificates from accredited Oregon academic institutions are eligible.

Benefits are paid while pursuing classroom instruction, home study courses, vocational training, licensing, and certificates from accredited Oregon educational institutions.

Eligibility and residency requirements:

- Served on active duty a minimum of ninety days and received an honorable discharge.
- Be a resident of Oregon.
- Served after June 30, 1958.

Be aware that funding has been suspended for this program through June 30, 2017.

PUERTO RICO

Puerto Rico Public Advocate for Veterans Affairs
Public Advocate for Veterans Affairs
P.O. Box 11737
San Juan, PR 00910-1737
(787) 758-5760

Benefit

- For those attending the University of Puerto Rico and its regional colleges, free tuition for veterans who have exhausted federal benefits before completing a degree. Verify qualifying criteria with the institutions.

SOUTH CAROLINA

http://va.sc.gov/benefits.html, (800)647-2434

Benefit

- Free tuition for children of veterans who have been awarded the PH for wounds received in combat. Award can be used at state-supported schools or technical education institutions.

Eligibility and residency requirements:

- Veteran must have been a resident at time of entry into the military and throughout the service period, or if veteran has been a resident of South Carolina for a minimum of one year and still resides in the state.

- Veteran was honorably discharged.
- Served during a war period.
- Student must be twenty-six years old or younger.

SOUTH DAKOTA

http://vetaffairs.sd.gov/benefits/State/State%20Education%20Programs.aspx

Benefit

- Free tuition for eligible veterans who have exhausted all federal education
  benefits they were eligible to receive.

Award is prorated on the veteran's qualifying military service (one month
for each qualified month of service, for a maximum of four years). Veteran
has twenty years from the end date of a qualifying service period to use the
entitlement.
  Eligibility and residency requirements:

- Veteran must be a resident of the state and qualify for resident tuition.
- Received an honorable discharge.
- Received a U.S. campaign or service medal for participating in combat
  operations outside the United States (e.g., an Armed Forces Expeditionary
  Medal).
- Veteran has a 10 percent (or more) disability rating with the VA.

TENNESSEE

https://www.tn.gov/collegepays/article/helping-heroes-grant

Benefit

- The Helping Heroes Grant for Veterans is available yearly to a maximum
  of 375 qualifying veterans.

The $1,000 per semester award is given on a first-come, first-served basis
to students completing a minimum of twelve credit hours per semester. Award
can be applied for until the eighth anniversary of the veteran's separation date,
or when the student has received the award for a total of eight semesters.

Eligibility and residency requirements:

- Be a Tennessee resident for one year prior to application.
- Be admitted to an eligible institution of higher education for an associate or bachelor's degree.
- Received an honorable discharge.
- Veteran received the Iraq Campaign Medal, Afghanistan Campaign Medal, or Global War on Terrorism Expeditionary Medal on or after September 1, 2001.
- Not be in default on any federal student aid programs or Tennessee student financial aid programs.
- Veteran does not have a bachelor's degree already.
- Is not in jail (that's right . . . you heard me—stated as such on the website).

TEXAS

http://veterans.portal.texas.gov/en/Pages/education.aspx

Benefit

- Hazlewood tuition waivers at state institutions

A list of eligible schools can be found under the Public School list at http://www.collegeforalltexans.com/. The award covers tuition, dues, fees, and other required charges up to 150 semester hours. The award will not cover room and board, books, student services fees, or deposit fees. The waiver can be used for undergraduate and graduate classes. Teacher certification fees, air craft flight training courses, and distance learning classes may also be covered (verify with the school).

Eligibility and residency requirements:

- At the time of entry into the military was a Texas state resident, designated Texas as home of record, or entered the service in Texas.
- Veteran served a minimum of 181 days of active duty.
- Received an honorable discharge and provide proof.
- Exhausted Post-9/11 GI Bill benefits.
- Veteran is not in default on state-guaranteed student loans.
- Must reside in Texas during the semester the exemption is being claimed (new rule started in fall 2011).

Note: Veterans are not able to double-dip with Post-9/11 and Hazlewood at the same time. Texas schools maintain a great amount of control over Hazlewood Act usage at its institutions. Always contact the vet reps at your institution of choice prior to making any final decisions.

Benefit

• Legacy Program

Children may be eligible to have unused Hazlewood benefits transferred to them. The award can only be used at state-supported institutions. A list of eligible schools can be found at http://www.collegeforalltexans.com/index. cfm?ObjectID=D57D0AC5-AB2D-EFB0-FC201080B528442A under the Public School list. The award covers tuition, dues, fees, and other required charges up to 150 semester hours. The award will not cover room and board, books, student services fees, or deposit fees.

Eligibility and residency requirements:

• Veteran was a Texas state resident when he or she entered the military, designated Texas as home of record, or entered the service in Texas.
• Child must be the biological child, stepchild, adopted child, or claimed as a dependent in the current or previous tax year.
• Be under the age of twenty-five at the beginning of any term for which the benefit is being claimed (some exemptions may apply).
• Make satisfactory academic progress.
• Provide proof of veteran's honorable discharge.

Benefit

• Combat Tuition Exemption (not currently funded)

Dependent children of service members deployed in combat zones receive tuition waivers (fees not exempted).

Eligibility and residency requirements:

• Child must be a resident of Texas, or entitled to receive the in-state tuition rate (dependents of military personnel stationed in Texas).
• Must be enrolled during the time the service member is deployed in combat zone.
• If out-of-state resident, child may need to provide copy of parent's orders.

Be aware that state reimbursement for this program is not available. It is up to each institution if they will grant this award.

UTAH

http://veterans.utah.gov/state-benefits/

Benefit

• Purple Heart recipients are eligible for tuition waivers at state schools.

Award works for undergraduate and graduate programs. Veterans who were eligible for this benefit should be able to complete a bachelor's and master's degree with little or no debt.
Eligibility and residency requirements:

• Show proof of Purple Heart.
• Be a Utah state resident.

VIRGIN ISLANDS

http://www.militaryvi.org/benefits/

Benefit

• Free tuition is offered for attendance at local public educational institutions and at the University of the Virgin Islands.

This program is for veterans who entered the Armed Forces while residing in the Virgin Islands. Contact the schools for more information.

WASHINGTON

http://apps.leg.wa.gov/RCW/default.aspx?cite=28B.15.621

Benefit

• Full or partial tuition waivers at state schools for undergraduate education for up to two hundred quarter credits (or equivalent semester credits).

Some schools offer the waiver for graduate programs (check with your institution). Full- or part-time enrollment is eligible. Award may work at some private institutions. Be aware that the tuition may not be fully covered.

Eligibility and residency requirements:

- Make satisfactory academic progress.
- Have served in a war or conflict fought on foreign soil or in international waters or in another location in support of those serving on foreign soil or in international waters.
- Received an honorable discharge.
- Be a resident of the state

WEST VIRGINIA

http://www.veterans.wv.gov/programs/Pages/default.aspx

Benefit

- West Virginia Veteran's Re-Education Scholarship Program

Eligible veterans can receive $500 per term (part-time students: $250). Amount cannot exceed a total of $1,500 per academic year. Program funding may be used to cover professional exam costs as well. Eligible veterans may use the scholarship in tandem with the Workforce Investment Act (WIA) and/or Trade Adjustment Act (TAA) if program cost exceeds the amount allocated under the latter two programs.

Eligibility and residency requirements:

- Veteran must be a resident of the state.
- Received an honorable discharge.
- Served 181 consecutive days on active duty.
- Eligible for Pell Grant or unemployed.
- Veteran has exhausted all federal GI Bill money possibilities (including Vocational Rehabilitation, if eligible).

WISCONSIN

http://dva.state.wi.us/Pages/educationEmployment/Education.aspx

Benefit

- Wisconsin GI Bill tuition remission benefit program (WI GI Bill).

Remission of tuition and fees at state institutions (University of Wisconsin and Wisconsin Technical Colleges) for eligible veterans and dependents. The award is good for a maximum of eight semesters (or 128 semester credits), undergraduate and graduate education, and professional programs. There are no income restrictions or delimiting periods. Many fees are not covered, such as books, meals, room and board, and online fees. Award cannot be combined with federal benefits.

Eligibility and residency requirements:

- Veteran must have served since September 10, 2001, and entered the service from Wisconsin.
- Must apply for Post-9/11 GI Bill benefits first, if eligible. (*Note*: Talk to an education counselor or the veterans' representatives before you elect which GI Bill you will use!)
- Children and spouses of veterans with a combined rating of 30 percent or greater from the VA may be eligible for the award.
- Child must be the biological child, stepchild, or adopted child, or any other child who is a member of the veteran's household.
- Child must be at least seventeen but no older than twenty-six, and must be a resident of the state.
- Spouse must be a resident of the state for tuition purposes.
- Spouse has ten years from the date of the veteran's VA rating to use the benefit.

The State of Wisconsin does not allow veterans to double-dip on federal and state-based benefits. However, if veterans paid into MGIB and if the MHA under Post-9/11 at the school they want to attend is less than what they would have received under MGIB, the school will reimburse the veteran for the difference. Talk to the veterans' representatives at the institutions for more information.

Benefit

- The Veterans Education (VetEd) Grant (http://dva.state.wi.us/Pages/educationEmployment/Vet-Ed-Reimbursement-Grant.aspx).

Reimbursement grant program. Reimburses veteran after successful completion of coursework (University of Wisconsin locations, Wisconsin

Technical Colleges, or a private institution of higher education in Wisconsin or Minnesota) at the undergraduate level only. Reimbursement is prorated based on aggregate length of qualifying active-duty service. Veterans with a minimum of 30 percent of qualifying disability from the VA are reimbursed at 100 percent.

Eligibility and residency requirements:

- Veteran entered active duty as a Wisconsin resident, or lived in Wisconsin for twelve months prior to entering the service.
- If veteran was discharged more than ten years ago, only reimbursement at the part-time rate is possible.
- Must exhaust all other benefits first (including Wisconsin State GI Bill).
- Maximum income limit applies (annual income of veteran and spouse cannot exceed $50,000, plus $1,000 for each dependent beyond two).
- Provide proof of income (adjusted gross income [AGI] from the current tax return).
- Must not already possess a bachelor's degree.
- Must not be delinquent on child support payments.
- Must maintain a 2.0 GPA.

WYOMING

http://www.communitycolleges.wy.edu/Data/Sites/1/commissionFiles/Programs/Veteran/_doc/statue-19-14-106.pdf

https://sites.google.com/a/wyo.gov/wyomingmilitarydepartment/veterans-commission/res#TOC-Tuition-Assistance-for-Veterans-and-Surviving-Dependents

Benefit

- Free tuition and fees for overseas combat veterans

Award can be used at the University of Wyoming and the state community colleges. Eligible veterans can receive ten semesters of schooling through this benefit.

Eligibility and residency requirements:

- Veteran must have had residency in state for a minimum of one year prior to entering service.
- Home of residence on DD214 states Wyoming.
- Must have an honorable discharge.

- Received the Armed Forces Expeditionary Medal or campaign medal for service in any conflict in a foreign country (list of qualifying medals found at: http://www.communitycolleges.wy.edu/Data/Sites/1/commissionFiles/Programs/Veteran/_doc/expeditionary-medal-list--2-jul-07.pdf).
- Maintains a 2.0 GPA.
- Veteran has eight years from date of acceptance into program to use.
- State-based education benefits based on severe levels of disability/or death.

STATE-BASED EDUCATION BENEFITS BASED ON SEVERE LEVELS OF DISABILITY/OR DEATH

There are other states besides those listed above that offer education benefits for spouses and/or children. In the case of these states, the veteran must be severely and permanently disabled, or have died while on active-duty service (in many cases, in combat or combat-related situations). I am not going to cover the specific details of these benefits, but below you will find a list of the states that offer this benefit and the links to their websites.

Alabama: http://www.va.state.al.us/gi_dep_scholarship.aspx
Alaska: http://veterans.alaska.gov/education-benefits.html
Arkansas: http://www.veterans.arkansas.gov/benefits.html#edu
California: https://www.calvet.ca.gov/VetServices/Pages/College-Fee-Waiver.aspx
Delaware: http://veteransaffairs.delaware.gov/veterans_benefits.shtml
Florida: http://floridavets.org/?page_id=60
Iowa: http://www.in.gov/dva/2378.htm
Kentucky: http://veterans.ky.gov/Benefits/Documents/KDVAInfoBookletIssueAugust2010.pdf
Louisiana: http://vetaffairs.la.gov/Programs/Education.aspx
Maine: http://www.maine.gov/dvem/bvs/VDEB_2.pdf
Maryland: http://veterans.maryland.gov/wp-content/uploads/sites/2/2013/10/MDBenefitsGuide.pdf
Massachusetts: www.mass.gov/veterans/education/for-family/mslf.html
Michigan: http://www.michigan.gov/documents/mistudentaid/CVTGFactSheet_271497_7.pdf
Minnesota: http://www.mdva.state.mn.us/education/SurvivingSpouseDependentInformationSheet.pdf
Missouri: http://mvc.dps.mo.gov/docs/veterans-benefits-guide.pdf
Montana: http://montanadma.org/state-montana-veterans-benefits
Nebraska: http://www.vets.state.ne.us/waiver.html

New Hampshire: http://www.nh.gov/nhveterans/benefits/education.htm

New Jersey: http://www.state.nj.us/military/veterans/programs.html

New Mexico: http://www.dvs.state.nm.us/benefits.html

New York: http://www.veterans.ny.gov/

North Carolina: http://www.milvets.nc.gov/

North Dakota: http://www.nd.gov/veterans/benefits/nd-dependent-tuition-waiver

Ohio: https://www.ohiohighered.org/ohio-war-orphans

Oregon: http://www.oregon.gov/ODVA/Pages/index.aspx

Pennsylvania: http://www.pheaa.org/funding-opportunities/other-educational-aid/postsecondary-educational-gratuity.shtml

South Carolina: http://va.sc.gov/benefits.html

South Dakota: http://vetaffairs.sd.gov/benefits/State/State%20Education%20Programs.aspx

Tennessee: http://www.state.tn.us/veteran/state_benifits/dep_tuition.html

Texas: http://www.tvc.texas.gov/Hazlewood-Act.aspx

Utah: http://veterans.utah.gov/state-benefits/

Virginia: http://www.dvs.virginia.gov/veterans-benefits.shtml

Washington: http://www.dva.wa.gov/benefits/education-and-training

Wisconsin: http://dva.state.wi.us/Ben-education.asp#Tuition

West Virginia: http://www.veterans.wv.gov/programs/Pages/default.aspx

Wyoming: https://sites.google.com/a/wyo.gov/wyomingmilitarydepartment/veterans-commission/res

SCHOLARSHIPS

Although quite a bit of scholarship money is available for veterans, you must be pro-active in your pursuit of a scholarship. No one is going to hand you the money without you making an effort. Applying for scholarships is not as difficult as it seems. Oftentimes, you can reuse information, so keep everything you write. Most education centers have financial aid packets available for you to pick up in their offices and some have the packets posted on their websites. These packets offer a good place to start conducting search.

Try to remember that the active-duty TA money only goes so far. TA does not cover books, tools, computers, and so on. You should run the numbers before you start. For example, CSULB, estimated the 2015–2016 school year book costs at $1,860. Currently, if a veteran is attending school full-time, the maximum book stipend awarded under the Post-9/11 GI Bill is $1,000 per academic year. That leaves a gap of $860 for the veteran attending CSULB to cover out of pocket. In either case, applying for scholarships is a wise move, although not your only option.

Scholarships come in all shapes and sizes. You will need to determine which scholarships may apply to you. Do not narrow yourself to simply veteran-based possibilities. You can apply for civilian scholarships as well. Most break down into specific categories, such as pursuit of study, age, gender, race, disability, state-based, or school-based options.

You will also need to inquire into whether the scholarship only pays tuition or perhaps goes into your pocket similar to FSA. If you have decided to use the Post-9/11GI Bill and all of your tuition is already covered, applying for scholarships that pay tuition might not be beneficial, but if you are using the MGIB that means you can keep more of the $1,789 monthly stipend in your pocket each month.

When you begin your search, remember it will take some time to find and determine eligibility. Start by making a quick search on your school's website. Many schools list scholarships specific to their institution right on their own web pages. Check with your school's veterans' representatives, the financial aid department, and the local education center on your base for possible scholarship opportunities. Libraries are also an underused resource for scholarship opportunities. Check opportunities based on options outside your military experience; then, check opportunities based on options within the military community.

Most scholarships will require an essay, so prepare the best essay possible, and then see if someone in the education center is willing to proofread it for you. Always start far, far in advance. Most scholarships are due during the spring semester in order to pay out for the following fall.

Be very careful of organizations demanding you pay money in order to be eligible for a scholarship. Scholarship information is widely available, and you should not have to pay to find, receive, or complete an application. Most certainly, *never* give any credit card information. If you need help, contact your school's financial aid department.

Applying for scholarships can require a lot of legwork and many students are not willing to put in the effort. This limits the pool of competitors and increases the chances of you being awarded a scholarship. Additionally, many veterans will not bother to explore other options outside of the GI Bill to increase their sources of funding, so military-related scholarships can have even less potential competitors. Use this to your advantage.

Lastly, remember that once you apply for a scholarship each subsequent scholarship becomes easier. Many essay requirements are similar and share a common theme of "How will you use your education to make better or change the world?" Essays can be modified slightly and used multiple times. Plus, once you have been through the process of filling out an application, listing information and extracurricular activities, you can just copy and paste the same answers for each subsequent application. If transcripts are required, perhaps to demonstrate a GPA or degree progression, the same copy can usually be used repeatedly. Keeping these tips in mind will give you the psychological edge required to endure the legwork far beyond your potential competitors to hopefully receive a financial reward.

Military Service–Related Scholarships

The following are just a few of the scholarships available to service members. Take a look and see what might be relevant to you. At the end of the section there are several scholarship search sites listed.

MILITARY-BASED SCHOLARSHIPS

The Air Force Aid Society

http://www.afas.org/background

The Air Force Aid Society (AFAS) is the official charity of the United States Air Force. According to their website, AFAS promotes the Air Force mission by helping *"to relieve distress of Air Force members and their families and assisting them to finance their education."*[5]

As a nonprofit organization, AFAS has helped countless members of the Air Force community since its creation in 1942. Strong support for AFAS programs and objectives is reinforced each year by the substantial personal contributions made by the active force, all of which are used solely for emergency assistance. Although AFAS receives no appropriated or nonappropriated funds, close ties are maintained between the society and Air Force officials. AFAS is governed by a Board of Trustees which includes key Air Force leaders. The Board provides policy direction for AFAS operations and for control and disposition of AFAS property and funds.

General Henry H. Arnold Education Grant Program

AFAS has been committed to helping Air Force members and their families realize their academic goals since their inception in 1942. The General Henry

H. Arnold Education Grant program is a centerpiece of the Society's education initiatives. As of March 2015, 102,244 grants have been disbursed since the first awards were made for the 1988–1989 academic year.

This grant program is competitive in its need-based selection criteria, uniquely tailored to recognize the proper weighing of family income and education cost factors. Grants of at least $2,000 are awarded to selected sons and daughters of Active Duty, Title 10 AGR/Reserve, Title 32 AGR performing full-time active duty, retired, retired reserve and deceased Air Force members; spouses of active-duty members and Title 10 AGR/Reservists; and surviving spouses of deceased personnel for their full-time undergraduate studies.

AFAS has contracted with Scholarship America, an independent, not-for-profit organization to provide administrative support services through their Scholarship Management Services (SMS) division.

AFAS Merit Scholarship

The AFAS awards a minimum of ten $5,000 merit-based scholarships to incoming freshman who have completed both phases of the General Henry H. Arnold Education Grant application, and therefore, have already been reviewed for eligibility and had their Grade Point Average (GPA) verified. These scholarship candidates, regardless of whether or not they receive the need-based Arnold Grant, will be directly contacted by AFAS HQ in May of each year. Selection is based on cumulative GPA, SAT/ACT scores, transcripts, and an essay on a specified topic. Winners will be announced in July, with funds disbursed directly to the universities and colleges in early August.

AFAS Supplemental Education Loan Program

The AFAS also offers an interest-free loan to help reimburse families for incidental college expenses such as books, fees and supplies that can pose a hardship for families already coping with high tuition and room and board costs. This loan is open only to dependents of regular Active Duty, Title 10 AGR/Reserve on extended active duty, Title 32 Air national Guard members (AGR) performing full-time active duty, regular Retired and Retired Reserve with 20+ years of creditable service who applied for the 2015–2016 General Henry H. Arnold Education Grant, as their eligibility has already been verified through the grant application process, *and* AFAS has the ability to collect repayment by allotment directly from the members' military/retired pay.

Maximum dollar amount for each full-time dependent undergraduate student is $1,000, regardless of whether or not they received the need-based Arnold Grant. AFAS provides the loan applications to identified applicants in August, with an application deadline of October 1. Checks will be disbursed by AFAS no later than mid-October. Repayment by allotment will be automatically started by AFAS and run for a ten-month period beginning November 15 for Active Duty, and December 1 for Retirees. Only incoming freshman who complete the Arnold Grant preliminary application, Family Financial Data Form and GPA verification will be considered for the Merit Scholarship.

Air Force Sergeants Association Scholarship Program

http://www.hqafsa.org/scholarships.html

The Air Force Sergeants Association (AFSA, not to be confused with AFAS) scholarship program began in 1968 with one $1,000 scholarship. According to their website, today's AFSA has awarded more than 550 scholarships totaling more than $800,000 in scholastic financial aid.

The scholarships are funded by donations from AFSA members, the association's field activities, and memorials. Scholarships are awarded in each program based on the applicant's academic record, character, leadership skills, writing ability, versatility, and potential for success. Financial need is not a consideration, but sponsors must be AFSA members. The awards are typically between $1,500 and $2,500 amounts.

Chief Master Sergeant of the Air Force Scholarship Program

http://www.hqafsa.org/scholarships.html

The CMSAF Scholarship Program was created in 1987 upon the death of CMSAF Kisling. It was renamed in 1997 following the passing of CMSAFs Andrews and Harlow. The program is funded by donations, memorials, and speaking honorariums. One unique aspect of the CMSAF Scholarship Program is the opportunity for an applicant to submit additional information he or she believes should be considered. Examples include student disabilities, parent POW/MIA/KIA status, extreme financial hardship, or other extenuating circumstances. Applicants simply complete the "additional information" form included in the application. Since 1988, the fund has awarded more than 250 scholarships valued at more than $350,000. The fund is governed by a committee appointed by the incumbent Chief Master Sergeant of the Air Force. CMSAF Sam Parish served as the committee chairman.

Airmen Memorial Foundation Scholarship Program

http://www.hqafsa.org/scholarships.html

In past years, the Airmen Memorial Foundation (AMF) Scholarship Program has provided scholarships to include scholarships to include:

$2,000—one Richard Howard Scholarship, and five Memorial Scholarships in the names of Sharon Piccoli, Julene Howard and Sgt. James R. Seal.

$1,500—five Basic Military Training scholarships.

$1,000—ten academic scholarships, one Memorial Scholarship for Audrey Andrews and five USAA scholarships. The AMF scholarships are funded by contributions received through the annual Combined Federal Campaign, the AFSA Parade of Checks, and other donations.

AFSA International Auxiliary Education Grant Program

http://www.hqafsa.org/scholarships.html

The Air Force Sergeants Association International Auxiliary conducts a program to financially help AFSA Auxiliary members with a valid need of assistance to enhance their income potential through formal education and/or training. The AEG program is designed for AFSA Auxiliary members to obtain effective education and/or training to acquire improved marketable skills. Since 1990, the AFSA Auxiliary has awarded grants and scholarships totaling over $117,000. Grants are awarded based on available funds, but will not exceed $2,000 per person. Grant funds will be mailed to the applicant's school/educational institution with instructions for use. The monies may be used for tuition, fees, books and supplies, child care, meals and transportation in commuting to and from school. The funds are not transferable from one school to another at any time during the semester or term.

Eligibility requirements for the AFSA International Auxiliary Education Grant (AEG) Program are as follows:

• Applicants must have been an AFSA Auxiliary member for at least one year at the time application is submitted and must continue as a member for two additional years after award is presented.
• Must be nineteen years of age or older.
• The applicant must be able to demonstrate a financial need for assistance.
• Applicant must be accepted to an accredited institution.
• At the conclusion of the course, class, or program, the applicant must receive a certificate, diploma, or degree.
• The applicant must show that he or she is acquiring or enhancing marketable skills that will increase his or her economic security.

Airman and Family Readiness Centers are located on each major Air Force Installation. In conjunction with the Education Center, they are the focal points for local opportunities for dependent scholarships. Examples include the local Chiefs Group, Enlisted Top Three Council, the Officer's Wives Club as well as local universities such as Troy University in Alabama.

American Legion Auxiliary

www.alaforveterans.org/Scholarships/Non-Traditional-Student-Scholarship/

Approximately five scholarships at $2,000 each are awarded to applicants who are members of the American Legion, American Legion Auxiliary, or Sons of the American Legion. Members must have paid dues for a minimum of two years prior to applying. Applicants must be nontraditional students (going back to school after an absence or starting later in life). Applications are due by March 1.

American Veterans (AMVETS)

http://www.amvets.org/pdfs/programs_pdfs/scholarship_application_veteran.pdf
(877) 726-8387

Award amount is $4,000 over four years. Applicant must be pursuing full-time study at the undergraduate, graduate, or certification level from an accredited institution. Three scholarships awarded annually. Application is due by April 15. Applicant must be a veteran, be a U.S. citizen, and have financial need. Required materials include the veteran's DD214, official school transcripts, a completed (and signed) 1040 form, a completed FAFSA application, an essay of fifty to one hundred words addressing a specific prompt (see website), a résumé (see website), and proof of school-based expenses.

American Veterans (AMVETS) National Ladies Auxiliary

http://www.amvetsaux.org/assets/14-15national-scholarship-applicationoct.pdf
(301) 459-6255

Two scholarships at $1,000 each and up to five scholarships at $750 each may be available. In order to be eligible, applicant must be a current member of the AMVETS Ladies Auxiliary; a son or daughter; stepchild; or grand-child or step grandchild of a member. Application can be filled out starting in the eligible individual's second year of undergraduate study at an eligible institution. Required documents include a personal essay of two hundred to five hundred words (see website for more information), three letters of rec-ommendation, official transcripts, a copy of the member's membership card, and all required paperwork from the Ladies Auxiliary. Applications are due by July 1.

Armed Forces Communications and Electronics Association (AFCEA)

http://www.afcea.org/education/scholarships/undergraduate/military.asp
(703) 631-6100

The AFCEA has six different categories of scholarships that pertain to undergraduate and graduate-level studies. Students must be attending four-year colleges or universities within the United States and may only apply in one category. The different categories include: War Veterans Scholarship (Afghanistan and Iraq War Veterans), STEM Majors Scholarship for Diver-sity Students, ROTC Scholarships, STEM Teachers Scholarship, and the STEM Majors Scholarship. See the above-listed website for more informa-tion pertaining to each option.

The War Veterans Scholarship (http://www.afcea.org/education/schol-arships/undergraduate/military.asp) is merit-based. Varying amounts can be awarded to persons on active duty in the uniformed military services, to honorably discharged U.S. military veterans (including Reservists and National Guard personnel). Students must be currently pursuing classes at the part-time or full-time rate of pursuit and in an eligible degree program at an accredited four-year college or university in the United States.

The STEM Majors Scholarship for Diversity Scholarship (http://www.afcea.org/education/scholarships/undergraduate/HBCUScholarship.asp) has two options, $5,000 awards for award winners attending an undergraduate course of study at Historically Black Colleges or Universities (HBCU) and $3,000 awards for eligible (women and minority students) award winners pursuing graduate degrees. Majors must support the mission of the AFCEA Educational Foundation.

The ROTC Scholarships (http://www.afcea.org/education/scholarships/rotc/) are only for those enrolled in ROTC, at least in their second year of college, enrolled full-time as a sophomores or juniors with an overall 3.0

GPA or above, and must be attending a four-year accredited college or university at the time of application submittal. Awards range from $2,000 to $3,000 and students must be enrolled in specific majors, such as biometry/biometrics, computer engineering, or cybersecurity (see website for other fields).

The STEM Teachers Scholarship awards (http://www.afcea.org/education/scholarships/undergraduate/TeachersScholarship.asp) are $5,000. Students must be actively pursuing a graduate-level degree or teaching credential in a STEM field.

The STEM Major Scholarship (http://www.afcea.org/education/scholarships/undergraduate/STEMMajorScholarshipUndergrad.asp) is for undergraduate and graduate-degree students who are majoring in STEM fields. Undergraduate students must be in at least their second year of college and have a minimum of a 3.0 GPA. Graduate-level students must be enrolled in at minimum their second semester of study and have a 3.5 or higher GPA.

*Scholarship awards are subject to availability of funding. Scholarship awards are restricted to tuition and mandatory fees.

Disabled American Veterans (DAV) Auxiliary

http://auxiliary.dav.org/membership/Programs.aspx
(877) 426-2838, ext. 4020

Life members with the DAV Auxiliary who are attending a college or vocational school full-time can participate in the scholarship program. The scholarship maxes out at $1,500. Part-time pursuit of study may be eligible for $750. Applicants must maintain a minimum of twelve credit hours per semester to remain eligible. Renewals are not guaranteed.

Leave No Veteran Behind

http://www.leavenoveteranbehind.org/
312.379.8652

A retroactive scholarship that is designed to assist with student debt that was incurred prior to entering military service. Winners get their loan amounts paid off in full. In return for the award, selectees must commit to one hundred to four hundred hours of community service. The community service work must take advantage of the awardees military skills and civilian education. Applicants must suffer from economic hardship, have student loans, have completed some degree of higher education, and have been honorably discharged.

Military Order of the Purple Heart (MOPH)

www.purpleheart.org/scholarships/Default.aspx
www.purpleheart.org/Downloads/Forms/ScholarshipApplication.pdf
(703) 642-5360
scholarship@purpleheart.org

Be aware that this scholarship demands a $15 payment at time of submittal. Applicant must be a Purple Heart recipient and a member of the Military Order of the Purple Heart, or the spouse, widow, child (step and adopted), or grandchild. Student must currently be a high-school senior or attending college as an undergraduate student full-time (or attending trade school), and have a minimum 2.75 GPA on a 4.0 scale. Applicant must submit an essay of two hundred to three hundred words (see site for prompt), two letters of recommendation, all other required materials, and the $15 fee (check or money order).

Pat Tillman Scholarship

http://pattillmanfoundation.org/
(480) 621-4074
info@pattillmanfoundation.org

Award amount varies every year. Active duty, veterans, and spouses of both categories are eligible to apply. Applicant must be attending school full-time at a four-year university or college (public or private) at the undergraduate or graduate level. This scholarship is a great opportunity for graduate school students, because options at that level are more difficult to find. Applicant must apply for Federal Financial Aid (FAFSA). Digital files of the applicant's DD214 or personal service record and résumé will be required in order to submit, as well as responding to the two essay prompts. Those who proceed further will need to turn in their financial aid award letter (from attending institution), SAR report from FAFSA, and a photo highlighting the applicable individual's military service. Application opens in January and closes the following month. Check the website for more information.

Veterans of Foreign Wars (VFW)

http://www.vfw.org/Scholarship/
(816) 756-3390, ext. 220

For VFW members who served or are currently serving in one of the branches. Scholarship awards are $5,000, are limited to one per family per semester, and must be used by the end of the semester for which the veteran applied. Scholarships are broken into fall and spring options. Check website for due dates and eligibility factors.

Veterans United Foundation Scholarship

http://www.veteransunited.com/about/scholarships/

This scholarship awards a maximum of twenty scholarships per year with an award amount of $2,000 to assist with tuition and books each semester. Essays are required for submission.

Eligible applicants must be pursuing an associate, bachelor, master, or doctoral degree, or be planning on attending school the following academic year. A connection to the United States Military must be demonstrated through one of five specific pathways.

Applicant must be:

- A current active-duty service member
- A veteran of the United States Armed Forces
- A spouse of a service member or veteran
- Surviving spouse or child of a fallen service member
- A child of a service member or veteran

Applicants must also maintain a cumulative 2.5 grade point average on a 4.0 scale at all times.

It is common for private organizations on Air Force bases to offer scholarships to graduates of the Community College of the Air Force. On Maxwell Air Force Base for example, the local Chief's Group, Enlisted Top Three, and Air Force Association all fund scholarships for graduates of the CCAF at the April and October graduation ceremonies. The organizations have panels that determine criteria and select scholarship recipients. Troy University also awards scholarships to CCAF graduates at these ceremonies. The scholarships range from $300 to $500 per student. This section is double spaced but the others are single spaced.

SCHOOL-BASED SCHOLARSHIPS

Many schools offer internal scholarships. Speak to the financial aid department of your chosen institution to find out about opportunities. This section demonstrates just a few of the scholarships available around the country.

Colorado

Colorado State University

Liniger Honor, Service and Commitment Scholarship
http://alvs.colostate.edu/liniger-scholarship
   Applicants must be an undergraduate or graduate student and enrolled in CSU at the full-time or part-time rate of pursuit. Applicant must be a combat veteran and have been awarded the Campaign Medal (Afghanistan, Iraq, Kosovo), Armed Forces Expeditionary Medal, Vietnam Service Medal or a service combat medal, or a Purple Heart.

Florida

Santa Fe College

Jeffrey Mattison Wershow Memorial Scholarship
http://m.sfcollege.edu/development/index.php?section=info/JeffreyMattison
WershowMemorial
   Applicant must have received an honorable discharge (but can still be on active duty) and must maintain a 2.5 GPA for award renewal. Award amount is $1,600 per year, or $800 per semester. Application demands a thousand-word essay pertaining to student's education (see website) and three letters of recommendation (see website).

Idaho

Idaho State University

Iwo Jima Scholarship
http://www.isu.edu/veterans/scholarships.shtml
   The Iwo Jima Scholarship may be available to a descendant of World War II veterans (preference for those who served at Iwo Jima). Applicant must

have a 3.0 GPA to be eligible, and preference is given to engineering majors. Personal statement and discharge papers are required (see website).

Kansas

Kansas Military Service Scholarship

http://www.kansasregents.org/students/student_financial_aid/scholarships_ and_grants

The scholarship is open for students attending public schools and is available for the payment of tuition and fees. Student must have served in military service in international waters or on foreign soil in support of military operations and received at least ninety days of hostile fire pay after September 11, 2001, or served less than ninety days due to injuries received during that time frame. Must have received an honorable discharge and complete a FAFSA.

Michigan

Michigan State University

MSU Disabled Veteran's Assistance Program
http://finaid.msu.edu/veterans.asp

New and returning undergraduate veterans with a military-related disability who are Michigan residents and working on their first baccalaureate degree potentially qualify for an aid package that covers all costs.

Minnesota

University of Minnesota Duluth

LaVerne Noyes Scholarship
http://www.d.umn.edu/onestop/student-finances/financial-aid/types/scholarships/umd-current.html

This scholarship is available to students attending the University of Minnesota Duluth. Applicant must be a direct blood descendant of a military member who served in the U.S. Army or Navy in World War I and died in service or received an honorable discharge. Applicant must demonstrate financial need. Award is $1,000.

New York

Cornell University Law School

Dickson Randolph Knott Memorial
http://www.lawschool.cornell.edu/alumni/giving/endowed_funds/scholarships_g-l.cfm
Applicant must be a military veteran enrolled in the law school (see website for more information).

Monroe Community College

Donald W. Holleder Endowed Scholarship
https://monroecc.academicworks.com/opportunities/1223
Applicant must demonstrate financial need, and preference is given to Vietnam veterans and their dependents. Award is for $600 per year.

Ohio

Cedarville University

James Cain Special Education Award
http://www.cedarville.edu/courses/catalog/2011-2012/financial-information.pdf
Full-time sophomore, junior, or senior students at the university majoring in special education (intent on teaching kids with special needs) may apply. Applicant must demonstrate financial need, and preference is given to certain populations, including those who have served in the military.

Texas

Angelina College

Disabled American Veterans Scholarship
http://www.angelina.edu/generalbulletin/scholarship-info/
Applicant must be a descendant of a member of the DAV. Award is $500 per semester for full-time study.

Texas Christian University

Adrienne Miller Perner Scholarship
http://www.dance.tcu.edu/financialaid.asp
(817) 257-7615

Amount varies. Applicant must be a child or grandchild of a career military service member. Applicant must also be female and majoring in ballet. Scholarship is based on talent or community work.

Utah

Westminster College

Doris Edwards Miller Endowed Scholarship
https://www.westminstercollege.edu/pdf/financial_aid_undergraduate/1314%20Scholarship%20List.pdf
This scholarship is available to veterans or their children, but both must demonstrate need. Full-time enrollment is mandatory in order to be eligible for this scholarship (eight at $3,500 each).

SCHOLARSHIP POSSIBILITIES FOR DEPENDENTS

Below is a list of scholarships available for spouses and dependent children. Always check with the Military Spouses Clubs at the base where you are stationed if you are still on active duty with the Air Force. The clubs usually have scholarship possibilities every year.

Ladies Auxiliary VFW

Continuing Education Scholarship
https://www.ladiesauxvfw.org/programs-page/scholarships/
Spouses, sons, and daughters of members may be eligible if they are pursuing a college degree or career pathway at a technical school.

Fisher House

http://www.militaryscholar.org/
Run by the commissaries. A minimum of one $2,000 scholarship is awarded through every commissary location, although more might be possible depending on funding. Award may be used for payment of tuition, books, lab fees, or other education-related expenses. Scholarship is open to children of active duty, retired, or reserve service members. Applicant must have a minimum of a 3.0 GPA on a 4.0 scale.

The Joanne Holbrook Patton Military Spouse Scholarships

https://militaryfamily.scholarships.ngwebsolutions.com/CMXAdmin/Cmx_
Content.aspx?cpId=561

For spouses of active duty, retired, and reserve service members. Award may be used for tuition, fees, or school room and board. The scholarship offers assistance for GED or ESL, vocational training or certification, undergraduate or graduate degrees, licensure fees, and clinical hours for mental health licensure. Applicants can attend face-to-face schooling or online.

American Legion

http://www.legion.org/scholarships
Samsung American Legion Scholarship

For high-school juniors who complete a Boys State or Girls State program. Applicant must also be a direct descendant of an eligible wartime veteran (see website for more information). Scholarship is for undergraduate study only and is based on financial need. It can be used for tuition, books, fees, or room and board. Applicants must have completed a Boys State or Girls State program, be direct descendants or legally adopted children of wartime veterans (must be eligible for American Legion membership), and be in their junior year of high school. Award is up to $20,000 for an undergraduate course of study. Winners are selected based upon academic record, financial need, and participation in community activities. Application requires several mini-essays.

Legacy Scholarship
http://www.legion.org/scholarships/legacy

Eligible applicants are children or adopted children of military members who died while on active duty on or after September 11, 2001; are high-school seniors or already graduated; and are pursuing an undergraduate degree.

The Baseball Scholarship
http://www.legion.org/scholarships/baseball
baseball@legion.org

Applicant must have graduated high school, be on a team affiliated with an American Legion post, and be on a 2013 roster filed with the National Headquarters. High-school transcripts, three letters of testimony, and a completed application must be filed.

National High School Oratorical Contest Scholarship
http://www.legion.org/scholarships/oratorical
oratorical@legion.org

Scholarship money (up to $18,000 for first place) can be used at any college or university within the United States. Scholarship has hundreds of small rewards involved at local levels.

Department of Michigan-American Legion Auxiliary

http://michalaux.org/scholarships/
Medical Career Scholarship

Applicants should be daughters, granddaughters, great-granddaughters, sons, grandsons, or great-grandsons of honorably discharged or deceased veterans of specific conflicts (World War I, World War II, Korea, Vietnam, Persian Gulf, etc.) and be living in Michigan. Award is $500 for tuition, room and board fees, books, and so on. Scholarship must be used at a school in Michigan, and applicants must be in their senior year of high school (top quarter of their class) and preparing to enter college. This is a need-based scholarship.

Scholarship for Nontraditional Students

One two-year scholarship of $500 per year will be awarded. Applicant must be the descendant of a veteran, over the age of twenty-two, and attending college or trade school for the first time or attending college after a significantly long break. The award may be used toward tuition and books at a school in the state of Michigan. Entries are due by March 15. Application includes short essays.

National American Legion Auxiliary

Children of Warriors Scholarship National Presidents' Scholarship
https://www.alaforveterans.org/Scholarships/Children-of-Warriors-National-
    Presidents--Scholarship/

Applicants must be daughters or sons, stepdaughters or stepsons, grandsons or granddaughters, step grandsons or step granddaughters, or step great-grandsons or step great-granddaughters of eligible American Legion members. Applicants should be in their senior year of high school and complete fifty hours of volunteer service. Check the website to determine when completed applications and all documentation (including an essay) are due to the local American Legion.

Spirit of Youth Scholarship

https://www.alaforveterans.org/Scholarships/Spirit-of-Youth-Scholarship-
    Fund/

Five awards at $5,000 each for this scholarship. Applicants must be seniors in high school and junior members of the American Legion Auxiliary for the past three years, hold current membership, and continue membership throughout awarding years. A 3.0 GPA is mandatory for individuals applying for this scholarship. Applications are due by March 1; winners are announced March 15. ACT or SAT scores, high-school transcripts, four letters of recommendation, a completed FAFSA application, and essays are required.

Other extremely noteworthy options:

The American Military Retirees Scholarships:
http://amra1973.org/Scholarship/

Federal sites for scholarship searches:

http://www.careerinfonet.org/scholarshipsearch/ScholarshipCategory.asp?se
    archtype=category&nodeid=22
http://studentaid.ed.gov/
https://studentaid.ed.gov/sa/types/grants-scholarships/finding-scholarships

Searches:

https://www.horatioalger.org/scholarships/index.cfm
http://www.collegescholarships.org/scholarships/army.htm
http://www.finaid.org/military/veterans.phtml
www.scholarships.com
www.collegeboard.org
http://www.scholarships4students.com/council_of_college_and_military_
    educators_scholarship.htm
http://scholarshipamerica.org/
www.careeronestop.org
www.collegedata.com
http://www.finaid.org/scholarships/
http://fedmoney.org/
www.militaryonesource.com

TEXTBOOK-BUYING OPTIONS

Who knew books could be so expensive? Welcome to college! The cost of books can often get out of control. The Post-9/11 GI Bill maxes out at $1,000 per academic year for books and supplies, and often that does not begin to cover the bill. If you are still on active duty, then you already know that TA does not cover books.

College books are notoriously expensive. Unlike high school, a year of college requires an incredible amount of books. Professors have to find supplemental materials to feed your brain and back up the information with proof. Books are still the most common, easiest way of accomplishing this task.

Now you know why you need them, but not why college books are so expensive. A few reasons come to mind: for example, copyrighted material, specialized material, and online supplements. College books can hold an incredible amount of copyrighted material. Publishers have to cover the copyright fees, as well as all other fees, within the cost of the book. Information within college books is usually quite specialized and often not found elsewhere. This means the books do not have another avenue for sales and contributes to a highly competitive market, driving the cost up. Many books also have online supplements attached to them, and those fees must also be included in the cost.

Last—although I hate addressing this reason, but I feel I (Jillian) must— many professors have written books. Can you guess which books could be included in your reading list? Terrible, I agree . . . since professors get royalties just like other authors. Let's think more positively about the situation. Sometimes these books can be some of your most informative and easily organized reference material. Professors often write books based on the knowledge they have derived from their years in the classroom and field experience to help themselves or others teach. Many schools take pride in having such accomplished professors on staff. Speaking from personal experience, getting published is no easy feat. This practice may sometimes help a professor cut down on the book expenses for his or her students because the book follows along closely with the class's learning expectations, thereby allowing the student to purchase one or at least fewer books than previously necessary.

Although many other reasons contribute to book costs, I'll get down to the reason you are reading this section: how to pay for them. The first trip to the bookstore can be excruciating as reality sets in. Do not stress yet; other options may exist. Since many books top the $100 range (sometimes closer to $200!), students should spend as much time as feasible trying to find books from alternate sources. I still recommend checking out the campus bookstore first. Some schools maintain significant used textbook sections. You will need to get to the store as early as possible to take advantage of this possibility; the discounted books will be the first ones to leave the shelves. Check to see if you can sell your books back at the end of the semester as well. Most likely, the amount the store will offer you will be greatly reduced. Try to think of it as a "Little cash is better than none," and you can roll that money into your textbooks for the following semester.

Next, you can try either renting or buying the books used online. Which path you choose depends on whether you want to keep the books. Personally, because books change every few years and the information within them becomes outdated at such a fast pace, I only kept my French books. The language was not going anywhere, so I figured I would hold on to them for future reference.

There is an astounding number of sites on the Internet that sell or rent used textbooks. Even some bigwigs have gotten into the game. Amazon has a used textbook section that may suit all of your needs. The section (at http://www. amazon.com/New-Used-Textbooks-Books/b?ie=UTF8&node=465600) enables users to refer friends and earn $5 credits. While it may not seem like much, if you are the first in your group to start referring friends, you could end up with a stash of extra money to help cover your own textbook expenses. Amazon also allows users to sell books back to the store for Amazon gift cards. If you would prefer to rent (yes, for a full semester!), the site has that option available to users. If you are an Amazon Prime member (payment required: join as a student and receive a discount), you can receive your shipment in two days; otherwise, orders over $35 receive free shipping but will run on regular shipment timeframes. Lastly, you can rent or buy Kindle Textbooks for Kindle Fire Tablets, or put the Kindle application on your iPad, Android tablet, PC, or Mac, and read it on your own device. You can rent the eTextbooks for an amount of time you specify. When you pick a book, Amazon lets you set the return date, although the price does go up the longer you keep the book.

Barnes & Noble offers the same services as Amazon (see http://www. barnesandnoble.com/b/textbooks/_/N-8q9). You can receive a check from the store and even get a quick quote by entering some easy information on the website. The eTextbooks offered through B&N can be viewed with a seven-day free trial before purchasing on your PC or Mac (not available for the actual NOOK device or mobile phones). This may come in handy if you are looking for an older version to save money. Make sure you compare the older version against a new version (find a friend!) before purchasing. The eTextbooks are viewed through NOOK Study (free app). You can highlight, tag, link, and conduct searches on textbooks downloaded with this app.

If I were currently attending school, I would ask for gift certificates to these two stores for every single holiday that came around. The generosity of family could keep me going with school textbooks for quite some time.

You may also want to check out the publisher's website. Very often the book's publisher will sell the ebook or text version for a greatly reduced rate. Sometimes there is no telling what pricing or distribution disputes are ongoing to affect the prices of textbooks from various vendors.

Now, these are not the only possible sources to rent or purchase textbooks. Below are just a few other possible sources. Always compare prices at different sites to make sure you are getting the best deal possible before you proceed.

- Amazon Student Website: www.amazon.com/New-Used-Textbooks-Books/b?ie=UTF8&node=465600
- Barnes & Noble: http://www.barnesandnoble.com/u/textbooks-college-textbooks/379002366/
- Compare book prices:
  http://www.bookfinder4u.com
  http://www.textbookrentals.com
- Rent, sell, or buy back books:
  http://www.chegg.com
  http://www.campusbookrentals.com
  http://www.bookrenter.com
  http://www.valorebooks.com
  http://www.skyo.com

Here are my last few ideas on this subject. You may be incredibly shocked to learn that sometimes the library is a good place to start. Check out both your college's library and your community library. The book may not be available for rental for the full semester, but if you only need a section or two, copy machines will work nicely. Or you can make friends with someone who already took the class and has not returned his or her book, and offer that individual a decent price. Check with the college's bookstore for class reading lists, or send a nice e-mail to the professor to find out the reading list in advance, then double-down on your mission.

FREE SUBJECT MATTER STUDY SUPPORT—MILITARY BASED

This section will be short and sweet. I packed it full of free websites and pre-paratory programs that can help in your educational pursuits. Often, all it takes is a little extra help, or a different explanation of the same material in order to clear the cobwebs and make progress in a subject. I find the websites listed below to have the best information/explanations to help promote learning.

Peterson's, a Nelnet Company

www.petersons.com/dod

Peterson's is a solid site for subject-matter proficiency exams and ASVAB test preparation. You can continue to use this site upon separation from the Air Force. Here is a basic rundown of what you and your dependents (free for them as well) can access on the site:

• CLEP prep (see the CLEP section for more info)
• DSST prep (see the CLEP section for more info)
• ASVAB prep
• OASC/CPST

This site also has options to help users narrow their searches—for example, by undergraduate and graduate school, vocational-technical school, or Service-members Opportunity Colleges (SOC). Under the undergraduate and graduate school search tabs are listed helpful articles that may give you more guidance in your pursuit of an appropriate school, an appropriate program, or preparing for the admissions process, which can be very long and time consuming.

Lastly, on the home page of Petersons is a link labeled OASC, Online Academic Skills Course. The program is intended to boost the user's read-ing comprehension, vocabulary, and math abilities. The preassessment will determine the user's strengths and weaknesses and help design an appropriate learning plan. As a user progresses through OASC, learning is supported by interactive exercises and quizzes.

eKnowledge Corporation & NFL Players

SAT & ACT test preparation
www.eknowledge.com/military
(770) 992-0900

LoriCaputo@eknowledge.com

This program is a combined effort of the Department of Defense and some patriotic NFL players. eKnowledge Corporation donates SAT and ACT test preparation software to military families and veterans. The software usually runs approximately $200, but it is free for service members and their families. The programs include classroom instruction, interactive learning participation, and 120 classroom video lessons. There is a small fee for the method of delivery of the materials.

Veterans Attending School with the GI Bill-Tutoring Available

Veterans attending school on a GI Bill at one-half time or more in a post-secondary program at an educational institution may be eligible for an extra tutoring stipend from the VA. The VA will pay up to $100 per month for tutoring on top of your regular GI Bill payments. The subject must be mandatory for program completion. Total amount cannot exceed $1,200. Students must need help in the subject, and even if currently receiving a passing grade, can receive the assistance if the current grade will not count toward program completion. Use the VONAPP system to fill out the DD 22-1990T and inquire with your school to see if they participate in this VA program. Often, tutors can be found for free at your school. Commonly, the tutors are students of the subject they give tutoring in and often receiving "tuition remission" or a deduction of their tuition costs. Regardless, even if fees are charged, rarely does it exceed $100 a month, unless you need extremely extensive tutoring.

Under Post-9/11, there is no entitlement charge (deduction of remaining months of benefit). Under MGIB, there is no entitlement charge for the first $600.

http://www.gibill.va.gov/resources/education_resources/programs/tutorial_assistance_program.html

NONMILITARY-SUPPORTED FREE SUBJECT MATTER HELP

Here is a list of free nonmilitary-related study websites I like to use when I need extra help. I have used all of them at some point and found each beneficial for one thing or another. Hopefully, you will find them constructive too.

Math

Khan Academy (www.khanacademy.org)

The very first website that should be on anyone's list for math is Khan Academy. This is far and away the most amazing math help available without paying for one-on-one tutoring. You can register for the site through Facebook or Google, and it is incredibly easy to use (and of course *free!*). Videos guide the user through different problems, and discussion question threads allow the user to ask questions. The site offers other subjects besides math. Science and economics, humanities, computer science, and some test prep help are available as well.

PurpleMath (www.purplemath.com)

Purple Math offers a wide array of math topics. You can find anything you might need on the site. The main page is a bit jumbled, and many of the links take you to external sites. Stick to the main Purple Math page. The examples are written step by step to show you how to proceed for each particular problem.

English

Grammar Bytes (www.chompchomp.com)

I (Jillian) dig this website. The layout is easy to understand without any mumbo jumbo to sort through. Each section has a print tab that organizes the material in an easily printed (no pictures or extra garbage to waste ink!), easy read manner. The subject matter is comprehensive, and the site even contains YouTube videos.

Purdue Owl (http://owl.english.purdue.edu/owl/)

As an English teacher, I love Purdue Owl. Everything I need is on this site. Plus the site offers instructive writing help, such as thesis statement development, dealing with writer's block, and creating an outline to start a paper. If you are in need of American Psychological Association (APA) or Modern Language Association (MLA) formatting help, go to this site. APA and MLA are formatting structures that most higher education classes demand be used in writing papers.

Guide to Grammar Writing (http://grammar.ccc.commnet.edu/grammar/)

This is a no-nonsense website that has all of the basics organized in a user-friendly manner. The Editing and Rewriting Skills section has a checklist that is similar to the one I use when writing and grading papers. The checklist also offers the user links to some of the most common grammatical problems facing writers.

The Grammar Book (www.grammarbook.com)

Another good no-nonsense English grammar website. The explanations are brief and easy to understand. The examples are to the point and easy to follow. The Quizzes tab also has two sections of comprehensive free activities to test your aptitude.

Citation Formatting for APA and MLA References

- http://citationmachine.net/index2.php
- https://www.calvin.edu/library/knightcite/

APA format guidance:

- American Psychological Association: www.apastyle.org
- Purdue Owl: https://owl.english.purdue.edu/owl/resource/560/01/

MLA format guidance:

- Cornell University Library: http://www.library.cornell.edu/resrch/citmanage/mla
- California State University Los Angeles: http://web.calstatela.edu/library/guides/3mla.pdf
- Purdue Owl: https://owl.english.purdue.edu/owl/resource/747/01/

Chapter 8

Prior Learning Credit

Prior learning credit is college credit that is granted for learning that occurred after a student completed high school. Many schools award prior learning credit even though it is not widely advertised. Institutions of higher learning often award prior learning credit to service members for training they completed while in the military. Employers and schools always demand evidence of the learning that took place. Typically, it is through a transcript that you would demonstrate this evidence. Job applicants or students seeking higher education will often use transcripts as a formal document to capture valuable academic qualifications. For enlisted airmen, that evidence is demonstrated through an evaluation of their Community College of the Air Force transcripts. The CCAF typically issues over 150,000 transcripts annually for use at other educational institutions or education validation for employment. If granted, these credits can result in service members expediting their college degrees. This chapter includes information on the following topics:

- Prior Learning and CCAF Transcripts
- Subject Matter Proficiency Exams (CLEP/DSST)

PRIOR LEARNING CREDIT AND CCAF TRANSCRIPTS

For enlisted airmen, prior learning credit is most often granted after reviewing the service member's CCAF transcript. Every active duty, Air Force Reserve and Air National Guard enlisted airman is automatically enrolled in a degree program upon completion of Basic Military Training (BMT). Airmen earn four semester hours of credit after completion of BMT, then attend a technical training course where they learn the initial technical skills for their jobs. If their school is among the 108 CCAF-affiliated schools, they accumulate college credit at a rapid rate. As many as seventy-nine semester hours can be earned from these accredited technical training schools. Air Force technical training is similar to attending college in this respect. Keep in mind that all of the degrees awarded by the CCAF are Associate in Applied Science degrees, meaning they are technical in nature. So every enlisted airman can obtain a free college transcript from the CCAF, even if they never set foot in a college classroom after completing technical training.

Upon completion of technical school, an airman can obtain either an official or unofficial transcript that captures this valuable college credit. This prior learning credit is reflected as semester hour credit and is accredited by the Southern Association of Colleges and Schools Commission on Colleges (SACSCOC). This is the same accreditation shared by some of the most widely recognized schools in the country such as the Universities of Georgia, Florida, and Alabama.

When an airman completes Air Force technical training, he is well on his way to completing an Associate of Applied Science degree, and in many cases has a significant head start on a baccalaureate degree. In order for the undergraduate credit earned from technical training to count toward a baccalaureate degree, it will need to apply specifically to the undergraduate requirements for the particular degree an airman pursues. This will vary between specific degree requirements and the institutions that award them. For example, an airman that graduates from the enlisted paralegal apprentice course at the CCAF-affiliated Judge Advocate school at Maxwell Air Force Base will find a host of colleges that accept full transfer for undergraduate requirements for a law degree. Aside from the SACSCOC accreditation, the American Bar Association also recognizes the curriculum. An airman that graduates an Avionics Systems course will also have the SACSCOC accreditation, but the coursework will not likely satisfy the undergraduate requirements for a law degree due to the different subject matter.

The CCAF will provide current and former students an official transcript for free and provide a fee-based option with expedited shipping. For members with a Common Access Card (CaC), unofficial transcripts can easily be obtained through the Virtual Education Center (AFVEC). When arriving at the AFVEC home page, click on the "CCAF View Progress Report" tab. This will enable you to view and print your unofficial transcript that often suffices for most purposes until your official transcript arrives. Official transcripts can be obtained by a written request with your personal information to the CCAF.

Like many colleges, the CCAF is known to have a wait time for outgoing transcripts. Another choice for current and former students is a third-party vendor such as Credentials Solutions found at www.credentials-inc.com. For students in a hurry, the Credentials Solutions option might be the best option but they do charge a rate according to the shipping method.

Veterans should inquire about prior learning credit at their schools. Assessment methods for prior learning credit typically fall into three different categories: coursework reflected on transcripts, such as CCAF or CLEP, portfolio-based assessment, and any other credit earned without examinations used to demonstrate proficiency.

Each school will have its own policies on this type of credit and they can vary greatly. Although prior learning credit is becoming more popular, double-check with the institution you are interested in to determine whether they will consider granting you credit based on your experiences.

Schools do not typically advertise their ability to offer prior learning credit, so it might not be widely detailed on their website. Veterans are often granted credit in this fashion, so it is wise to follow through. Contacting the school to determine whether the intuition will review your CCAF transcript might get you credit for accredited coursework that you have already completed. They may not realize that the CCAF is regionally accredited through SACSCOC, so it may save you time by supplying supporting documentation from the CCAF or Air University website. CLEP and DANTES exams are shown as "college level testing" without a grade or subject on the CCAF transcript. You will need to send a separate CLEP/DANTES transcript to the institution for consideration of this credit.

Why do you care if the school you have chosen awards prior learning credit? Because it will help fast-track your degree. You only have thirty-six months of GI Bill benefit available to use. Think about the flexibility you will have if you attend an institution that awards prior learning credit. You might be able to save some benefit for a master's degree, a certification program, or simply to build a small buffer into each semester's class load. Consider the process as a beneficial pathway to helping you achieve your degree, but don't pick a school based solely on this criterion. Remember, the point of going to school is to feed your brain.

SUBJECT MATTER PROFICIENCY EXAMS

Subject matter proficiency exams allow students to earn college credit by taking tests as opposed to sitting through the traditional class. The exams enable students to save money and time, prepare on their own timeline, and fast-track their degrees. All of these reasons are incredibly important for veterans who have to maintain a class load specified by the VA if they want to continue with full benefits.

The testing center at your education center offers the College Level Examination Program (CLEP) and the DANTES Subject Standardized Tests (DSST). The first exam in every subject is free for active-duty personnel. If an airman fails and would like to test again, he or she will need to wait three months and pay a fee to retest. Verify with your base what the retest fee is for that particular location. Retirees, dependents, and separated airmen can test for the same fee as well (be aware that test costs can increase in the future).

The first thing students should do prior to taking CLEP or DSST exams is to verify with their school that the institution accepts these exams, which version, and in which subjects. There is no point in taking exams for no reason. Many colleges and universities do accept subject matter proficiency exams, but they limit the amount of credit awarded through this pathway, and sometimes they limit which subjects they accept. CLEP exams are more widely accepted than DSST exams.

After verifying exam acceptance through your school, look at http://www.petersons.com/dod. The Peterson's website maintains free study material for all of the CLEP and DSST exams offered on the bases. Now it is time to study, study, study! After all, who wants to pay to test again? Sometimes, the bases will offer preparation classes based on demand but the frequency varies. For example, at Maxwell AFB, the Enlisted Top Three provide monthly classes to help prepare airmen.

Once you have determined that you are ready to test, contact the education center at the base and book an appointment. If the local center offers computerized testing, you will receive instant results for all exams except for the English essay component.

CLEP has thirty-three tests available in six different subject areas: English composition, humanities, mathematics, natural science, social sciences, and history. The exams cover material typically learned during the first two years of college. The College Composition exam is 120 minutes, but all other exams are ninety minutes. Most exams are multiple choice, although some, including the College Composition, have essays or other varieties of questions. CLEP essays are scored by CLEP or the institution giving the exam. If CLEP holds responsibility for scoring, essays are reviewed and scored by two different English composition professors. The scores are combined and then weighted with the multiple-choice section. Exams usually match college classes that are one semester in duration.

The DSST exam program has thirty-eight available tests. DSST exams cover lower- and upper-division classes. This is beneficial for students who have deep knowledge of certain subjects, as it will enable them to test further along the degree pathway. Testing further into a specific subject area may also enable a student to participate in classes that can usually only be accessed after prerequisites are completed. Two tests include optional essays, "Ethics in America" and "Technical Writing." Essays are not scored by DSST; they are forwarded to the institution that the test taker designates on his or her application and graded by the college or university. DSST exams are offered only for three-credit courses.

As I (Jillian) stated earlier, you will benefit greatly as a veteran using your GI Bill if you take and pass CLEP or DSST exams while still on active duty, because during that time you can test for free. Veterans should still consider paying for the exams; the result can get you into the workforce faster. Veterans who take and pass subject matter proficiency exams may reap two major benefits: build a buffer to the required semester credit load and graduate early.

The VA demands that students maintain a minimum of twelve credit hours per semester in order to rate the full housing and book stipend. Twelve credits equal four classes. Maintaining four classes per semester is not a difficult course load; however, if your goal is a bachelor's degree and you have no previous college credit, you will need to take five classes (which typically equals fifteen credit hours) every semester, which is the traditional credit load. Most bachelor's degrees demand 120 credit hours of predetermined courses (found on your degree plan) in order to graduate. Twelve credit hours each semester will total ninety-six credit hours, which is not sufficient to graduate, and you will be out of monthly benefits. If you can add some CLEP or DSST scores into each semester, you will have reduced your required course load.

Reaching graduation early can be a boost to many veterans, especially those with families. Veterans who have completed CLEP or DSST credit may be able to combine those exams with their JST credit and finish their degrees in less than the four years normally required. This enables students to get into the workforce faster or save GI Bill benefit for graduate school, certificate programs, and so on.

The Defense Language Institute Foreign Language Center (DLIFLC) is a school that select airmen may attend to become proficient in foreign languages. The DLIFLC produces the Defense Language Proficiency Tests (DLPT) that the DoD uses for military and other select personnel. These exams might be taken while on active duty if you speak a second language. DLPTs score the test takers' reading, listening, and real-life proficiency in a foreign language. If an airman is assigned a language job, he will receive an additional monthly pay amount that will vary depending upon his scores, the language tested, and his current assignment. The servicing education office will provide test scores to the airman shortly after the test and forward the scores to Military Personnel Flight, where the updates in the automated record system will be made. When the update is complete, airmen can view the scores online by looking at their record in the Military Personnel Data System.

Ask your school if the institution awards credit for DLPT exams. If you speak a second language and you are still on active duty, contact the local education center for more guidance regarding DLPT testing policies. For study materials, visit the DLIFLC website (http://www.dliflc.edu).

Airmen with families are always looking for ways to pursue higher education at a faster pace, ways that offer the least interruption to their working careers while they complete their degrees. This is a reasonable desire as they need to maximize their income-earning potential as quickly as possible after separation from the service. Passing CLEP, DSST, or DLPT exams while on active duty can have a major impact on the amount of time these service members must spend in the classroom later. Often, they take several CLEPs on active duty even if they do not elect to take classes until after they separate from the service. If airmen plan for long-term goals as well as accomplish what is possible at the moment they will gain solid insight into their future academic pathways.

Chapter 9

Troops to Teachers (TTT)

Troops to Teachers is a U.S. Department of Defense (DOD) program that may help eligible service members pursue a career as a teacher in the public K-12 school system.

The program has two pathways:

1. Counseling pertaining to credentialing pathways and resources to help the service member or veteran achieve success
2. Financial support to help obtain a credential (note that this pathway incurs a three-year payback commitment)

The thought process behind TTT is to empower service members and veterans to pursue secondary careers as public school teachers while filling teacher shortage needs, especially in subjects such as math and science. The program aims to supply schools that maintain populations of low-income families with highly qualified teachers.

While TTT itself does not train veterans to be teachers, the counselors do give guidance and direct eligible personnel toward appropriate credentialing programs. As a former language arts teacher, I have a few of my own ideas (which I will go into more depth on within this chapter).

In the past few years, education in this country has taken a beating. There have been massive teacher furloughs and big pay cuts in many states. This will hopefully change in the future, but there are no guarantees. Take a look at all possible options to protect your future—for example, private schools, community colleges (maybe a different education pathway!), teaching abroad (sounds like fun, right?), online teaching, and charter schools, just to name a few.

Any resource offered should be looked into as a possible information-gathering activity, including TTT. Check with your state's chapter (http://troopstoteachers.net/Portals/1/National%20Home%20Page/stateoffices.pdf) to determine exactly what they can offer you. Almost every state has a chapter. If your state does not, check with the national TTT department at (850) 452-1242 or (800) 231-6242, or via e-mail at http://troopstoteachers.net/EMailUs.aspx.

TTT can be used by eligible personnel while still on active duty; however, you must be within one year of retirement. Also, the program does not participate in job placement, but the website does offer the links to each state's teacher job banks for self-directed searching. If you are a veteran and have already exhausted your GI Bill, TTT may give you the money you need to pursue a teacher credential.

Before you follow through on your decision to be a teacher, read below and check out the TTT website (http://www.proudtoserveagain.com/) or the DANTES website on TTT (http://www.dantes.doded.mil/service-members/troops-to-teachers/index.html) for some good advice.

I (Andrew) have a close friend that recently used the TTT program to become a full-time teacher after a thirty-year career in the Air Force. On his retirement from active-duty service in 2010, Chief Master Sergeant Mark Brejcha, the former Command Chief for the 412th Test Wing at Edwards Air Force Base, began focusing on his next career move as an administrator in the civilian sector. As he and his family returned home to Big Rapids, Michigan, Mark decided to go back to college full-time at Ferris State University. After a chance meeting with the local principal from the middle school, Mark was asked to consider substitute teaching on his days off from college classes. It didn't take long for Mark to find his second vocational calling in life . . . teaching.

Indeed, lightning struck. The former Command Chief was back leading troops of a different sort; secondary students in a public school setting. He continued his college education to a second year to become certified in Social Studies with the state of Michigan. This time he enrolled in the Department of Defense TTT program and was soon entered into a database that networked across the country. TTT's mission is to locate and place former military members into classrooms predominately in rural and inner-city settings where the need is greatest. TTT also looks for qualified teachers in the STEM areas of Science, Technology, Engineering and Math. The program's requirement is not limited to these disciplines alone, as demonstrated with Mark's desire to be a social studies teacher.

The TTT job placement data base aligns the teacher's subject discipline within the state he or she is volunteering to teach in. For example,

Mr. Brejcha was considering moving to Wyoming to teach secondary social studies. The TTT coordinator for Wyoming is also a former military member, and he used their statewide network with Wyoming schools to notify prospective TTT candidates across the United States who wish to come to Wyoming. Mark was instantly notified of each and every opening that TTT Wyoming was aware of in the state, especially the tough assignments in the remote and high-poverty areas. Fortunately for Mark and his family, an opening at the Big Rapids Middle School for a sixth grade social studies teacher allowed him and his family to remain in the local area, again a high rural poverty area based on the number of free and reduced lunches.

TTT desires qualified candidates who, for the most part, are willing to take the tough assignments to make a difference in those communities and in the lives of those local students. The leadership skills learned, used, and honed in the military are often a perfect fit for the classroom. School administrators love former military members who have decided to use their leadership skills in the classroom to inspire the next generation of young Americans. Just having these highly qualified teachers as a presence in the school is inspiring to the staff and parents as well as the kids. Again, the beauty of the TTT program is the partnership with qualified teachers in a nationwide network and advocates for those candidates who raise their hand and say "Here I am. Send me."

THOUGHTS FOR TEACHER CREDENTIALING

Teacher-credentialing programs are next to impossible to complete while on active duty. They always require some form of student teaching, possibly ranging from six weeks to a full semester of school. If you are on active duty, would like to be a teacher, and do not have a bachelor's degree in an applicable subject, that should be your first goal.

Always contact the state credentialing authority first. You need to determine an appropriate pathway based on the information the state gives you. State governments usually maintain this information on their websites, which can be found with a quick Google search. Second, research the schools in that particular state, and determine the academic pathways they follow to obtain a teaching credential and/or bachelor's degree that leads in that direction. I work with many service members who attend their community colleges from back home online while on active duty. Check the Department of Defense Memorandum of Understanding website (http://www.dodmou.com) to see if your school is eligible for tuition assistance.

If you are unable to attend a school in your desired state, make an appointment at your local education center to find an available equivalent pathway in your current location, or complete your own search on the College Navigator website.

You can always consider the time you have left while on active duty. Maybe a better pathway for you if you are just getting started would be to attend a local community college and begin working toward the credit you will need in order to finish at a school back home. You cannot go wrong by starting with general education classes: math, English, arts, and humanities, social and behavior sciences, and natural sciences.

If this is the case, contact the four-year university you are interested in attending and obtain a degree plan for the academic pathway they recommend; bring it with you to meet the education counselor. He or she will help you find a college that you can attend while on active duty that will enable you to fulfill the prescribed parameters. Typically, a state community college will provide you with the safest transfer credit. After you find a local school to attend, you will need to contact the future school and ask about the transferability of the credits. Many schools have strict transfer guidelines.

Many teacher-credentialing programs take more time than just a bachelor's degree, but some do not. Check with the schools in the state where you want to earn a credential to determine the proper pathway. You also might prefer to complete a master's degree with an attached credentialing program. Typically, a master's degree will earn you more money as a teacher. You may get an extra yearly stipend, or you may get a push up the pay scale because it is college credit above and beyond a bachelor's degree.

Since both GI Bills only offer you thirty-six months of benefit, you may not have enough to finish a full bachelor's degree and credentialing program. So think ahead! Whatever you manage to get done while you are still on active duty is less work you will need to do after you separate. This pathway will save you time, money, and potentially some GI Bill benefit to use toward a master's degree at a later date. Many of the clients I have worked with prefer to finish their bachelor's degree while on active duty (if possible), and then use their GI Bill for a master's degree and/or a credentialing program after separation.

Chapter 10

Vocational Pathways

The federal GI Bills can be used for vocational training for those airmen who want to pursue a career pathway that is aligned to the skills needed for an occupation, trade, or profession. This type of training might include an apprenticeship or on-the-job training. The GI Bills offer great flexibility in the different types of programs that the benefits might be applied toward for those who earned them.

Some service members want to pursue career fields similar to the job they have been holding while in the Air Force, but civilian sector credentials or training are frequently needed. Some of these certifications can be gained while on active duty, like the Airframe and Powerplant Certification (chapter 5), but others must be pursued upon transition into veteran status. Oftentimes, federal benefits can be used to cover these pathways as well. More information on both pathways can be found on the GI Bill website: http://www.benefits.va.gov/gibill/onthejob_apprenticeship.asp.

This chapter includes information on the following topics:

- Total Force Training
- Apprenticeship Programs
- GI Bill and Training

TOTAL FORCE TRAINING AND APPRENTICESHIP PROGRAMS

The term Total Force (TF) Training includes Upgrade Training (UGT) and Qualification Training (QT). UGT is considered the key to the TF program

215

and leads to award of the higher skill level. OJT is designed to increase an airman's overall skills and abilities, while QT is designed to train for a specific position.

On-the-Job Training (OJT)

The U.S. Air Force operates a sizable part of the world's most advanced weapon systems. This takes highly capable airmen who have the training and discipline to ensure that the systems are maintained and working properly. Over the past few decades, many friendly foreign countries have sent delegations to examine Air Force (AF) training programs, especially aircraft maintenance. Unlike any other country in the world, the AF exclusively uses enlisted personnel to maintain aircraft and weapon systems. These skilled and trained personnel are the most critical aspect to the Air Force in providing a strong global defense capability.

The AF OJT Program is governed by Air Force Instruction 36-2201 volume three entitled Air Force Training Program, On the Job Training Administration. The program is designed to facilitate attainment of the knowledge and skill qualifications required for airmen to successfully perform duties in their specialty. The strategy of AF OJT is to develop, manage, and execute training programs that provide realistic and flexible training that produces a highly skilled, motivated force capable of carrying out all tasks and functions in support of the AF mission. These programs provide the foundation for AF national and global readiness.

The AF OJT program consists of knowledge and position qualification components. Career knowledge and general task knowledge is gained through a planned program of study involving Career Development Course (CDC) or technical references listed in the applicable Career Field Education and Training Plan (CFETP). The CFETP is a comprehensive core-training document. It identifies life-cycle education and training requirements, training support resources, and minimum core task requirements for each AF specialty.

The Specialty Training Standard (STS) is an Air Force publication that is inserted as part two of the CFETP. It describes an AF specialty in terms of tasks and knowledge that an airman in that specialty will be expected to know and perform on the job. It also identifies the training provided to achieve a three, five, or seven skill level within an enlisted AFS. The STS further serves as a contract between training providers and the functional user to show the overall training requirements for an AF specialty. It accurately reflects the subject matter taught in formal schools as well as what was covered in correspondence courses.

In order to be awarded Apprentice (three skill level) status, airmen must complete a resident initial skills training course for award of the three skill level. CDCs are published to provide the information necessary to satisfy the career knowledge component of OJT. These courses are developed from references identified in the CFETP correlating with mandatory knowledge items listed in Air Force Manual (AFMAN) 36-2108. CDCs must contain information on basic principles, techniques, and procedures common to an AF specialty.

The Journeyman (five skill level) requires completion of the mandatory CDC, all core tasks identified in the CFETP, and other duty position tasks identified by the supervisor. Trainees must also complete a minimum of fifteen months in UGT, meet mandatory requirements listed in the specialty description in AFMAN 36-2108 and CFETP, and be recommended by their supervisor for award of the five skill level.

For the award of the Craftsman (seven skill level) status, airmen must be at least a staff sergeant (SSgt=E5), complete mandatory CDCs, complete core tasks identified in the CFETP, and other duty position tasks identified by the supervisor. Airmen must also complete the seven skill-level craftsman course, meet mandatory requirements listed in the specialty description in AFMAN 36-2108, complete a minimum of twelve months in training, and be recommended by the supervisor for award of the seven skill level.

The highest skill level is the Superintendent or nine skill level. Promotion to Senior Master Sergeant (SMSgt=E9) is required for the award of the nine skill level.

The technology of today's AF weapon systems requires a high degree of rigor and precision associated with each skill level and all associated training provided. For example, the tactical aircraft maintenance career field (2A3X3) requires a total of 460 tasks to be certified prior to being upgraded to the seven skill level.

According to SSgt Aaron Holden, the Aviation Maintenance Degree Program Manager at the Community College of the Air Force, the five-level core tasks focus on typical day-to-day maintenance tasks such as pre-flight and basic postflight aircraft inspection and jet engine bay inspection. Later in an individual's career, the focus for the seven-level tasks is on major maintenance tasks or tasks that require an expert to supervise. Examples of these include operating the digital engine start system control and supervising the aircraft tow team.

Qualification Training (QT)

QT is actual hands-on task performance training designed to qualify an airman in a specific duty position. This training occurs during and after UGT and is conducted any time an individual is not fully qualified in a particular area. The airman's supervisor has the greatest single impact on accomplishing the training mission. They must share their experiences and expertise to meet mission requirements and provide a quality training program to the trainee. Supervisors must plan, conduct, and evaluate training.

Each AFS has an Air Force Career Field Manager (AFCFM) that oversees and manages training requirements at the higher headquarters level. The difficulty or criticality of some tasks requires certification by a third party. Certifiers will provide this third-party certification and evaluation on tasks identified by the AFCFM. The responsibility of the certifier is to conduct additional evaluations and certify qualification on those designated tasks.

The OJT you receive in the Air Force will ideally prepare you to thrive in the civilian sector, because the same strategies are often used in the civilian workforce. Some companies use OJT to tailor training to their specific workforce needs. In other cases they may use OJT to enhance an individual's preexisting skill set. Typically, a combination of tactics is used to train employees to operate functionally in their new or changing environment. OJT is a proven strategy that is used in almost all instances and is designed to assist in training employees who might not possess the required knowledge for the position. For example, you might already know how to install and maintain cable systems, but if you take that skill set to a civilian company they will want to train you to their standards for their specific applications. Oftentimes, in vocational fields, OJT is the form of training that will be used to accomplish this task.

Employers and employees reap numerous benefits from participating in OJT. OJT allows companies to use their preexisting environment to train new employees while instilling performance expectations at the same time. It is cost-effective, increases productivity, and produces employees that are taught to company-driven standards. Employers training employees using OJT promote a good public image through their commitment to the community, help create a more skilled workforce, and see immediate return on their investment. The skills, knowledge, and competencies that are needed to perform a specific job within a specific workplace are delivered from day one, typically by another employee or mentor (mandatory for the GI Bill) who can already perform his or her duties competently. Sometimes, special training rooms or equipment are used to demonstrate performance parameters. OJT is not like an apprenticeship program, because it does not have an instructional portion that requires you to attend classes. Many apprenticeship programs are covered by the GI Bills and will be discussed in the next section.

Employees also benefit from OJT. They begin earning wages as they learn a new skill, gain job experience, and develop a new marketable skill set oftentimes by earning certifications or journeyman standing. Productivity is increased on both sides as training progresses, as does trust as relationships develop through teamwork.

Some potential fields of employment for OJT are heating and air conditioning, law enforcement, welding, electrical work, machinist, tool and die maker, and construction and auto mechanics. If you are looking for a program that is VA approved, contact the state approving agency here: http://www.nasaa-vetseducation.com/Contacts.aspx, or search participating employers on the U.S. Department of Veterans Affairs at http://department-of-veterans-affairs.github.io/gi-bill-comparison-tool/.

If you were recently hired at a new job, and your employer does not currently participate in OJT programs with the VA, contact the State Approving Agency (http://www.nasaa-vetseducation.com/Contacts.aspx) to determine if it is possible to facilitate your OJT with the GI Bill. The State Approving Authority within each state approves OJT programs within its borders.

Apprenticeship Programs

The U.S. Department of Labor (DOL) oversees registered apprenticeship programs through its Employment and Training section. According to the DOL:

> Registered Apprenticeship programs meet the skilled workforce needs of American industry, training millions of qualified individuals for lifelong careers since 1937. Registered Apprenticeship helps mobilize America's workforce with structured, on-the-job training in traditional industries such as construction and manufacturing, as well as new high-growth industries such as health care, information technology, energy, telecommunications, advanced manufacturing and more.[1]

The DOL uses this department to connect potential employees to employers by working with a variety of different companies and organizations, such as community colleges, labor organizations, and state workforce agencies. The federal program has regional contacts in almost every state that can be found here: http://www.doleta.gov/oa/regdirlist.cfm. State-based apprenticeship searches on the DOL site can be conducted here: http://oa.doleta.gov/bat.cfm?start.

Like OJT, the GI Bill can be used toward apprenticeship training. Programs can last anywhere from one to six years, although most are geared toward four years, depending upon the technical field, and you work under a tradesman during that time before you earn the same status. Assessments throughout the program, mandatory testing, and work inspection conducted by a master tradesman are part of the apprenticeship process. Formal classroom training is part of an apprenticeship. Classes typically include general education, such as math and English, and classes pertaining to technical theory and applied skills. State-mandated licensing for many fields, such as plumbing, can demand numerous study hours and formal preparation prior to testing.

Apprenticeship programs are common in trades that are skill based, such as welding, construction, and electrical work. Oftentimes, skilled trades require formal licensure, which is obtained partly by working under a journeyman within the field. This is only the starting point; journeyman and master tradesman are the following two steps. Apprentices are overseen by a journeyman or master tradesman, who ultimately is responsible for your work at that time. The goal, over time and with continuing education, is to reach journeyman or master tradesman status. High-level tradesman status leads to higher pay.

Registered apprenticeship participants receive pay starting from the first day of the program. This pay will grow over time as the apprentice learns more skill. Many programs have mandatory college classes, usually at the local community college, built into the program. Typically, these classes are paid for by the employer. Participants in apprenticeship programs often finish without any education debt. Completing a registered apprenticeship program earns participants certification that is recognized across the country, making them highly portable career fields.

Apprentice-able occupations come in all shapes and sizes, including airfield management, automobile mechanic, welder, and cabinetmaker. Major companies such as UPS, CVS, Simplex-Grinnell, Werner Enterprises, and CN (railways) provide apprenticeship opportunities. Green technology has a bright future for growth. Areas such as recycling in the green technology field have some of the fastest-growing apprenticeship programs. Wind turbine technicians, hydrologists, and toxic waste cleanup specialists are all in demand.

The American Apprenticeship Initiative was launched in the fall of 2014. Through this initiative the DOL made $100 million "available for American Apprenticeship Grants to reward partnerships that help more workers participate in apprenticeships. This competition will help more Americans access this proven path to employment and the middle class: 87 percent of apprentices are employed after completing their programs and the average starting wage for apprenticeship graduates is over $50,000."[2] The new American Apprenticeship Grants competition centers on organizations that create apprenticeships in new, high-growth fields, align them with possibilities for more learning and career progression, and create models that work. More information on the initiative can be found here: http://www.doleta.gov/oa/aag.cfm. The competition has concluded and forty-six awardees have been named. To read more about the companies that were awarded grants check the following link: http://www.dol.gov/apprenticeship/pdf/AmericanApprenticeshipInitiativeGrantsAwardSummaries.pdf.

The U.S. DOL's website has a wealth of information regarding apprenticeship programs (http://www.doleta.gov/oa/). The DOL site has links to search for state apprenticeship agencies, all approved apprenticeship programs, and state-based program sponsors. Contacts can also be found on the National Association of State Approving Agencies (NASAA) website (http://www.nasaa-vetseducation.com/).

Career One Stop, covered in the Research Tools chapter (chapter 3) (http://www.careeronestop.org/) is a free resource tool that can help apprentice-seekers find career-based information and training pathways. I (Jillian) often use this resource during my counseling sessions. On the main page there are six main search tabs:

- Explore Careers
- Find Training
- Job Search
- Find Local Help
- Toolkit
- Resources For

All six sections host valuable information for apprentice-seekers, but "Find Training" is most informative regarding the topic at hand. After selecting "Education and Training" choose the "Apprenticeships" tab. This section allows for detailed exploration of apprenticeships including work option videos, a state-based search site, information from the Department of Labor, and a local job center search. Users can even target specific states for their apprenticeship research. For more information regarding Career One Stop, visit the "Research Tools" chapter of this book (chapter 3).

THE GI BILL AND TRAINING

Either the Montgomery GI Bill (MGIB) or Post-9/11 may be used for OJT. If you rate both, double-check with the institution within which you plan to work to determine the best pathway, or contact the VA directly (1-888-GIBILL-1).

The Post-9/11 GI Bill pays a scaled monthly housing allowance (MHA) if you are accepted into an eligible OJT or apprenticeship program. You will earn wages as well from the company training you, although normally wages are low while participating in OJT because both OJT and apprenticeship pay are usually not a percentage of (or related to) journeyman pay.

Post-9/11 payments for apprenticeship programs are:

- 100 percent of your applicable MHA for the first six months of training
- 80 percent of your applicable MHA for the second six months of training
- 60 percent of your applicable MHA for the third six months of training
- 40 percent of your applicable MHA for the fourth six months of training
- 20 percent of your applicable MHA for the remainder of the training

As your wages increase, the GI Bill payments decrease. A maximum of $83 per month for a book stipend can also be received during training.

MGIB payments as of October 1, 2015, are:

- First six months: $1,341.75
- Second six months: $983.95
- Remaining training time: $626.15

The VA maintains rules pertaining to how OJT must be run and whether a program is or can be eligible. For example, the length of the OJT program should be equivalent to what is normally required (for civilians), and the program must encompass the knowledge and skills demanded for the position. Participants should earn wages equal to a civilian partaking in the same program, and starting wages should be set with consideration of the previous experience of the participant. All records of the program need to be kept adequately and orderly to verify training with the VA. Using the GI Bill for OJT purposes is not allowed while on active duty, nor can spouses who have had GI Bill benefits transferred to them participate.

Most states list the available OJT and apprenticeship programs for residents on the state government website. Look through the DOL section as well as the state VA website. You can also contact your VA Regional Office for help: (http://www2.va.gov/directory/guide/map_flsh.asp).

On the NASAA website (http://www.nasaa-vetseducation.com/), under the "Programs" tab, you can search approved education and training programs, which include universities, certificate programs, flight school, correspondence school, and OJT-approved programs. You can also access the approved license and certification programs and approved national exams lists.

Chapter 11

VA Programs

The VA has several little-known programs available for veterans. Always check your eligibility because many stipulations apply, such as the disability rating for vocational rehabilitation. These programs may help you with academic preparation and support for school, funding sources for school, and part-time work. The following programs are discussed in this chapter:

- Veterans Upward Bound (VUB)
- Vocational Rehabilitation
- VA Work Study
- GI Bill Tutorial Assistance

VETERANS UPWARD BOUND (VUB)

Veterans Upward Bound (VUB; http://www.navub.org/) is a U.S. Department of Education program that assists and promotes veteran success within higher education. The free program aids veteran students who have not been to school for a long time, or simply need a refresher by assisting in academic preparation. The programs are conducted on college campuses. "The primary goal of the program is to increase the rate at which participants enroll in and complete postsecondary education programs."[1]

Participants in VUB may receive academic skills assessment and refresher courses to enhance their college-level skills. The courses consist of subjects such as math, science, English, computers, and foreign languages. Veteran education services may also be available—for example, assistance completing college admissions applications or GI Bill applications, academic advising, tutoring, or cultural field trips.

In order to qualify, veterans must:

- Have completed a minimum of 180 days of active service, or have been discharged prior to that point because of a service-connected disability *or* have been with a reserve component that served on active duty on or after September 11, 2001, for a contingency operation
- Have any discharge other than dishonorable
- Be low income (based upon family income and number of household dependents) *or* be a first-generation college student (parents do not have degrees)

If you feel that your school-based skills are rusty, VUB will help boost the deficient areas. Participating in a program will create a more solid foundation for you to begin your studies and achieve success.

Not every school hosts a VUB program, but you can attend a program at a school where you are not enrolled as a student. To find a VUB program in a specific state, check http://www.navub.org/VUB-Program-Information.html and contact the program director. Information about the program can also be found on the Department of Education's website, http://www2.ed.gov/programs/triovub/index.html.

Here are just a few of the schools that offer VUB programs:

- Santa Ana Community College, CA (https://www.sac.edu/StudentServices/VUB/Pages/default.aspx)
- Boise State University, ID (http://education.boisestate.edu/vub/)
- Wichita State University, KS (http://www.wichita.edu/thisis/home/?u=veteransupwardbound)
- LaGuardia Community College, NY (http://www.lagcc.cuny.edu/veterans/programs1.html)
- University of Massachusetts, MA (http://www.mass.gov/veterans/education/vet-upward-bound/umass-boston.html)
- University of Pennsylvania, PA (http://www.vpul.upenn.edu/eap/vub/Staff.php)
- Georgia State University, GA (http://oeo.gsu.edu/precollege-programs/veterans-upward-bound/)
- University of New Mexico, NM (http://taos.unm.edu/veteransupwardbound/index.html)
- Roosevelt University, IL (http://www.roosevelt.edu/Education/CommunityOutreach/VeteransUpBound.aspx)

VOCATIONAL REHABILITATION AND EMPLOYMENT

The VA Vocational Rehabilitation and Employment program (Voc Rehab; http://www.benefits.va.gov/vocrehab/index.asp) may assist eligible service-connected veterans with job training, job skills, education, or employment accommodations. The ultimate goal of Voc Rehab is to make you as employable as possible while considering any potential limitations of your disability. Voc Rehab counselors will work with individuals to determine career interests, skills, and existing abilities. They will help participants find jobs, on-the-job training, or apprenticeship programs. Formal education through an institution of higher learning might also be a necessary component to the retraining program.

Veterans with severe disabilities can seek assistance through Voc Rehab to find help for independent living. Voc Rehab often pays for new laptops for studying or equipment and uniforms needed for school.

Voc Rehab can be a very generous program, but remember that all benefits are meant to lead to successful employment in the field of your choice. Employment plans must be reviewed by Voc Rehab counselors in order to be approved. If a plan is not determined to be a viable option, then it must be modified before it can be accepted and implemented. Veterans using Voc Rehab will not have the same level of flexibility in choosing their programs as they would under the MGIB and Post-9/11 GI Bills.

Eligible service members must meet the following parameters:

- If still on active duty, must be expecting to receive an honorable discharge, becoming service connected at a minimum of 20 percent.
- Veterans must receive a discharge that is anything other than dishonorable, and receive a VA service-connected disability rating of 10 percent with a serious employment handicap or 20 percent or more with an employment handicap.

After a veteran receives a service-connected rating, he or she must apply for Voc Rehab and schedule an appointment with a counselor. The vocational rehabilitation counselors (VRCs) will complete an evaluation to determine final eligibility. If eligible, the VRC and the veteran will work together to determine the appropriate retraining pathway for the desired career outcome.

Potentially, Voc Rehab can cover far more than any of the current GI Bill benefits in regard to education. Voc Rehab also comes with a housing allowance that is similar to the Monthly Housing Allowance (MHA) under the Post-9/11 GI Bill, but the allowance is not particularly generous. The monthly amount for institutional training is currently set at $605.44 (as of October 1, 2015) for a veteran without dependents. Current payment rates can be found here: http://www.benefits.va.gov/vocrehab/subsistence_allowance_rates.asp. Depending upon the how many dependents the veteran has, the amount can go up. Check current rates on the following website: http://www.benefits. va.gov/vocrehab/subsistence_allowance_rates.asp.

In some instances you might be able to borrow the MHA rate from your Post-9/11 GI Bill and use it to replace the Voc Rehab rate if you have any remaining benefits. Combining the two programs in this manner is very often the best way to maximize the total amount of money that can be made while attending school.

I must emphasize that meeting with a VRC is necessary. Only these specialists can determine an appropriate pathway for you and help you achieve the desired results. They can even help evaluate your interests and skills in order to determine your best employment pathway.

Some institutions of higher learning have partnered with Voc Rehab to maintain a counselor on the school campus and are referred to as a VSOC counselor or VetSuccess on Campus Counselor. VSOCs are valuable sources of information for the veteran and active-duty population in attendance at the school as they can assist in navigating the maze of available federal education benefits. To see if your school of choice has a VSOC counselor check here: http://www.benefits.va.gov/vocrehab/vsoc.asp.

To apply for Voc Rehab, visit the VONAPP website (under the "Apply for Benefits" tab) on eBenefits and fill out Vocational Rehabilitation Form 28-1900. eBenefits: http://www.vba.va.gov/pubs/forms/VBA-28-1900-ARE.pdf.

VA WORK-STUDY

VA Work-Study (http://www.benefits.va.gov/gibill/workstudy.asp) is a part-time work program available to veterans who currently attend school at the three-quarter pursuit rate or higher. The program offers an opportunity for veteran students to earn money while pursuing education. Work-Study payments are tax free. Participants work within a community of peers and build skills for résumés. All services rendered within the program relate to work within the VA. Eligible participants may not exceed 750 hours of VA Work-Study per fiscal year.

Selected participants receive the federal minimum wage or state minimum wage, depending on which is greater. Sometimes, positions at colleges or universities are paid an extra amount by the school to make up the difference in pay between the institution and the VA Work-Study program.

Students are placed in a variety of positions depending upon availability, institution of attendance, and local VA facilities, such as Department of Veterans Affairs (DVA) regional offices or DVA medical offices. Priority may be given to veterans who have disability ratings of 30 percent or higher. Selection depends on factors such as job availability and a student's ability to complete the contract prior to exhausting his or her education benefits. Positions can include processing VA documents, assisting in VA information dispersal at educational institutions, and working at a local VA facility.

Veterans must be using one of the following programs in order to be eligible:

- Post-9/11 (including dependents using transferred entitlement)
- Montgomery GI Bill (MGIB) active or reserve
- Raising the Educational Achievement of Paraprofessionals (REAP) participants
- Post–Vietnam Era Veterans' Educational Assistance Program
- Dependents' Educational Assistance Program
- Dependents who are eligible under Chapter 35 may use Work-Study only while training in a state
- Vocational Rehabilitation participants

To apply for VA Work-Study, visit the VA link at http://www.vba.va.gov/pubs/forms/VBA-22-8691-ARE.pdf or check with the local processing center at http://www.gibill.va.gov/contact/regional_offices/index.html.

GI BILL TUTORIAL ASSISTANCE

If you are a veteran and you are having trouble in one of your classes, tutorial assistance is available under MGIB and Post-9/11. Veterans eligible for this assistance have a deficiency in a subject or prerequisite subject that is required for his or her degree plan. The assistance is a supplement to your selected GI Bill. To be eligible, you must be pursuing education at a 50 percent or greater rate, have a deficiency, and be enrolled in the class during the term in which you are pursuing tutoring.

The cost cannot exceed $100 per month or the cost of the tutoring if less than $100. If the eligible student is under MGIB, there is no charge to the entitlement for the first $600 of tutoring received. If the eligible student elected the Post-9/11 GI Bill, there is no entitlement charge.

VA Form 22-1990t, "Application and Enrollment Certification for Individualized Tutorial Assistance," must be completed by the eligible student, the tutor, and the VA certifying official to apply for the benefit. The form must be signed, dated, and filled out either monthly or after a combination of months.

More information can be found on the VA website, http://www.benefits.va.gov/gibill/tutorial_assistance.asp. For application and enrollment certification for individualized tutorial assistance, see http://www.vba.va.gov/pubs/forms/VBA-22-1990t-ARE.pdf.

Chapter 12

Programs Designed to Assist Active Duty, Veterans, and Dependents

Many programs are available for veterans and dependents to assist in education and career development. Some of the programs are volunteer-based; others are run on set schedules through institutions of higher learning. Several service members I know (Jillian) have gone through the programs listed in this chapter, and all speak highly of their experiences.

In this chapter, we will discuss:

• Programs Available for Active-Duty Personnel, Veterans, and Dependents
• Military Spouse Career Advancement Accounts (MyCAA)
• General Advice for Spouses

PROGRAMS AVAILABLE TO ACTIVE-DUTY PERSONNEL, VETERANS, AND DEPENDENTS

I (Jillian) have run across a few organizations and programs that service members have found especially beneficial over the past few years. I am sure many more wonderful programs are available, but these are the few I use almost daily. Usually, we discuss the organizations that have been around for a while, such as the Veterans of Foreign Wars (VFW), Disabled American Veterans (DAV), and American Veterans (AmVets), mainly because the organizations have very established, credible programs.

Volunteering is a great way for veterans to continue to serve after they leave the service and build skills for their résumés. Staying active with others in the community can give veterans a sense of purpose. Many service members I counsel enjoy volunteering after separating from the service and sometimes while still on active duty.

Oftentimes younger service members prefer some of the newer organizations. Mostly, they cater more specifically to Iraq and Afghanistan veterans, such as Iraq and Afghanistan Veterans of America (IAVA). Team Rubicon and The Mission Continues are interesting possibilities for those interested in hands-on participation; the programs handle disaster relief and community building.

The first few organizations listed in this section offer services and programs for veterans and their immediate families. The last few are volunteer-based organizations.

Syracuse University Institute for Veterans and Military Families (IVMF)

http://vets.syr.edu/

Syracuse University, partnered with JPMorgan Chase & Co., has several programs available through the IVMF to assist transitioning Post-9/11 service members with future career plans depending upon their interests and pursuits. Many of the programs consist of free online courses that users can access from any location at any time to promote veteran preparedness and understanding of the civilian sector. Other courses are offered in a face-to-face format that lasts roughly two weeks, and they are now available in several different locations. IVMF offers courses for veterans, active duty, active-duty spouses, and disabled veterans.

The programs currently offered by IVMF include the following:

- EBV: Entrepreneurship Bootcamp for Veterans with Disabilities
- EBV-F: Entrepreneurship Bootcamp for Veterans' Families (caregivers and family members)
- V-WISE: Veteran Women Igniting the Spirit of Entrepreneurship for veteran women, female active duty, and female family members
- E&G: Operation Endure & Grow for guard and reserve members and family
- B2B: Operation Boots to Business: From Service to Startup for transitioning service members
- Veterans' Career Transition Program (VCTP): Great program for active duty to gain industry-level certificates in high-demand career fields.

Entrepreneurship Bootcamp for Veterans with Disabilities (EBV)

http://ebv.vets.syr.edu/

EBV is designed to help post-9/11 veterans with service-connected disabilities in the entrepreneurship and small business management fields. Syracuse University, Texas A&M, Purdue University, UCLA, University of Connecticut, Louisiana State University, Florida State University, and Cornell University currently participate in EBV. EBV promotes long-term success for qualified veterans by teaching them how to create and sustain their entrepreneurial ventures (http://whitman.syr.edu/ebv/). All costs associated with EBV are covered by the program, including travel and lodging.

Entrepreneurship Bootcamp (EBV-F)

http://vets.syr.edu/education/ebv-f/

Entrepreneurship Bootcamp for Veterans' Families is offered through Syracuse University's Whitman School of Management and the Florida State University College of Business. The cost-free (including travel and lodging) one-week program assists family members in their pursuit to launch and maintain small businesses.

Eligible spouses include the following:

- A spouse, parent, sibling, or adult child who has a role supporting the veteran (health, education, work, etc.)
- A surviving spouse or adult child of a service member who died while serving after September 11, 2001
- An active-duty service member's spouse

V-Wise

http://whitman.syr.edu/vwise/

Veteran Women Igniting the Spirit of Entrepreneurship is a joint venture with the U.S. Small Business Administration (SBA). The program helps female veterans along the entrepreneurship and small business pathway by arming them with savvy business skills that enable them to turn business ideas into growing ventures. Business planning, marketing, accounting, operations, and human resources are covered. The three-phase approach consists of a fifteen-day online course teaching the basic skills pertaining to being an entrepreneur, a three-day conference with two tracks (for startups or those already in business), and delivery of a comprehensive listing packet that details the community-level resources available to participants.

Eligible participants are honorably separated female veterans from any branch of the military from any time. Female spouses or partners of veteran business owners are eligible as well. Hotel rooms and taxes are covered, but other fees apply, such as travel.

Endure & Grow

http://vets.syr.edu/education/endure-grow/

Operation Endure & Grow is a free online training program open to National Guard, reservists, and their family members. The program has two tracks, one for startups and the other for those who have been in business for more than three years. The tracks are designed to assist participants in creating a new business and all related fundamentals, or to help an operating business stimulate growth.

Operation Boots to Business: From Service to Startup (B2B)

http://boots2business.org/

B2B is a partnership with the Syracuse University Whitman School of Business and the SBA. The program goal is to train transitioning service members to be business owners through three phases. Phases 1 and 2 are taken while the service member is still on active duty, preparing to transition to the civilian world and attending the Transition Readiness Seminar (TRS). The third phase is accessible if veterans elect to continue and consists of an intensive instructor-led eight-week online "mini"-MBA.

Active-duty service members and their spouses or partners are eligible to participate in B2B during the separation process. The entire B2B program is free. Speak to your career planner about electing the Entrepreneurship Pathway during TRS.

Veterans' Career Transition Program (VCTP)

http://vets.syr.edu/education/employment-programs/

The VCTP offers numerous classes for career training and preparation. Many of the courses lead to high-demand industry-level certifications. This free online program is available to eligible Post-9/11 veterans. The program is geared to help veterans understand corporate culture in the civilian business world. VCTP is a three-track program that includes professional skills, tech, and independent study tracks.

The professional skills track aims at training veterans in "soft" skills—mainly how to prepare for and implement job searches by conducting company research and creating cover letters and résumés. Foundations for advanced-level courses in Microsoft Office Word, Excel, PowerPoint, and Outlook can be achieved within this track. If a veteran participates in this track, he or she becomes an official Syracuse University student and receives a noncredit-based certificate upon completion.

The tech track is geared to prepare participants for careers in operations or information technology (IT). Industry-level certifications are offered in this level, and, where applicable, VCTP will cover exam fees. Participants also become Syracuse University students and receive noncredit-awarding certificates upon completion. Certificates include proficiency in subject areas such as Comp TIA (Server+, Network+, and A+), Oracle Database 11G, CCNA with CCENT certification, and Lean Six Sigma Green Belt.

The independent study track hosts a large library of online coursework. Coursework includes subject matter pertaining to professional and personal development, leadership, IT, and accounting and finance. Coursework is determined by veterans' demands and learning needs. Students will not be considered Syracuse University students. Veterans must be within eighteen months of their date of separation (front or back) to be eligible. Active-duty spouses and spouses of eligible veterans are now eligible as well.

American Corporate Partners (ACP)

http://www.acp-usa.org/
http://www.acp-advisornet.org

ACP is a New York City–based national nonprofit organization founded in 2008 to help veterans transition from active duty into the civilian workforce by enlisting the help of business professionals nationwide. Through mentoring, career counseling, and networking possibilities, ACP's goal is to build greater connections between corporate America and veteran communities. ACP has two available programs: ACP AdvisorNet, which is open to service members and their immediate family members; and a one-on-one mentoring program for post-9/11 veterans. ACP AdvisorNet is an online business community that offers veterans and immediate family members online career advice through Q&A discussions. The mentoring program connects employees from ACP's participating institutions with veterans or their spouses for mentoring options, networking assistance, and career development. More than fifty major companies are participating in ACP's mentoring program, and success stories and videos are available on ACP's website.

Hiring Our Heroes

http://www.uschamber.com/hiringourheroes

The U.S. Chamber of Commerce Foundation launched Hiring Our Heroes in 2011 to help veterans and spouses of active-duty service members find employment. The program works with state and local Chambers as well as partners in the public, private, and nonprofit sectors. Hiring Our Heroes hosts career fairs at military bases. The program offers transition assistance, personal branding, and résumé workshops.

Google for Veterans and Families

http://www.googleforveterans.com/

Google offers a wide range of help for active-duty and veteran military members. It has tools to help families stay in touch during deployments, record military deployments, explore life after service (including résumé-building opportunities), and connect with other veterans.

Vet Net on Google+

https://plus.google.com/+VetNetHQ

VetNet was launched by the U.S. Chamber of Commerce's Hiring Our Heroes program, the IVMF, and Hire Heroes USA as a partnership program. The program is set up similar to the TRS with different pathways designed to help transitioning service members find a more tailored approach to their specific needs. VetNet has three different pathways depending upon your goals: basic training, career connections, and entrepreneur. The site hosts live events and video seminars designed to provide information from those who have gone before them and to generate group discussions about civilian career and entrepreneur challenges. You can find many VetNet videos on YouTube.

Iraq and Afghanistan Veterans of America (IAVA)

http://iava.org/

IAVA offers service members another way to maintain the brotherhood while actively participating in an organization that promotes veteran well-being. The nonprofit, nonpartisan organization is strictly for veterans of the Iraq and Afghanistan campaigns. IAVA actively generates support for veteran-based policies at the local and federal levels while assisting members through programs related to health, employment, education, and community resources. Its aim is to empower veterans who will be future leaders in our communities.

IAVA sponsors several academic and career-related programs for its members. Many of the service members I work with have sought out IAVA for assistance. One active-duty E-7 I worked with was accepted to the Culinary Command program offered through IAVA's Rucksack. Culinary Command is a six-week, intensive, top-tier culinary arts program in New York with all costs covered, including travel and accommodations. Many other interesting programs are available for participation, including the War Writer's Campaign (http://www.warwriterscampaign.org/), my personal favorite. Programs are offered for online or on-the-ground participation depending upon members' needs.

The Mission Continues

http://missioncontinues.org/

The Mission Continues promotes community service and brotherhood through fellowships with local nonprofit organizations. The program empowers veterans to achieve post-fellowship full-time employment or pursue higher education while continuing a relationship with public service. The Mission Continues has several different options available for veterans to research and decide what might be best for them: fellowships, service platoons, service missions, and fundraising opportunities. The program also aims to bridge the military-civilian divide and allow veterans to connect with the community to feel a sense of belonging.

Team Rubicon

http://teamrubiconusa.org/

Team Rubicon unites veterans in a shared sense of purpose through disaster relief assistance by using the skills they have learned in the military. Volunteering veterans reintegrate into society and give back to communities in desperate need. Veterans are the perfect group of trained individuals to cope with the destruction seen in many places hit by natural disasters because many of the circumstances are similar to the conditions that service members were trained to handle while on active duty. Team Rubicon uses the combat skills that many veterans have already cultivated to facilitate greater momentum during disaster relief operations.

The Veterans Posse Foundation

http://www.possefoundation.org/veterans-posse-program

The Veterans Posse Program aims to support veterans who are interested in attending bachelor's degree programs at prestigious institutions across the country. The program creates cohorts of veterans and prepares them to matriculate into select schools. The Veterans Posse Program is currently working with schools such as Vassar College, Cornell University, Dartmouth College, and Wesleyan University (http://www.possefoundation.org/our-university-partners/participating-schools). Selectees will attend a monthlong, all-inclusive, precollege summer training program designed to foster leadership and academic excellence. The schools then guarantee that selectees' full tuition will be covered even after GI Bill and the Yellow Ribbon Program funding run out.

Warrior-Scholar Project

http://www.warrior-scholar.org

The Warrior-Scholar Project is a two-week intensive program designed to promote veteran academic success. Through classes, workshops, discussions, and one-on-one tutoring sessions, veterans are taught how to transition into higher education, challenged to become leaders in their classes at their institutions, and prepared to overcome challenges and embrace new learning experiences. Yale, Harvard, and the University of Michigan host the program. Be aware that some cost is involved with this program.

Student Veterans of America (SVA)

http://www.studentveterans.org/

The SVA organization is a nonprofit designed to help veterans succeed in higher education. Groups of student veterans on school campuses across the country have gotten together to create member chapters. The goal of these chapters is to help veterans acculturate to college life by offering peer-to-peer support. Chapters organize activities and offer networking opportunities.

SVA develops partnerships with other organizations that also aim to promote veteran academic success. Through these partnerships, the SVA has helped to create several new scholarship opportunities. In late 2014 the organization created its thousandth chapter on a college campus in the United States. According to CHEA, there are about 8,300 campuses in the United States, so there is a one-in-eight chance that your future school will have a chapter.[1] Even if it does not, you can always organize and start your own. Check the website for more information.

MILITARY SPOUSE CAREER ADVANCEMENT ACCOUNTS (MYCAA)

https://aiportal.acc.af.mil/mycaa

Military One Source facilitates the MyCAA program. The program offers $4,000 to eligible spouses of active-duty military members to be used for education, either traditional or nontraditional. MyCAA is good for an associate degree, a certification, or a license. The program cannot be used toward a bachelor's degree, but it can be used for programs after a spouse receives a bachelor's degree. For example, I (Jillian) used the program for a supplementary teaching credential offered through the University of California, San Diego, after completing a master's degree in education when I qualified through my husband's rank.

MyCAA aims to increase the portable career skills of active-duty service members' spouses by developing their professional credentials to help them find and maintain work. Military One Source counselors can help eligible spouses find specific programs or schools that participate in the program. Counselors can also help spouses identify local sources of assistance, such as state and local financial assistance, transportation, and child care. They can also help with employment referrals.

Eligible spouses must be married to active-duty service members in the following ranks:

- E1–E5
- O1–O2
- WO1–CWO2

MyCAA will *not* cover the following:

- Prior courses
- Books, supplies, student activities, and the like
- Prepayment deposits
- Audited courses or internships
- Nonacademic or ungraded courses
- Courses taken more than one time
- College Level Examination Program (CLEP) or DSST exams

- Associate of arts degrees in general studies or liberal arts
- Personal enrichment courses
- Transportation, lodging, and child care
- Course extensions
- Study abroad

To apply, visit https://aiportal.acc.af.mil/mycaa or call (800) 342-9647 to speak with a Military One Source Counselor.

GENERAL ADVICE FOR SPOUSES

Unfortunately, besides MyCAA, no other direct financial assistance is available for spouses to pursue their education. If spouses are just beginning their education and willing to attend the local community college, MyCAA will typically cover an associate degree, depending upon the cost of the school. Many community colleges offer associate degrees fully online, which may also offer spouses with children more flexibility.

Past the associate degree, scholarship options (chapter 7) and in a few cases transferring GI Bill benefits from the active-duty spouse are the best bets. Many universities and colleges offer tuition discounts to spouses of active-duty service members but usually not enough to fully alleviate the financial burden.

Spouses should also apply for Federal Student Aid through the Free Application for Federal Student Aid (FAFSA). More information on Federal Student Aid can be found in chapter 7, "Cost and Payment Resources." Many spouses receive all or a portion of the Pell Grant money (chapter 7), which does not need to be paid back.

Spouses are entitled to receive in-state tuition rates at state schools in whatever state they are stationed with their active-duty service member. The Higher Education Opportunity Act (H.R. 4137) signed into law on August 14, 2008, guarantees this benefit. This law eliminates all out-of-state tuition fees and at least eases the financial burden of pursuing higher education. Be aware that many schools will want to see a copy of the service members' orders to verify in-state tuition.

Some states offer low-income tuition waivers to residents, usually through the state-based community colleges. Because spouses are eligible for in-state tuition (so are active duty), they may be eligible for this type of waiver as well.

For example, California offers the Board of Governor's (BOG) Fee Waiver (http://home.cccapply.org/money/bog-fee-waiver) through the state community colleges. Many spouses stationed in California with their active-duty service member are attending community colleges in California and receiving this waiver, and they do not pay to attend school.

Always check with the local community colleges first if you are a spouse and are just getting started. In most cases, it is hard to beat their low tuition rates and the flexible class offerings. Community colleges typically also offer vocational programs at drastically reduced prices when compared to private institutions. They should be your number one starting point!

The Officers' Spouses' Clubs on the different bases offer scholarships for the dependents of airmen. If you can write an essay and watch the deadline dates, that is usually a decent option for a funding source. As a last resort, you may want to discuss GI Bill transferability with an education counselor at your base. Just remember, if you go that route, that those are benefits your active-duty spouse will not have later. For more information regarding eligibility and the process to transfer the GI Bill visit chapter 7, "Cost and Payment Resources."

Transferring the GI Bill to a spouse so that he or she can use it while the service member is on active duty is not my first goal in most cases. Spouses are not eligible for the housing stipend while the airman is still actively serving, but children are eligible. For example, consider the following case:

An airmen transfers his GI Bill to his spouse while still active duty. She uses the benefit to attend California State University, San Marcos (CSUSM). Although she will receive the book stipend, she will not receive the housing allowance. Her school is paid for, and she has some extra money for books. Another airman transfers his GI Bill to his daughter. His daughter attends the same institution and receives the book stipend as well as the housing stipend, which is currently $2,341 per month. At the end of a nine-month school year, the monthly stipend totals $21,069. That is the amount of money the spouse did *not* get while using the benefit. Now consider the same monthly amount (even though it receives cost-of-living adjustments) over a four-year bachelor's degree: $84,276.

For this reason, only in very few circumstances do I recommend spouses using transferred GI Bill benefits while the airman is still on active duty. Obviously, this does not take into account different variables. For example, maybe the couple does not plan to have children, maybe the airman has attained the maximum level of education he or she is interested in pursuing, or maybe the children are very young and the spouse has no other resources. In the end, the decision is personal and all outlets should be pursued.

Notes

CHAPTER 2

1. Kimberly Griffin and Claire Gilbert, Center for American Progress, "Easing the Transition from Combat to Classroom," http://www.americanprogress.org/wp-content/uploads/issues/2012/04/pdf/student_veterans.pdf (last modified April 2012, accessed June 2, 2013).

2. Nisha Money, Monique Moore, David Brown, Kathleen Kasper, Jessica Roeder, Paul Bartone, and Mark Bates, "Best Practices Identified for Peer Support Programs," Defense Centers of Excellence, January 1, 2011, http://www.dcoe.mil/content/Navigation/Documents/Best_Practices_Identified_for_Peer_Support_Programs_Jan_2011.pdf (accessed October 10, 2014).

3. The University of Alabama Student Affairs, "Veteran and Military Affairs," http://vets.ua.edu/ (accessed January 7, 2015).

CHAPTER 3

1. Bryan Cook and Terry W. Hartle, "Why Graduation Rates Matter—and Why They Don't," Spring/Summer 2011, http://www.acenet.edu/the-presidency/columns-and-features/Pages/Why-Graduation-Rates-Matter%E2%80%94and-Why-They-Don%E2%80%99t.aspx (accessed June 29, 2015).

CHAPTER 4

1. Health, Education, Labor, and Pensions Committee, "For Profit Higher Education: The Failure to Safeguard the Federal Investment and Ensure Student Success,"

http://www.help.senate.gov/imo/media/for_profit_report/PartI.pdf (last modified July 30, 2012).

2. Sandy Baum and Jennifer Ma, "Trends in Higher Education 2014," College Board, https://secure-media.collegeboard.org/digitalServices/misc/trends/2014-trends-college-pricing-report-final.pdf (accessed October 21, 2014).

3. National Association of Independent Colleges and Universities, "Independent Colleges and Universities: a National Profile," http://www.naicu.edu/docLib/20110317_NatProfile-Final4.pdf (accessed August 1, 2015).

4. Judith Eaton, "An Overview of U.S. Accreditation," Council for Higher Education Accreditation, http://www.chea.org/pdf/Overview%20of%20US%20Accreditation%202012.pdf (last modified August 2012).

5. Barbara Brittingham, Mary Jane Harris, Michael Lambert, Frank Murray, George Peterson, Jerry Trapnell, Peter Vlasses, Belle Wheelan, Ralph Wolff, Susan Zlotlow, and Judith Eaton, "The Value of Accreditation," Council for Higher Education Accreditation, June 1, 2010, http://www.chea.org/pdf/Value of US Accreditation 06.29.2010_buttons.pdf (accessed July 21, 2015).

CHAPTER 5

1. The Air University. 2015. "Mission," http://www.au.af.mil/au/barnes/ccaf/index.asp (last modified August 10, 2015).

2. The Air University. 2015. "Vision," http://www.au.af.mil/au/barnes/ccaf/index.asp (last modified August 10, 2015).

3. Carl Collins, e-mail message to author, March 5, 2015.

4. The Air University. "Welcome to the CCAF Credentialing Programs Flight." Last modified December 29, 2015. http:www.au.af.mil/au/barnes/ccaf/certifications.asp.

CHAPTER 6

1. U.S. Air Force Academy. "About Us," http://www.academyadmissions.com/about-the-academy/about-us/mission/ (accessed December 29, 2015).

CHAPTER 7

1. Federal Student Aid, "School Costs and Net Price," https://studentaid.ed.gov/prepare-for-college/choosing-schools/consider#school-costs-and-net-price (accessed August 7, 2015).

2. Federal Student Aid, "How Aid Is Calculated," https://studentaid.ed.gov/fafsa/next-steps/how-calculated (accessed August 7, 2015).

3. Federal Student Aid, "How Aid Is Calculated," https://studentaid.ed.gov/sa/fafsa/next-steps/how-calculated#what-does-cost-of-attendance-mean (accessed August 7, 2015).

4. Federal Student Aid, "For Members of the U.S. Armed Forces," https://studentaid.ed.gov/sites/default/files/military-student-loan-benefits.pdf (last modified October 2014).

5. "Background and Our Relationship with the USAF," Air Force Aid Society, http://www.afas.org/background (accessed September 2, 2015).

CHAPTER 10

1. "Registered Apprenticeship." United States Department of Labor Employment and Training Administration. January 7, 2010. June 28, 2015. http://www.doleta.gov/oa/aboutus.cfm#admin.

2. "American Apprenticeship Initiative." United States Department of Labor Employment and Training Administration. December 11, 2014. Accessed July 29, 2015. http://www.doleta.gov/oa/aboutus.cfm#admin.

CHAPTER 11

1. "Veterans Upward Bound Program," U.S. Department of Education, http://www2.ed.gov/programs/triovub/index.html (last modified March 19, 2015).

CHAPTER 12

1. Council for Higher Education Accreditation, "Database of Institutions and Programs Accredited by Recognized United States Accrediting Organizations." January 1, 2015. Accessed January 5, 2015. http://chea.org/search/default.asp.

Bibliography

Air Force Virtual Education Center. "Air Force COOL." Accessed December 29, 2015. https://afvec.langley.af.mil/afvec/Public/COOL/Default.aspx.

The Air University. 2015. "Mission." Last modified August 10, 2015. http://www.au.af.mil/au/barnes/ccaf/index.asp.

American Council on Education. "Military Guide Frequently Asked Questions." Accessed June 29, 2015. http://www.acenet.edu/news-room/Pages/Military-Guide-Frequently-Asked-Questions.aspx.

Baum, Sandy, and Ma Jennifer. College Board. "Trends in Higher Education 2014." Accessed July 11, 2015. https://secure-media.collegeboard.org/digitalServices/misc/trends/2014-trends-college-pricing-report-final.pdf.

Brittingham, Barbara, Mary Jane Harris, Michael Lambert, Frank Murray, George Peterson, Jerry Trapnell, Peter Vlasses, Belle Wheelan, Ralph Wolff, Susan Zlotlow, and Judith Eaton. "The Value of Accreditation." Council for Higher Education Accreditation. June 1, 2010. Accessed July 21, 2015. http://www.chea.org/pdf/Value%20of%20US%20Accreditation%2006.29.2010_buttons.pdf.

Career One Stop. "Get Credentials." January 1, 2015. Accessed July 8, 2015. http://www.careeronestop.org/EducationTraining/KeepLearning/GetCredentials.aspx.

College Board. "Veterans and College Admissions: FAQs." Accessed June 22, 2015. https://bigfuture.collegeboard.org/get-in/applying-101/veterans-college-admission-faqs.

Collins, Carl. E-mail message to author, March 5, 2015.

The Council for Higher Education Accreditation. "Database of Institutions and Programs Accredited by Recognized United States Accrediting Organizations." January 1, 2015. Accessed January 5, 2015.

The Council for Higher Education Accreditation. "The Fundamentals of Accreditation." Last modified September 2002. Accessed August 22, 2015. http://www.chea.org/pdf/fund_accred_20ques_02.pdf.

Council of Regional Accrediting Commissions. "Regional Accreditation and Student Learning: Principles for Good Practice." Last modified May 2003. http://www.msche.org/publications/Regnlsl050208135331.pdf.

Defense Activity for Non-Traditional Education Support. "Troops to Teachers." Accessed August 2, 2015. http://www.dantes.doded.mil/service-members/troops-to-teachers/index.html#sitemap.

Eaton, Judith. The Council for Higher Education Accreditation. "An Overview of U.S. Accreditation." Last modified August 2012. http://www.chea.org/pdf/Overview%20of%20US%20Accreditation%202012.pdf.

Federal Student Aid. "For Members of the U.S. Armed Forces." Last modified October 2014. Accessed December 2, 2014. https://studentaid.ed.gov/sites/default/files/military-student-loan-benefits.pdf.

Federal Student Aid. "How Aid Is Calculated." Accessed August 7, 2015. https://studentaid.ed.gov/fafsa/next-steps/how-calculated.

Federal Student Aid. "School Costs and Net Price." Accessed August 7, 2015. https://studentaid.ed.gov/prepare-for-college/choosing-schools/consider#school-costs-and-net-price.

Federal Trade Commission. "Choosing a Vocational School." Last modified August 2012. http://www.consumer.ftc.gov/articles/0241-choosing-vocational-school.

General Education Mobile. "Frequently Asked Questions." Accessed December 29, 2015. http://www.au.af.mil/au/barnes/ccaf/publications/GEM_FAQ.pdf.

Griffin, Kimberly, and Claire Gilbert. The Center for American Progress. "Easy the Transition from Combat to Classroom." Last modified April 2012. Accessed June 26, 2013. http://www.americanprogress.org/wp-content/uploads/issues/2012/04/pdf/student_veterans.pdf.

Health, Education, Labor, and Pensions Committee. "For Profit Higher Education: The Failure to Safeguard the Federal Investment and Ensure Student Success." Last modified July 30, 2012. http://www.help.senate.gov/imo/media/for_profit_report/PartI.pdf.

Kleinman, Rebecca, Annalisa Mastri, Davin Reed, Debbie Reed, Samina Sattar, Albert Yung-Hsu Liu, and Jessica Ziegler. Mathematica Policy Research. "An Effectiveness Assessment and Cost-Benefit Analysis of Registered Apprenticeship in 10 States." Last modified July 25, 2012. http://wdr.doleta.gov/research/FullText_Documents/ETAOP_2012_10.pdf.

Kurtzleben, Danielle. "Apprenticeships a Little-Traveled Path to Jobs." *U.S. News and World Report.* January 13, 2013. Accessed March 4, 2013. http://www.usnews.com/news/articles/2013/01/13/apprenticeships-a-little-traveled-path-to-jobs.

Maryland Higher Education Commission. "The Importance of Accreditation." Accessed October 29, 2014. http://www.mhec.state.md.us/highered/colleges_universities/accreditation.asp.

Money, Nisha, Monique Moore, David Brown, Kathleen Kasper, Jessica Roeder, Paul Bartone, and Mark Bates. "Best Practices Identified for Peer Support Programs." Defense Centers of Excellence. Last modified January 1, 2011. http://www.dcoe.mil/content/Navigation/Documents/Best_Practices_Identified_for_Peer_Support_Programs_Jan_2011.pdf.

National Association of Independent Colleges and Universities. "Independent Colleges and Universities: a National Profile." Accessed August 1, 2015. http://www.naicu.edu/docLib/20110317_NatProfile-Final4.pdf.

National Skills Coalition. "On-the-Job Training Recommendations for Inclusion in a Federal Jobs Bill." Last modified January 2010. http://www.nationalskillscoalition. org/resources/publications/file/issue-brief-cte.pdf.

Peterson's. "Colleges and Universities: Choosing the Right Fit." Accessed October 29, 2014. http://www.petersons.com/college-search/colleges-universities-choosing-fit.aspx.

State of California Employment Development Department. "Workforce Investment Act." Accessed December 1, 2014. http://www.edd.ca.gov/jobs_and_Training/ Workforce_Investment_Act.htm.

United States Air Force Academy. Accessed December 29, 2015. http://www.usafa. af.mil/.

United States Department of Education. "Accreditation in the United States." Last modified December 1, 2014. http://www2.ed.gov/admins/finaid/accred/accredi-tation_pg2.html and http://professionals.collegeboard.com/guidance/college/ community-college.

United States Department of Education. "Career Colleges and Technical Schools-Choosing a School." Last modified June 18, 2013. http://www2.ed.gov/students/ prep/college/consumerinfo/choosing.html.

United States Department of Education. "Federal Versus Private Loans." Accessed November 15, 2014. http://studentaid.ed.gov/types/loans/federal-vs-private.

United States Department of Education. "Learn about your college and career school options." Accessed August 24, 2015. https://studentaid.ed.gov/sa/ prepare-for-college/choosing-schools/types.

United States Department of Education. "Veterans Upward Bound Program." Last modified March 19, 2015. http://www2.ed.gov/programs/triovub/index.html.

United States Department of Labor: Employment and Training Administration. "Registered Apprenticeship: A Solution to the Skills Shortage." Accessed February 02, 2014. http://www.doleta.gov/oa/pdf/fsfront.pdf.

United States Department of Labor. "Unemployment Insurance." Accessed November 20, 2014. http://www.dol.gov/dol/topic/unemployment-insurance/.

United States Department of Labor. "Unemployment Compensation for Ex-servicemembers." Accessed June 28, 2015. http://workforcesecurity.doleta.gov/ unemploy/ucx.asp.

United States Department of Labor: Employment and Training Administration. "American Apprenticeship Initiative." June 28, 2015. Accessed July 29, 2015. http://www.doleta.gov/oa/aboutus.cfm#admin.

United States Department of Labor Employment and Training Administration. "Registered Apprenticeship." January 07, 2010. Accessed June 28, 2015. http://www. doleta.gov/oa/aboutus.cfm#admin.

United States Department of Veterans Affairs. "On-the-Job Training and Apprenticeship." Last modified November 4, 2014. Accessed November 20, 2014. http:// www.benefits.va.gov/gibill/onthejob_apprenticeship.asp.

United States Department of Veterans Affairs. "Tuition Assistance Top Up." Last modified December 2, 2014. http://www.benefits.va.gov/gibill/tuition_assistance. asp.

United States Senate: Health, Education, Labor, and Pensions Committee. "For Profit Higher Education: The Failure to Safeguard the Federal Investment and Ensure Student Success." Last modified July 30, 2012. http://www.help.senate.gov/imo/media/for_profit_report/PartI.pdf.

University of Alabama. "Veteran and Military Affairs." January 1, 2009. Accessed July 5, 2015. http://vets.ua.edu/.

Index

About the Authors

Jillian Ventrone works as a servicemember's higher education counselor aboard a federal installation, which allows her to work with combat veterans who aspire to pursue higher education. Her family's service background extends from World War I through the current war in Afghanistan, with family serving in numerous capacities from Air Force pilots to the Marine Corps Infantry; two of them received Purple Hearts. Ventrone has a passion for veterans and their higher education benefits, and writing this book has enabled her to disseminate much needed information.

Andrew Hollis is the vice commandant of the Community College of the Air Force (CCAF), the world's largest multi-campus community college. He manages the daily operations and strategic direction of the CCAF, supervising over 318,000 students, 6,300 faculty, 2,100 courses of instruction, and 2.8 million student records at 108 affiliated schools worldwide. Hollis serves as a liaison to universities and public and private colleges, as well as a liaison to international, national, congressional, and Department of Defense leaders, as he works to develop enlisted education initiatives and opportunities while keeping advisees informed of the College's operations and effectiveness. Over the past 28 years he has served in several education and training positions, most notably as the chief of education and training at Air Mobility Command headquarters. Hollis has also served as a recruiter, career advisor, and senior enlisted advisor at the unit and group levels.